D0175439

Special Educator's Consultation Handbook

Lorna Idol-Maestas

University of Illinois
at Urbana-Champaign

AN ASPEN PUBLICATION®
Aspen Systems Corporation
Rockville, Maryland
London
1983

Library of Congress Cataloging in Publication Data

Idol-Maestas, Lorna.
Special educator's consultation handbook.

Bibliography: p. 329
Includes index.
1. Mainstreaming in education. 2. Communication
in education. 3. Teacher participation in personnel service. 4. Parent-teacher conferences. I. Title.
LC4019.I36 1983 371.9′046 82-18445
ISBN: 0-89443-926-X

Publisher: John Marozsan
Editorial Director: Curtis Whitesel
Managing Editor: Margot Raphael
Editorial Services: Eileen Higgins
Printing and Manufacturing: Debbie Collins

Copyright © 1983 by Aspen Systems Corporation

Library of Congress Catalog Card Number: 82-18445
ISBN: 0-89443-926-X

Printed in the United States of America

1 2 3 4 5

Table of Contents

Acknowledgments

The strength of this book lies in the consultation projects that were done by Resource/Consulting Teachers studying at the University of Illinois. The names of these individuals appear with the projects that are reported in Chapters 5, 6, 7, 8, 9, and 10. The consultation strategies reported are the work of these individuals, as well as all program graduates from 1979, 1980, 1981, and 1982. It is due to the willingness and openness of these students that various strategies have been brought to the attention of the author.

The quality of these field-based projects also depended on the expert field supervision of the following individuals: Sandy Lloyd, Shirley Ritter, Louise Givens-Ogle, Mary Pilosof, Steve Rock, Janice Schreck, and Lisa Fleisher.

Professors Joe Jenkins (now at the University of Washington) and Steve Lilly (University of Illinois) were instrumental in the initial development of the Resource/Consulting Teacher Program at the University of Illinois. The basic groundwork they laid has served as an impetus for the consulting teacher component of this program. Professor Laura Jordan (University of Illinois) provided information for and feedback on Chapter 2. This input was extremely valuable and greatly appreciated.

Ricardo Maestas, my husband, graciously donated his time for reading of rough drafts and checking for possible errors. Beth Anderson provided loving care for my child during some of the hours that I prepared the manuscript. Mary Walle and Glenna MacCallum carefully prepared the many tables within this book.

Finally, the classroom teachers and parents whose names are unheralded and who collaborated with the teacher consultants played an essential role in the development of the consultation projects.

To all of these individuals, I express my appreciation.

Lorna Idol-Maestas
December 1982

Chapter 1

The Need for Consultation

As a result of litigation efforts and legislative mandates at both the state and federal levels, increasing numbers of mildly handicapped students are returning to regular classes. Returning these pupils to the mainstream of regular education without systematic planning is potentially a serious problem. Desired skill levels of students must be thoughtfully structured in order to prepare them for successful performance in regular classes. These skill levels should include academic behaviors, social behaviors, or a combination of the two.

Desired behaviors attained in the resource room must be methodically transferred to the regular classroom. Once the desired behaviors are occurring in the regular classroom, they must be monitored to ensure that they are maintained in the new setting. Consequently, support personnel and classroom teachers must work together to effect such changes.

As the numbers of special children attending regular classes increase, the likelihood of child and group management problems increasing is probable. Support can be provided for academic and behavioral assessment, appropriate academic placement, child management systems, and utilization of data-based instruction to ensure academic and behavioral growth of all students. This assistance is valuable for students, regardless of whether or not they carry a special education label. Thus, support, for the purposes of this book, is defined as *consultation*. Consultation is support provided to regular classroom teachers to assist with academic and social behavior problems of mildly handicapped students. The support can come from a variety of personnel who are concerned with the advancement of mildly handicapped students.

THE INTENDED AUDIENCE

This book is primarily written for special educators who offer resource support for mildly handicapped students. (Throughout the book, the term *mildly handicapped* describes students who exhibit mild academic and/or social behavior problems in regular classroom settings.) Also, there are several types of educators and professionals who work closely with mildly handicapped students and who may find that their current positions either include some consultative work or could be easily redesigned to include consultation. This handbook will prove to be a valuable source of information for resource teachers, remedial teachers, teachers at the preservice level, regular classroom teachers, self-contained special education teachers, school psychologists, school counselors, speech and language therapists, social workers, special education program coordinators, and building principals.

Resource Teachers

Most special educators who provide resource support to mildly handicapped students work in direct service settings. They instruct students in a one-to-one teacher/pupil tutorial setting and/or in small group settings in a classroom separate from the students' regular classrooms. The students usually receive resource services anywhere from one hour per day to one-half of the school day. The remainder of students' time is spent in the regular classroom. Because of this partial integration, resource teachers usually work closely with regular classroom teachers. This working together may be limited to coordinating time schedules and signing the Individualized Educational Program (IEP), which has been completed by the resource teachers. It may be more collaborative in nature and include some systematic planning of the instructional program by both teachers. This consultation handbook is offered as a means of assisting and expanding teacher collaboration.

In order to accommodate such collaborative efforts, the role of the resource teacher requires some alteration. Resource room teachers should begin to assume a consultant role as well. Their professional time can be scheduled in order to encompass direct instruction in the resource room and consultation time with other teachers. To measure degree of consultation needs, Evans (1980) surveyed the opinions of 48 resource teachers randomly selected to represent a southwestern state. Eighty percent saw consultation actually making up five percent or less of their professional time. Resource teachers, regular educators (n = 144), and principals (n = 48) agreed that the time spent in consultation was one-half of what it should be. Truly effective mainstreaming may mean that consultative time should constitute 20 to 40 percent of the resource teacher's time rather than the approximate 10 percent agreed upon by these survey respondents.

In addition, most resource room teachers have not had training in consultation. A report by Brown (1977) supports the need for specific training in consultation. Brown interviewed approximately 200 candidates for teaching positions for emotionally disturbed (ED) and learning disabled (LD) students in a public school system. Most of the applicants wished to be consulting teachers, yet only ten could provide data or descriptions of how they had successfully intervened on behalf of a child with problems. Only three had even tried the consulting role, and none had been specifically trained in the consultation process.

Remedial Teachers

Remedial teachers provide support services to students having academic difficulties. The two most common service delivery models are Title I programs for reading and/or mathematics instruction and remedial reading programs. These teachers have contact with regular classroom teachers, but they may not collaborate to the extent they might if they had a consultation framework from which to operate.

The amount of consultation need not be different than that offered in a special education resource room. Resource/consulting teachers at the University of Illinois train in a variety of field sites—Title I classrooms included—as part of their noncategorical training (Idol-Maestas, Lloyd, & Lilly, 1981). These teachers-in-training complete a specified number of projects, regardless of the type of direct service program they work in. The academic skill deficits of students served in this program have been found to be strikingly similar across Title I, learning disabled, and behavior disordered categorical labels (Idol-Maestas, Lloyd, & Lilly, 1981).

Teachers at the Preservice Level

Instruction and practice in classroom consultation is a viable component that should be added to teacher preparation programs for the mildly handicapped. The majority of special education programs for instruction of the student with mild handicaps (learning disabilities, mild behavior disorders, and mild mental retardation) offer training in the resource room model. Use of a consultation handbook for resource room teachers is a viable means of altering such training models to include consultation.

Some of the strategies offered in Chapters 3 through 8 can be used by elementary and secondary educators at the preservice level. Also, some of the reading consultation projects in this handbook may be useful to students who are selecting reading instruction as an area of expertise. At the University of Illinois, some program coordinators are investigating the benefits of requiring collaborative consultation projects by students preparing to be regular classroom teachers and students preparing to be resource/consulting teachers. Offering collaborative consultation experience during teacher preparation could affect the expectations that regular classroom teachers have about consultation and, more importantly, those they hold for mildly handicapped students.

Regular Classroom Teachers

The outcomes of classroom consultation projects as presented in the latter part of this volume may be of interest to all classroom teachers, especially those interested in assisting special students in regular classes. It is important to demonstrate that mildly handicapped students can be effectively managed and taught in regular classrooms. It is much more important to report to teachers the particular strategies and methodologies that were used to obtain positive results. These strategies will be more successful if they are used by teachers who are interested in aiding effective regular class placement for special students.

School Psychologists

The following are five factors that characterize some major job responsibilities of school psychologists:

1. They are assigned to serve as consultants to particular school buildings.
2. They serve as counselors for students with social behavior problems.
3. They work as special education program consultants.
4. They are involved in program placement decisions for special education students.
5. They serve as members of multidisciplinary teams to plan IEPs for special students.

All of these factors should involve working closely with the teaching staff (regular and special education) responsible for the education of these students. Developing expertise in consultation could prove to be beneficial to school psychologists and to the teachers with whom they might consult.

An underlying strength of the reported consultation projects in this book is that student behaviors are specifically defined. Sometimes the professional language used by classroom teachers is different from that used by school psychologists. These differences are particularly evident when the discussion topic is student assessment results. As school psychologists become more accustomed to using specific, behavioral definitions to describe child behavior, they may also improve communication with the teaching staff. They could also provide a needed service to teachers, giving them specific suggestions for instructing and managing special and/or problematic students. Also, the active involvement of school psychologists on the consultation model could decrease the numbers of students who are referred for special education services. If fewer students were referred by teachers as a result of consultative work with school psychologists, psychologists would spend less time doing formal assessments and would be more available to work directly with students and their teachers.

School Counselors

Consultative skills are also useful to school counselors, especially those who work with students with mild social behavior and academic problems. School counselors should work directly with regular and special educators, not only with problem students. It is essential that all concerned professionals know what is being done with a particular student. It is just as essential that the student know that all concerned adults are communicating with one another. The social behavior-change projects in this handbook may be of interest to school counselors whose caseloads include problematic students.

Speech and Language Therapists

Speech and language therapists are assigned to various schools and, often, to special programs. It is not unusual for them to be assigned to more than one school and, as a result, provide therapy within an itinerant service delivery model. A caseload dispersed over two or more geographical locations may mean therapists do not see students as frequently as they might prefer.

Thirty years ago it was documented (McGeorch & Irion, 1952) that retention decreases as a function of time lapse between practice sessions. Mowrer (1972), in a timely piece advocating accountability in speech therapy, pointed out two factors that probably have an effect upon the accuracy of response: the length of time between instructional sessions and the amount of practice given to each task.

With large caseloads, therapists often move to group instructional models that decrease the amount of response time for individual students. Lack of time and lack of practice are good reasons why speech therapists may want to consider gaining some consultative skills in order to increase practice in classroom settings. Also, therapists may be interested in effecting transfer of remediated speech and language problems to regular classrooms. Students may reach a point at which they respond correctly with the therapist but continue to respond incorrectly in the classroom or with another adult. By consulting with classroom teachers and special teachers, the therapist may be able to increase the instances in which students may practice a skill. They may also be able to offer suggestions for increasing the desired linguistic behavior and ensuring successful transfer to new settings.

Social Workers

Social workers who act as support persons to special education students may be particularly interested in consultation strategies for use in the home environment. Chapter 9 focuses on this aspect of consultation. These illustrated home consultations were accomplished by special teachers and parents working together. The most effective style of home consultation may be for social workers, parents or guardians, and special education and classroom teachers to plan home programs together. The social worker could assume major responsibility for giving feedback to parents, collecting home progress data, and sharing it with school personnel. Offering strategies and possible solutions to parents through consultation may provide positive support to parents of problematic students. This kind of hands-on, positive assistance could alter parental perceptions of social workers. Parents may feel like the social worker is more of a support person and less of a social agency watchdog.

Serving as a member of the multidisciplinary team is another effective role that social workers could play in the lives of special children. Social workers could enhance their supportive position to parents by acting as liaisons between parents and school personnel. They also could attend school meetings with the parents as interested friends. They could then make certain that any educational jargon was restated in clear terms. Finally, they could help develop constructive parental input into the IEP by including home consultation work within IEP goals statements.

Special Education Program Coordinators

Coordinators of educational programs for the mildly handicapped must be familiar with different types of consultation models, some of which are defined in Chapter 3. Information about models may spark an interest in redefining special education delivery models to include an element of consultation. If this interest ignites, the program coordinator must be prepared to serve as an advisor to program teachers. The guides and examples provided in the second half of this handbook should be useful aids in this preparation process.

The likelihood of a given school district incorporating consultation into its special support systems is much greater if that request for change comes from program coordinators as opposed to individual, enthusiastic teachers. Well-informed people can create an impression. United, well-informed people can have an impact. Also, the higher people are on the hierarchical structure of a system, the more quickly and efficiently an impact is felt. United program coordinators who are informed about the long-term benefits and cost efficiency of adopting consultation can have this kind of impact. Details regarding the long-term benefits and cost efficiency of consultation are contained within Chapter 2.

Building Principals

The educational position most easily molded to include consultation is that of building principals. Principals often serve as confidants to teachers who are having difficulty with students. They are often on the receiving end when teachers remove problematic students from classrooms. They are frequently left to deal with the problem and select the best intervention. It is not unusual for this to result in child punishment. If building principals were to become actively involved in consultation, benefits would be reaped by all. Principals would be in a more viable position to offer suggestions and ideas for use of positive social reinforcers, rather than using punishment as a solution to a problem that reaches them too late.

Teachers would be in a position of collaborating with principals, rather than admitting that they can no longer handle the problem by referring students to the office. As teachers become more open to consultative work with principals, they may feel less threatened about having principals in their classrooms. Sometimes teachers feel that if a principal visits their classroom, it is for teacher evaluation. If teacher/principal consultations were occurring, this feeling of *evaluation* = *threat* could be reduced.

As principals become a more integral part of classroom happenings, they are also in a better position to give helpful, constructive feedback to teachers. This is surely preferred to offering formal evaluations once a year, which are sometimes viewed as critical feedback.

Parents may experience school attitudinal changes as a result of seeing teachers and principals working closely together for the benefit of their children. Most crucial, however, is the effect consultation can have on the students. Students may be less likely to play principals and teachers against one another. They will experience more consistency in behavioral consequences between the principal's office and their classrooms. Also, some students are afraid of principals, and, to reinforce this, principals are often forced to interact more with problem students than with those who are experiencing no difficulties. Principals actively consulting in classrooms could enhance the quality of principal/student interaction in general.

Building principals may also be interested in Chapter 3, which presents different types of consultation models. This information might serve as a useful tool for advocating changes in existing service delivery models for students with academic/behavioral difficulties. Principals who view the classroom teacher as the central person in the school program may see consultation as a necessary support to offer on a formal basis to teachers. Principals could serve an extremely important function by guiding teachers to support personnel who could provide long-term consultation. An important resulting benefit is that principals may begin to consider hiring consulting teachers or transform resource positions into resource/consulting positions.

EFFECTS OF INDIVIDUAL DIFFERENCES ON THE NEED FOR CONSULTATION

Least Restrictive Environment for the Mildly Handicapped

A current issue in special education is the concept of least restrictive environment (LRE). Despite difficulties in determining what is least restrictive for individuals, LRE roughly means selecting the most normal educational setting in which a special education student can profit from learning opportunities that afford the maximum amount of progress in the least amount of time.

For the vast majority of mildly handicapped students, LRE means the regular classroom. The further away these students are from good role models in the regular classroom, the more likely they might be to appear deviant. This important consideration must be examined prior to special education placement. For example, students in classrooms for behavior disorders are surrounded by other students with behavior disorders. The more time the student spends in the special environment, the less time there is available for observing and interacting with preferred models. A situation where one deviant student is surrounded by many positively conforming students may create a more efficient environment in which to instruct preferred behavior than group instruction of deviants.

A second consideration is that there is evidence to support the premise that perceptions of adults who work with students may be altered by special class placement. Foster, Schmidt, and Sabatino (1976) reported an investigation of teacher expectancies created by the term "learning disabilities." Forty-four elementary teachers viewed a videotape of a normal fourth-grade boy. The boy was taking achievement tests, performing perceptual/motor tasks, and engaging in free play. Teachers were randomly assigned to two groups. One group was told that the student had been evaluated by a clinical team and was considered normal. The second group was told that the student had been classified as learning disabled. Both groups viewed the videotape and were then asked to complete a referral form based on the behavior they had viewed. Teachers who viewed the boy as learning disabled viewed the behaviors significantly more negatively than those who believed the boy was normal.

Foster and Salvia (1977) have also demonstrated that, when teachers were asked to assess academic and social behaviors of a labeled versus a nonlabeled student, a bias against special education labels emerged. When one group of teachers assessed behavior of a student labeled learning disabled, they rated the student as being academically less able and socially disruptive. When a second teacher group rated the same student with the same behavior, without the label, they rated the student as someone who could "fit" into their classes. This differential attitude has been observed in special educators as well as regular educators.

Gillung and Rucker (1977) gave brief descriptions of behaviors of students who were labeled mentally retarded, emotionally disturbed, or learning disabled. Some of the descriptions did not include the labels indicating the type of handicap. Regular educators ($n = 176$) and special educators ($n = 82$) were asked to choose what they felt was the most appropriate educational placement for each described child. The results indicated that regular and special education teachers had lower expectations for labeled children with identical behaviors of unlabeled children. For the special education teachers, most teachers with the label-related expectancies had high levels of teaching experience. Those with less than seven years did not have lowered expectations for labeled children.

If, not labeling students, has an effect upon the attitudes of classroom teachers then educators must begin to consider regular class placement as the preferred alternative for mildly handicapped students. Consultative collaboration between special and regular educators is a mechanism by which this alternative can be accomplished.

Child management strategies that are effective for the special student can be implemented. It is not unusual for these strategies to be effective for other nonlabeled students in the same class as well. Chapter 8 contains examples of this type of consultation.

For effective planning and educational programming to occur, particular emphasis must be placed on the working relationship of the regular class teacher and the special teacher (or any personnel providing supportive services). It is easy for an interested and concerned teacher to be working toward individual goals for a special student that are different than those projected by colleagues working with the same student. In some instances these goals may not only be different, they may be totally uncorrelated.

For example, the following situation was discovered in an elementary school. A boy who carried an LD label was mainstreamed (integrated) into a regular fourth-grade classroom. He went to an LD resource room for academic instruction for math and reading. At another time during the day, he saw a remedial reading teacher for further reading instruction. He was in the fourth-grade classroom when group reading instruction was in progress, as well as for the remainder of the day. In the resource room, the special educator was using a multisensory approach to teaching sounds and letter recognition, as well as practice on visual and auditory memory tasks.

In the remedial reading room, the boy was reading isolated words printed on cards, with no accompanying contextual materials. He was not reading in any materials or books. In the regular classroom, he was off-task during most of the reading period. The expected task was to read orally before the group in a fourth-grade basal reader. Out of frustration, the fourth-grade teacher had given the boy a handwriting task to work on during reading period. The worksheet consisted of copying cursive letters using a teacher-made letter as a model.

A synopsis of the boy's reading program is as follows: in the resource room, a modified phonics approach was used; in the remedial class, a sight word approach was used; and oral reading was expected in the classroom. Aside from the discrepancy between remedial reading approaches, there had been no effort to teach sound blending within the phonics program. There were no attempts to practice words in phrases, sentences, or context in the sight word program. Most essential, there was little correlation between what was taught in the two remedial settings and what was expected in the regular classroom.

The IEP is an ideal mechanism by which these teachers could have collaborated in their educational plans for this student. With this document, they could have delineated the necessary components of the reading program and an accompanying curriculum, selected a consistent method of instruction, and determined which teacher would be responsible for each instructional component(s).

Selecting a curriculum is an essential element of this multidisciplinary team plan. A central theme of the consultation strategies presented in this book is to use the regular class curriculum whenever possible as the source of remediation material. One alternative for selecting curriculum is to train the student in the curriculum that is used in the regular class. This usually means placing the student in the same series but at a lower level. Two excellent reference sources for this type of strategy are found in Lovitt and Hansen (1972) and Blankenship and Lilly (1981). Another alternative is to make modifications in the existing curriculum in order to accommodate individuals needs better. Either of these two strategies could also benefit other children who are having academic difficulties in a classroom.

The Individualized Education Program

To follow through with the example provided earlier that illustrated an instance of poor team-teacher planning, a section of an IEP is presented in Figures 1–1 and 1–2 to demonstrate how a team-teaching plan might look. Some noteworthy changes were made in this student's reading program. Although it may be unusual for a student to have access to both an LD resource teacher and a remedial reading teacher, both teachers continued to provide service because the student was two years below grade level and needed intensive direct instructional services.

A major change was to use the basal series as the source of remediation material. The student was criterially placed (Lovitt and Hansen, 1976a) in the level at which he could most optimally read. He read orally every day at this level, and the tutorial practice involved reviewing sounds, vocabulary, and error words associated with each story he read.

A second major change was to restructure the reading class to include three reading groups. The first group constituted the majority of the class. They read in the 4.0 reader *(Silver Twist)* of the *Economy Series* (1975) *(Keys to Reading)*. The majority of the students were in this group. Members of the second group read at least one year above grade level. They read some stories out of *Silver Twist* and spent the remainder of the time reading independently selected books. A minority of the students were either in this group or in the third group. These students read a year or more below the fourth grade. Their major source of reading material was the 3.1 reader *(Air Pudding)* of the *Economy Series*. These students preselected and rank ordered 50 percent of the stories in this reader; thus, they had a list of preferred stories. For every story they read that they met teacher approval on (this included group attending by sitting quietly and keeping the place), they were allowed to skip one of the stories of the remaining 50 percent of the reader. (See Lovitt and Hansen [1976b] for more details on skip and drill contingencies for reading.)

Billy was a partial member of this group. He participated in the oral reading activity. When he missed a word, the teacher supplied the word. When the group did silent reading activities, Billy silently read the story

Figure 1–1 Sectional Sample of an IEP Illustrating Multidisciplinary Cooperation and Short-Term Instructional Objectives for Regular Class Participation

Individualized Education Program   Academic Subjects: Reading

Present Level of Educational Performance: Billy is reading orally with 95% word accuracy at 50 cwpm (correct words per minute) with 80% correct comprehension in the 2.1 reader (Curbstone Dragons) of the Ecomony (1972) reading series on 9-15-81.

Annual Goal: Billy will have completed the 3.2 reader (Mysterious Wysteria) of the Economy (1972) reading series at the above-stated criterial performance level by May 31, 1981.

Educational Services Provided:

Type	Initiation Date	Number of Minutes per Day	Number of Days per Week
fourth grade class	9-25-81	240	5
LD resource room	9-25-81	30	5
remedial reading	9-25-81	30	5

he had previously read (in the 2.1 reader) with the remedial reading teacher and completed the written comprehension questions as stated on the IEP.

A third major change was that the auditory/visual memory tasks were discontinued in the resource room. A minor change was that the LD resources teacher selected the letter sounds for the student to practice from the stories to be read orally in the 2.1 reader with the remedial reading teacher. Also, the phonetically irregular words and new vocabulary words contained in the story to be read were offered for instructional practice. The remedial reading teacher discontinued word practice and devoted the session to oral reading and comprehension practice. A daily timed reading sample was taken to determine whether Billy had passed the story or would reread the same story in the following session. This teacher was also responsible for supplying the comprehension questions for Billy's stories (2.1 reader) to the classroom teacher.

Assistance from the Consulting Teacher

Three primary areas in which regular class teachers may need assistance are (1) programming, (2) management, and (3) monitoring.

Figure 1–2 Sectional Sample of Short-Term Instructional Objectives for an IEP for Support Services

Sample IEP

Instructional Area: Academics - Oral Reading   Student's name: Billy

Goal Statement: Billy will read orally everyday   Implementor: Remedial Reading Teacher
with 90% accuracy at 50 correct words per
minutes with 80% comprehension. He will
progress through four readers.

Condition	Behavior	Criteria	Materials	Evaluation/ Schedule	Date Objective Mastered
(3) Will read at least one story daily. A 100-word timed sample will be taken near the end of the story. Story is passed if criteria are met.	Read orally.	90% accuracy 50 correct words per minute	2.1 reader (Curbstone Dragons) 2.2 reader (Magic Mushrooms) 3.1 reader (Air Pudding) 3.2 reader (Mysterious Wysteria)	Direct, daily measurement	
(4) Ten oral comprehension questions for each story will be asked when each story is completed.	Oral response to comprehension questions. Partial sentences responses will be corrected by teacher modeling a complete sentence and Billy imitating the model.	80% correct	10 Teacher-made comprehension questions (6 factual, 2 sequential and 2 inferential questions)	Same	

Programming

Programming is the identification and implementation of the educational program for the students in a classroom that includes the special needs student. Within the programming framework would probably be included some individualization of instruction and work assignments.

A given fact in every group of students is that individual students have differing skills and abilities. A heterogeneous grouping such as a typical classroom has a wide range of skill levels across students. Some students may be at high levels in all skills; some students' skills may be dispersed from high to medium, high to low, or medium to low; and other students may be at lower levels for all skill areas. If this degree of heterogeneity exists, it is essential to place students appropriately in the curriculum.

Appropriate curricular placement involves the following: (1) determining how the curricular skills will be measured; (2) sequencing the curriculum in a hierarchical order that consists of levels; (3) establishing criteria to define whether or not students have mastered a level; (4) testing students on various levels; and (5) placing students within the curriculum at levels they can begin to master. Some examples of this type of curriculum-based assessment (CBA) are explicated in Blankenship and Lilly (1981).

This process to determine appropriate curricular placement is one in which a consulting teacher can offer invaluable assistance both in CBA construction and administration. A consultant assigned to a single school may establish CBAs for the major curricular areas in the school. These CBAs can be used by various teachers in various grade levels. CBAs could also be used on a districtwide basis if the curriculum content is consistent. Consulting teachers can form an excellent networking system between schools in which they can share established CBAs. Then they can spend more time defining new areas of curricular assessment and not waste time reinventing a CBA that has been established by another teacher.

CBAs may be used more with special needs students, but they may also be a useful instrument for higher skill level students as well. How they are used may depend on the subject matter. For example, individualized CBAs may be given to all students in reading at the beginning of the year. In contrast, spelling CBAs might be administered to the entire group simultaneously. Math assessment might entail primarily large group testing and some individual testing of a few skill levels at times dispersed over the entire year.

Management

Once the major assessment hurdle has been cleared, the collaborating teachers must define some student and group management plans. These management strategies must be organized in order to glean the utmost out of the curricular assessment data that have been gathered.

Iano (1972) in a paper investigating alternatives to special class placement, suggests flexible grouping as one strategy for accommodating special needs students in regular classes. Flexible grouping is a key to organizing classrooms for best individualized instruction. This entails forming skill level groups, but the membership of the groups may change depending on the instructional content area being covered. For example, during the first two months of school, three math groups may have been formed in a third-grade classroom. As time goes on, the teacher may discover that some students in groups two and three need more review of addition facts. These students would then be formed into a temporary grouping where they could practice addition facts. They may continue to be members of their primary math groups, and some students may attend the addition fact practice group longer than others depending on individual speed of mastery. Flexible grouping can be used in any areas in which more than one student is having the same difficulty.

Groups may remain more static with a subject area such as reading. The same third-grade classroom may have three groups for reading. Students may move from group to group depending on reading progress, but the movement may not be as frequent as in a flexible grouping system. For students who also receive remedial assistance for reading, careful planning must go on between the special teacher and the classroom teacher. This type of consultation might include placing the student in the same curricular series that is used in the classroom even though instruction occurs in a special setting at a lower level. The collaborating teachers would define the level at which students will be performing when they return to the classroom for instruction. Some examples of these classroom-transfer, consultation projects are offered in Chapter 5.

Another important area of management occurs during transition of students from one area of the classroom to another or from one subject to another. Consulting teachers can observe during these transition periods, watching for best possible solutions, or they may temporarily take over instruction so the classroom teacher has time to observe students. Examples of small and large group management strategies used by teachers in consultation are presented in Chapters 7 and 8.

Monitoring

Monitoring of pupil progress is an area in which consulting teachers can and must gain expertise. They can then guide classroom teachers in developing efficient systems of observing and recording pupil progress.

The actual means of measuring pupil progress are usually tied directly to the CBAs. The CBA criteria used to determine optimal performance will probably remain constant throughout instruction. A recommended practice is to take daily or at least frequent measurement of pupil performance. An excellent rationale and discussion of the importance of this is offered in Lovitt, Schaff, and Sayre (1970). In essence, a constant measure of performance is obtained. In reading, some examples of measurement are the percentage of accurately read words, the number of correct words read per minute, and the percentage correct for comprehension. Some math examples are the number of pages completed with a particular percentage correct, number of problems completed per minute, and number of problems that were self-corrected. Some examples of measuring completion of independent words are the number of minutes to complete a silent reading assignment, number of sentences written correctly over time, number of homework assignments completed at a specified level of correct performance, and number of workbook pages completed with acceptable performance defined. The list can go on and on. As the examples imply, performance over time may be a crucial factor. In fact, a student may have mastered the skill area being tested, but the time it takes to complete the task is too long for efficient student and class management.

One important characteristic of direct and continuous measurement is that the behaviors that are measured are clearly specified so that they convey the same message to all observers and observees. Another important characteristic of frequent, behavioral measurement is that acceptable levels of performance (known as criterion levels) are succinctly defined. These predetermined criteria can be used to ascertain whether the student has or has not mastered the lesson.

Issues Concerning School Consultation

If a consultation model is selected, then decisions must be made as to the amount of time spent for consultation. Consulting teachers in Vermont are employed on a full-time basis as consultants. In Kentucky, Nelson and Stevens (1981) reported time spent in consultation ranging from 31.4 percent in 1977–1978 and 26.9 percent in 1978–1979. At the University of Illinois, resource/consulting teachers (R/CTs) are encouraged to secure positions that devote one-third to one-half of the professional day to consulting. A factor to be considered is whether a district will hire some consulting teachers or whether current resource positions will be redefined to include a consultation component.

If a district chooses the resource-transformation alternative, then individual consulting teachers must make decisions concerning scheduling of consultation time. The majority of R/CT graduates schedule consultation time using one of two options. The first option is to select set time frames for a portion of the school day. This is beneficial to the teachers who need support during those established time frames. This is problematic, however, for teachers who may have classroom management problems during a part of the day that is different than the time the teacher consultant is available. A possible solution to this dilemma is to disperse the time frames intermittently throughout the school day. For example, consulting services might be provided from the hour to the half-hour of each day and resource services from the half-hour to the hour.

A second option that R/CTs have used is altering the schedule every other day of the week. For example, resource services might be provided from 8:00 until 10:30 A.M. and 2:00 until 3:00 P.M. on Mondays, Wednesdays, and Fridays, and 10:30-2:00 on Tuesdays and Thursdays. The remaining time would be used for consulting teaching. This alleviates the difficulty of problems occurring at times of the day in which a consultant is unavailable. It does require a little more initial planning for the resource service schedule. It can be advantageous in that some classroom teachers prefer not to have students leave their classes for resource services at the same time each day.

Another set of issues surrounding consultation concern teacher attitude. Classroom teachers may feel threatened by the idea of having support personnel in the classroom. They may be concerned that requests for assistance will result in lowered evaluations of their teaching performance. There may be teachers who are initially unreceptive to the idea of consultation and/or the idea of mainstreaming handicapped students in regular classes. The following are some suggestions that are useful in altering teacher perceptions and receptivity:

- Ensure that the building principal offers strong support to the consultation model and positively communicates this to the teaching staff. Consultation should be communicated to teachers as a service that is available and one that the administration encourages them to use.
- Teacher consultants should not become involved in any type of teacher evaluation.
- Teacher consultants and/or other district personnel can offer inservice workshops that address such topics as the role of the consulting teacher, mainstreaming in the regular classroom, behavior management, construction of curriculum-based assessments, and so on.
- At the beginning of the year, teacher consultants should send memos to all staff members describing the available services.
- Teacher consultants can offer a brief presentation of consultation services at a faculty meeting at the beginning of the year.
- Initially teacher consultants should emphasize the quality of consultation projects done rather than the quantity of contacts. The word will spread quickly if the consultant is doing a good job. It will spread like wildfire if the consultant's service is of poor quality.
- Results of successful consultation should be shared with the teaching staff. Teachers will be particularly interested in strategies that produce results.

Some other issues that are pertinent to the consultation process have been addressed in a survey (Idol-Maestas & Jackson, 1981) that was conducted to collect reactive responses of classroom teachers who were the recipients of consultation by R/CT trainees. Thirty-one classroom teachers were surveyed. This was an intact group that totaled all recipients of consultations during the spring of 1981. Twenty-nine teachers returned the survey, resulting in a response rate of 93 percent. Seventy-four percent of the consultations were initiated by the R/CTs. The R/CTs had a specified number of consultation projects to complete during the semester, which explains the high percentage of R/CT contacts. As consulting teachers become immersed in the school system, the percentage of classroom teachers' initiations should increase. It is promising that even with consulting teachers-in-training, 26 percent of the projects were initiated by classroom teachers.

The remaining questions and the response data are displayed in Table 1–1. The responses have been tallied by total number of responses, and percent and frequency of "Yes" and "No" responses for each question. The data are promising. All but one respondent found the consultation to be beneficial, and 11 consultations resulted in not referring those students for special services. The consulting teachers seemed to be providing an atmosphere of positive exchange (items 4, 5, and 6). Item 6 is especially reassuring because all of the consulting teachers were in their twenties. It has been a concern of this author that young consulting teachers may not be acceptable to classroom teachers. Items 7, 8, and 9 address the issue of whether data collection procedures are bothersome to classroom teachers and students, and the majority of the responses indicate that this does not have to be a matter of concern.

Items 10, 11, and 12 provided space for written comments as well as for "Yes-No" responses. In most cases, where consultation services were available, they were provided by either Title I teachers or R/CTs previously trained in this model. In two instances consultation was provided by the school social worker, while in two other instances, consultation was available with University of Illinois graduate students in programs other than the Resource/Consulting Teacher Training Program.

The survey also indicated that many teachers were introduced to data-based instruction for the first time. Many indicated that charting both academic and social behaviors was new. One teacher indicated that learning to identify specific behaviors rather than something general was new and useful. The manner of specifying baseline and intervention data was new and provided a graphic picture of behavior change and the effectiveness of behavior modification techniques. Lastly, many teachers indicated that the use of contingent reinforcement was a new concept. One teacher summarized her newly acquired skills most aptly by saying, " . . . gave me an opportunity to see behavior modification in action!"

For the majority of the respondents, the consulting teacher offered new ideas. One teacher who saw the survey results said that the R/CT may not have necessarily offered a new idea, but certainly may have reminded classroom teachers of a strategy or an idea that they had once studied in school but never implemented. This type of reaction would have probably resulted in a "No" response. One new idea was reinforcing a student contingent on behavior. Teaching children to manage their own behavior and to self-record was a valuable idea. The use of skipping pages as a

Table 1–1 Survey Questions and Responses of Classroom Teachers Who Collaborated With Consulting Teachers

QUESTION	N	YES %	YES FREQ.	NO %	NO FREQ.
1. Are consultation services beneficial to you?	28	96	27	4	1
2. Did this consultation project remediate a problem in your classroom so that you didn't have to refer the student for special services?	23	48	11	52	12
3. Did the R/CT actively listen to what you said?	29	97	28	3	1
4. Did the R/CT give you positive feedback regarding your ideas?	28	96	27	4	1
5. Did you find the charted data helpful?	25	88	22	12	3
6. I have confidence in the R/CT who consulted with me?	28	100	28	0	0
7. The observation and recording which was done was disruptive to the students.	28	4	1	96	27
8. The observation and recording which was done was disruptive to me.	29	0	0	100	27
9. Has consultation been provided to you in the past?	28	46	13	54	15
10. Did you learn any new skills from the R/CT which you can apply in your classroom at a later time?	24	50	12	50	12
11. Did the R/CT offer any innovative ways of managing child behavior or selecting academic interventions?	23	61	14	39	9

contingency for work accuracy was new to some teachers. Using a changing performance criterion so that a child could meet success immediately was specified as a new idea by one teacher. She indicated that quite often teachers expect a total change all at once, whereas working for a goal in gradual steps made sense. Finally, one teacher indicated that the ideas suggested by the consulting teacher were rather simple, but ones that had not been tried prior to the R/CT systematically setting up the project.

The range of consultations included academic and social child-change projects. Some examples of the academic projects were:

- timed reading to improve speed
- increase in math accuracy
- increase in spelling accuracy
- improvement of reading and writing skills
- preparation for book report conferences
- use of contingency skipping to increase rate of completion in math

Examples of social behavior projects were:

- increasing on-task behavior
- following directions
- completing work independently
- decreasing inappropriate language and name calling
- improving class structure based on behavioral observation

WHO BENEFITS FROM CONSULTATION?

Students of any school age with academic and/or social behavior problems who attend regular classes can profit from consultation. These students may have been assigned special education labels, but this need not necessarily be the case. If collaborating teachers devise more systematic and efficient means of instructing and managing students, then many students will reap the benefits. Some of these recipients may even be gifted and talented students who could profit from individualized instruction and efficient time management systems. For the handicapped student, consultation can facilitate effective remediation strategies in both the direct service setting (that is, resource rooms and self-contained classrooms) and the indirect service setting (the regular classrooms). Consultation can certainly pave the way for designing systematic plans for returning special students to the least restrictive environment.

Consultation can be beneficial to classroom teachers. Through this type of service delivery, teachers can receive direct assistance with classroom problems. This is powerful when compared to receiving professional recommendations for best practice but no assistance in implementing the recommendations.

Parents may also profit from consultation efforts. Consulting teachers can offer assistance and suggestions for child management programs in the home. Some examples of this type of consultation are presented in Chapter 7. Consulting teachers, especially those who use data-based instruction, can also give parents more detailed and understandable feedback concerning the progress of their children.

The long-term benefits of consultation may prove to be especially attractive to schools and administrators. From a school budget point of view, the numbers of students receiving special assistance can be increased without the usual accompanying cost increase. If consulting teachers use a data-based framework, administrators can have access to quantifiable records that contain pupil progress data and results of child-change consultations.

Chapter 2

Special Services for Mildly Handicapped: Are They Effective?

We now have what may be called the six-hour retarded child—
retarded from 9 to 3, five days a week, solely on the basis of an
IQ score, without regard to adaptive behavior, which may be
exceptionally adaptive to the situation and the community in
which the child lives . . .

*Adapted from the President's
Commission on Mental Retardation, 1969*

Attitudes of special educators toward the preferred service delivery
model for students with mild learning and behavior problems have under-
gone some basic alterations during the last 50 years. The first, most commonly used means of providing special instruction was through segregated,
self-contained classes. As people began to question the efficacy of special
class placement, the service delivery trend moved toward a resource room
model. Some students continued to attend special classes; others attended
resource rooms for a portion of the school day and remained in regular
classes for the remaining school time. After resource services were implemented, evaluative questions were again raised regarding the impact of
these services. Some professionals began to think in terms of least restrictive educational placement. For many students this type of thinking meant
that the regular classroom was the most preferred model of service delivery. This inclusion of some special students in regular classes has been
described as mainstreaming. Mainstreaming has had a tremendous impact
upon some school districts, and, therefore, consultation service has been
conceptualized as a preferable alternative to nonintegrated special education services.

THE EFFICACY OF SPECIAL CLASS PLACEMENT

Some school districts are adopting policies that encourage regular class integration of many special class students. Such integration efforts call for careful planning and teacher collaboration. This collaboration should include both systematic transfer from special education to regular education of students presently receiving special classes and support for students enrolled in regular classes. For school districts still using the self-contained classroom model for delivery of services to mildly handicapped students, the question must be raised as to whether this is the most efficacious model for supporting all of these students. Many students currently attending special classes may perform as well or better in regular classes with resource and/or consultation support. A useful strategy for selecting optimal service delivery models is to examine the research literature that pertains to the effectiveness of special placement.

Between 1932 and 1965, comparative studies, commonly known as "the efficacy studies," were conducted to compare academic gains and social competence of students labeled educable mentally retarded (EMR) who attended special classes with equally low scoring students in regular classrooms. Tables 2–1 and 2–2 contain a summation of the primary findings of ten of those studies. These ten studies were consistently reviewed in the majority of seven literature reviews (Cegelka & Tyler, 1970; Corman & Gottlieb, 1978; Guskin & Spicker, 1968; Kaufman & Alberto, 1976; Kirk, 1964; Quay, 1963; Semmel, Gottlieb, & Robinson, 1979). The tables also contain the conclusions for the individual studies, a list of variables that were controlled (usually by matching procedures), and a list of uncontrolled variables that cast a conservative light on the conclusions. The studies are separated by the direction of the findings. The studies in Table 2–1 are those in which academic gains of EMR students attending regular classes were superior to those of similar students in special or self-contained classes. Table 2–2 contains the studies in which there are no significant differences between academic gains made in self-contained classes and those made in regular classes. There were no studies in which the majority of academic gains were made by students attending special classes.

Subject Selection

The primary criticism of these studies has been how the students in the two comparative educational settings were selected. Most studies were conducted by an *in situ* approach where intact groups already created by school districts were studied. Thus, eight of the studies (Ainsworth, 1959; Bennett, 1932; Blatt, 1958; Cassidy & Stanton, 1959; Elenbogan, 1957;

Table 2-1 Efficacy Studies in which Academic Gains Were Superior in Regular Classes When Compared to Self-Contained Classes

Year	Investigators	Variables Controlled	Conclusions	Variables Not Controlled
1932	Bennett (Baltimore)	Chronological age Mental age Intelligence	• Regular class students were superior to special class students on four types of reading, arithmetic computation and reasoning, arithmetic total, and spelling.	• Initial group differences for educational achievement and physical characteristics • Selection factor not controlled
1936	Pertsch (New York City)	Chronological age Mental age Intelligence Sex Race	• Regular class students were superior on reading comprehension, arithmetic computation and reasoning, and personality adjustment.	• Students with more serious problems were referred to special classes.
1957	Elenbogan (Chicago)	Chronological age Intelligence Sex School district	• Regular class students were superior in paragraph meaning, word meaning, and arithmetic computation and reasoning. (Arithmetic reasoning was not statistically significant.) • Special class students were superior in social adjustment.	• Selection factor not controlled • Different curriculum in special class than in regular class
1959	Cassidy & Stanton (Ohio)	Chronological age Intelligence	• Regular class students were superior in educational achievement. • Special class students were superior in some aspects of personality and social adjustment.	• Special class teachers were more interested in social adjustment than academics.

Table 2–1 continued

Year	Investigators	Variables Controlled	Conclusions	Variables Not Controlled
1961	Mullen & Itkin (Chicago)	Chronological age Intelligence Sex Socioeconomic status Reading achievement School attendance Foreign languages Adjustment appraisal Presence or absence of brain injury	• Regular class students were superior in arithmetic gains for first year, reading gains after two years, and ratings of overall classroom work for second year.	• Regular students had higher scores on Chicago Test of General Information and Comprehension. • Subjects were matched at beginning of study, not upon entrance to special education. • Students placed on waiting lists had more serious problems.

Table 2-2 Efficacy Studies in which There Were No Significant Differences Between Academic Gains Made in Self-Contained Classes and Regular Classes

Year	Investigators	Matched Variables	Conclusions	Variables Not Controlled
1958	Blatt (Pennsylvania)	Chronological age Mental age Intelligence	• No group differences in educational achievement, personality, or physical status. • Special class improved more in reading from one year to the next.	• Groups were selected from different school systems: one with special classes and one without. • Special class had more uncorrected or permanent physical defects. • Selection factor not controlled
1959	Ainsworth (Georgia)		• All groups made educational achievement progress during one-year period. • No significant group differences for achievement, social adjustment, or behavior.	• Kirk (1964) criticized the study for its short duration of one year. • Selection factor not controlled
1959	Wrightstone, Forlano, Lepkowski, Sontag, & Edelstein (New York City)	Chronological age Intelligence Sex Ratings of social maturity and emotional stability Teachers' ratings of educability Test (level and form)	• No major group differences for academic achievement. • Of 40 separate comparisons for academic achievement, one favored special class and six, regular class. • Low level EMR had more difficulty in social adjustment and speech.	• Groups were not discrete. • Two-thirds of population was lost through attrition during first year.

Table 2-2 continued

Year	Investigators	Matched Variables	Conclusions	Variables Not Controlled
1959	Thurstone (North Carolina)		• On Stanford Achievement Test (SAT) regular class students scored higher except on arithmetic computation. • For low IQ group, gains were higher in special class (except arithmetic computation). • No group differences for gain scores except for extreme deviates. • Social adjustment was superior in special class.	• Selection factor not controlled • Low EMR were more likely to be referred to special class. • IQ differences between groups were significant.
1965	Goldstein, Moss, & Jordan (Illinois)		• Regular class students scored higher in reading (no differences by fourth year), word discrimination (by the fourth year), and arithmetic (only the first year). • No group differences for social knowledge, but less social interaction in special classes • More mothers thought special class students were doing well. • Special class students were superior on verbal tests of orginality, fluency, and flexibility of thought; tried to answer more questions.	

Mullen & Itkin, 1961; Pertsch, 1936; Wrightstone, Forlano, Lepkowski, Sontag, & Edelstein, 1959) contain a matching procedure. Students in regular classes were matched to special class students on such variables as chronological age, mental age, intelligence test score, sex, race, and socioeconomic status. Tables 2–1 and 2–2 present additional matched variables unique to individual studies.

Regardless of various combinations of matched variables, there were probably initial group differences for the subjects. For example, in the Bennett study (1932), educational achievement and physical characteristics were superior in the regular class students. The regular class students in the Blatt study (1958) were from school districts that had no special classes. Here, too, special class students had more physical defects. In the Mullen and Itkin study (1961), the matching procedures were done at the onset of the study, not upon entrance to special education. This procedure could nullify effects of special class instruction prior to the study. In the Wrightstone and others study (1959), the groups were not orthogonal to one another. Two special class groups, one made up of high level students and one of low level students, as defined by academic test scores, were compared to regular class grouping with a mixture of low and high level students. The two special class groups were not homogeneous in that there were some high level students in the low group and vice versa. In the Pertsch study (1936), regular class students were selected by building principal recommendation, with the principals identifying students they thought might benefit from special education.

Another problem concerning group selection is presented by the Mullen and Itkin (1961) study. After the first year, Mullen and Itkin tested 140 pairs of students who were matched on a total of nine variables. After the second year, they retested only 64 of these pairs. This attrition rate of more than 50 percent could indicate a serious problem with subject selection.

Attempted Solutions for Subject Selection Problems

In order to compensate for the subject selection factor, Cassidy and Stanton (1959) selected a random sample of special class students by stratifying five geographic locations in the state of Ohio. However, in order to obtain a sufficient sample of regular class students, they selected those students from the ten largest cities from each of the five regions.

Goldstein, Moss, and Jordan (1965) constructed the most problem-free design regarding the subject selection factor. They randomly assigned first-grade students to special and regular classes. This should have eliminated the problem of special class students having had more problems and thus having been more likely to be referred to special classes. However, even with randomization, the special class students as a group were lower initially on several scores than were the comparison students. No significant differences between academic gains made in special or regular classes were found in the Goldstein et al. (1965) study. It is important to note that there were better reading gains in the regular classes after the first year; by the end of the fourth year these differences had dissipated.

Effects of Curricula and Teachers

An aspect of the Goldstein et al. (1965) study that must be taken into consideration was that a curriculum guide was used in the special classes. The focus of the guide included instruction in both socialization training and academics. The special teachers were trained and supervised. This curriculum guide approach is superior to approaches in some previous studies where the curriculum was simply different from that used in regular classes, although this still yields only minimal information on actual course of study. The degree of teaching expertise in this study, as in all others, remains undocumented.

Elenbogan (1957) describes some characteristics of the special classes in his study. The special classes had smaller memberships, two special curricula, and teachers trained to work with EMR children. These characteristics were probably generally true of most of the special class efficacy studies. The different curriculum offered in special classes is illustrated in the study reported by Cassidy and Stanton (1959). The special class teachers were more interested in social adjustment than academics. In this particular study, the special class students scored higher on some aspects of personality and social adjustment. Since these data came from teacher reports, the question of teacher interest and tolerance is a confounding variable. This superiority of sociability is also reported by investigators who did not look at differences in academic gain (Baldwin, 1958; Johnson, 1950; Johnson & Kirk, 1950). These special class characteristics raise the question of why efficacy studies should compare academic gains of students exposed to regular class curricula to special class students who receive different curricula and different teacher expectations?

Differential Student Placement

Examination of sample population and curricular differences certainly leads to cautious interpretation of the findings of these comparative studies. However, if they are examined from the position that lower ability children have been more likely to be placed in special classes and their higher ability counterparts have had a better chance of remaining in regular classes, their respective academic progress is informative. In the Ainsworth study (1959), progress of the following groups was considered: (1) the special class; (2) the regular class; and (3) the regular class plus an itinerant teacher. This was one of the studies in which no academic gain differences occurred across groups. As this *in situ* research would seem to indicate, the higher level students were in regular classes; the itinerant support was used for students in regular classes who needed it; and the students with serious problems were placed in special classes.

Perhaps this type of preplanned grouping indicates that as a first option educators should attempt to remediate referred problems in regular classrooms. If the problem is such that the teacher needs assistance in remediation, then the itinerant teacher approach is the next logical option to take. (What was conceived as an itinerant teacher in 1959 had most likely developed into a consulting teacher approach by the late 1970s and early 1980s.) Only when a student's problems are so severe that neither option one nor two has been successful, should a special class placement be considered. A principle to apply in determining which type of service delivery is best is to begin with the least possible amount of change in the regular classroom and make changes only when necessary.

EFFICACY OF RESOURCE SUPPORT

The recurring negative results of studies investigating the efficacy of special class placement may have had an effect upon the development of resource room models during the 1960s and 1970s. Many students taught in special classes during the 1950s and 1960s would have been more likely to have attended resource rooms during the late 1960s and 1970s. This movement was stimulated in part by Dunn (1968), who published a classic article in the special education literature reminding special educators that many of the educational services provided for the mildly retarded should have been obsolete if regular classes were the best they could have been. Services were redefined for many students who had previously received academic instruction via self-contained, special education classes. More students were assigned to regular classroom teachers, but the students spent a portion of their day working in a resource setting under the tutelage of special education teachers.

Sindelar and Deno (1978) published a review of 11 studies, conducted between 1967 and 1976, that examined the efficacy of resource rooms as a service delivery model for mildly retarded, learning disabled, and behavior disordered students. Sindelar and Deno reviewed only studies that compared groups of students receiving instruction in special classes and/ or regular classes versus those receiving instruction in resource rooms. Sindelar and Deno noted similarities between the design problems that occurred in the special class efficacy studies and those associated with the resource efficacy studies. They concluded that a definitive statement could not be made regarding the efficacy of resource placement for academic or personal-social domains.

The 11 studies they reviewed for comparative academic achievement are displayed in Table 2–3. Four studies compared academic achievement of mildly retarded subjects in resource rooms to those in special classes (Budoff & Gottlieb, 1976; Carroll, 1967; Jenkins & Mayhall, 1976; Walker, 1974) with differentiated results. In the Budoff and Gottlieb study, academic gains were similar regardless of placement. In the Walker study, the resource program group made significantly higher gains in word reading and vocabulary than the special class group. In contrast, in the Carroll study, the special class group made greater gains on word recognition (reading subtest of the Wide Range Achievement Test [WRAT]). In the Jenkins and Mayhall study, resource students improved at a faster rate than special or regular class groups.

Seven studies compared performance of mildly retarded (Smith & Kennedy, 1967), learning disabled (Jenkins & Mayhall, 1976; Sabatino, 1971), and behavior disordered students (Glavin, 1973, 1974; Glavin et al., 1971; Quay et al., 1972) to that of similar students in regular classes. Five studies used the California Achievement Test (CAT) to measure performance; two (Glavin, 1974; Smith & Kennedy, 1967) showed no group differences and three (Glavin, 1974; Glavin et al., 1971; Quay et al., 1972) favored resource programming. Two studies used the Weschler Intelligence Scale for Children (WISC) to measure group differences (Sabatino, 1971; Smith & Kennedy, 1967). One reported no significant differences (Smith & Kennedy, 1967), and one reported more significant gains on some subtests of the WISC for children in special classes and resource rooms than 11 children in regular classes (Sabatino, 1971). Two studies used the WRAT as a measure of performance (Jenkins & Mayhall, 1976; Sabatino, 1971). Both favored the resource room for producing better reading gains.

In spite of the differential results reported in the Sindelar and Deno (1978) review, they concluded that the most carefully designed studies supported the effectiveness of resource programming over regular class placement for behavior disordered (Glavin et al., 1971; Quay et al., 1972), learning disabled (Jenkins & Mayhall, 1976; Sabatino, 1971), and mildly retarded students (Jenkins & Mayhall, 1976). Three factors must be taken into consideration. First, the measures most predominantly used in these studies were group achievement tests. A group test is a less precise and

Table 2–3 Studies of Academic Achievement

Author(s)/Date	Population/N/Assignment	Comparisons	Duration	Measures	Results
Carroll (1967)	Mildly retarded N = 39 In naturally existing groups	Resource program with special class	1 school year	Wide Range Achievement Test (WRAT)	1. Children in both treatments realized significant gains. 2. Special class group made greater gains on reading subtest than resource group.
Smith & Kennedy (1967)	Mildly retarded N = 96 Randomly assigned	Resource program (45 min./day) with control activity (45 min./day) with regular class placement	Unclear (Authors cite "short period of time" as major limitation—pretests 9/61; posttests 4/63.)	California Achievement Test (CAT) Wechsler Intelligence Scale for Children (WISC)	1. There were no significant differences among groups on either measure.
Walker (1974)	Mildly retarded N = 58 Matched on CA, IQ, and reading level	Resource program with special class placement	2-year program, 1st and 2nd evaluations	Word reading, vocabulary, and arithmetic subtests of Stanford Achievement Test (SAT)	1. Resource program group scored significantly higher in word reading and vocabulary than special class group. 2. There was no difference in arithmetic.
Budoff & Gottlieb (1976)	EMR N = 31 Randomly assigned	Resource program (45 min./day minimum) with special class placement	3 Evaluations (1) pretest (2) 2 months after assignment (3) 9 months after assignment	Metropolitan Achievement Test	1. At time 2 and 3, there were no significant differences attributable to placement.

Table 2–3 continued

Author(s)/Date	Population/N/Assignment	Comparisons	Duration	Measures	Results
Glavin, Quay, Annesley, & Werry (1971)	Behaviorally disruptive or overtly withdrawn Experimental, N = 27 Control, N = 34 Random assignment of teacher identifications	Resource program with regular class placement	2-year program, 1st-year evaluation	CAT	1. Resource program group scored significantly higher on reading comprehension and arithmetic fundamentals than regular class group.
Quay, Glavin, Annesley, & Werry (1972)	(as above)	Evaluation following 2nd year of the program described	2-year program, 2nd-year evaluation	CAT	1. Resource program group scored significantly higher than regular class group on reading vocabulary, total reading, arithmetic fundamentals, and total arithmetic.
Glavin (1973)	Same as: Glavin, Quay, Annesley, & Werry (1971)	First-year evaluation following termination of program	2-year program, 1st-year postcheck	CAT	1. Resource program group scored significantly higher than regular class group on arithmetic fundamentals only.
Glavin (1974)	(as above)	Second-year evaluation following termination of program	2nd-year program, 2nd-year postcheck	CAT	1. There were no significant differences between groups.

Study	Sample	Design/Treatment	Duration	Measures	Results
Sabatino (1971)	Learning disabled N = 114 Matched on CA, sex, IQ, and perceptual impairment	Special class with resource program A. (1 hr./daily); resource program B. (½ hr./twice weekly); regular class placement	1 school year	14 selected subtests of WRAT, WISC, and Illinois Test of Psycholinguistic Abilities (ITPA)	1. All 3 "special" groups gained significantly more than regular class group. 2. Resource program. A group was superior to both resource program B and special class groups, which did not differ.
Affleck, Lehning, Brow (1973)	Learning disabled N = 29 Within-subject comparisons	Interpolated historical rates of improvement with rate of improvement in resource program	1 school year	Spache Diagnostic Reading Scales	1. Ss made significant pre- to posttest gains. 2. Ss rates of progress significantly improved during resource program placement.
Jenkins & Mayhall (1976)	A. EMR and LD N = 6 and N = 24 Random assignment	Special class vs. special class and resource program for EMRs; resource program vs. regular class	A. 3½ months	WRAT	1. Resource program group improved at a significantly faster rate than either special or regular class group.
	B. LD, N = 28 ½ randomly assigned, lowest 7 of remaining ½	For LDs: resource program (for reading only) vs. regular class placement	B. 1 school year	WRAT	1. Resource program group significantly outgained regular group on reading subtest. 2. There was no difference on arithmetic subtest.

Source: Reprinted from "The Effectiveness of Resource Programming" by P.T. Sindelar and S.L. Deno with permission of *Journal of Special Education,* (see 1978, 12(1), pp. 20–21).

accurate measure of performance gain than an individualized test. Second, variable performance of students who are exhibiting academic and behavioral difficulties on group tests must be considered. A preferred measure of performance might be to consider measurement of curricular progress on an individual basis. A third factor is that students performed at least as well in regular classes as with resource services in three studies. This occurrence may indicate that some students perform best in regular classes. With such inconclusive research data, a true continuum of services (Deno, 1970) for the mildly handicapped must be offered that includes the regular class as the least restrictive placement for many mildly handicapped students.

ARE THERE BENEFITS TO LABELING SPECIAL STUDENTS?

A recurring theme throughout all of the reviewed efficacy studies is that students may be different depending on the setting. Environments that are less restrictive may be naturally selected by school personnel for less problematic students. However, another issue to consider is that students may change as the method of service delivery changes. For instance, when the majority of the special class efficacy studies were conducted, the most usual instructional alternative for mildly handicapped students was the special class. As the trend moved toward a resource approach, more students received assistance through these programs. A common label used to categorize special students during the special class era was mildly mentally retarded. Those students with higher IQs were more likely to remain in regular classes.

During the resource movement, students were described by a more finite system of categorization: learning disabled (LD); emotionally disturbed (ED); or behavior disordered; and educationally handicapped as well as educably handicapped or retarded. In Gajar (1980) some research is described in which characteristics of exceptional categories were analyzed. The subjects were 198 students previously identified by school districts as EMR, LD, or ED. Certain significant measures were identified that distinguished between these types of exceptional children about 82 percent of the time, that is, IQ score, reading achievement, test-score scatter, presence or absence of a conduct disorder, and a score on a personality problem measure. As would be expected, EMR students demonstrated lower IQs than LD and ED subjects. Learning disabled students had lower achievement scores than did ED students, and they had a higher incidence of scattered scores than was true of the other groups. The ED students scored higher on measures of conduct-disorder and personality problems. Similar overall results were reported in an earlier study (Gajar, 1979). These two studies described a system of classification of mildly handicapped students that is not unlike classification practices used in many school districts. Most states include most of these differences in the content of state rules and regulations for special education, so school districts must adhere to classification differences. Succinctly, these general differences are the following:

- EMR—lower IQ scores, coupled with low achievement
- LD—lower academic achievement with variability on test performance indicating high and low skill areas
- ED—conduct and personality problems that may or may not be accompanied by academic problems

Are these distinguishing characteristics educationally relevant? This question has been raised by others (Bruininks & Rynders, 1971; Forness, 1974; Hallahan & Kauffman, 1976; 1977; Lilly, 1970; Reynolds, 1970), as well as by Gajar (1979) herself.

SERVICE DELIVERY IN LEAST RESTRICTIVE ENVIRONMENTS

One philosophical solution to the categorical issue that was suggested (Bruininks & Rynders, 1971; Reynolds, 1970) almost ten years before the Gajar studies was that less emphasis be placed on conceptualizing the educational difficulties of handicapped children in terms of categories, unless these classifications could be translated into effective educational treatments. This philosophy has been advocated by some through use of noncategorical resource rooms (Culkin, Mooney, & Tremulis, 1972; Deno & Gross, 1973; Hammill & Wiederholt, 1972; Idol-Maestas, Lloyd, & Lilly, 1981; Reger & Koppmann, 1971; Wiederholt,1974), although this is not to say that whether a resource is categorical or noncategorical makes much difference in terms of educational advancement. A more important consideration is how close the match is between curricular content and child management procedures in the resource setting versus the regular classroom.

Another solution to both the categorical issue and the question of resource/ regular class match is to mainstream mildly handicapped students into regular classrooms. Lilly (1971) referred to this service model as a *zero reject model,* meaning that "Once a child is enrolled in a regular education program within a school, it must be impossible to administratively separate him [or her] from that program for any reason" (p. 745). Lilly maintained that two goals were accomplished through zero reject: (1) responsibility for failure was placed on teachers rather than students; and (2) educators could deny themselves the possibility of ultimate failure with a child.

An example of zero reject implementation has been described by Hewett (1975), in a report on the Madison School Plan in the Santa Monica Schools, which includes a strategy for compulsory reintegration of the educationally handicapped (ED and LD) students into regular classes. In June of each year, each student in a special class for educationally handicapped was reassigned to a regular classroom at chronological grade level. Exceptions were made only for seriously deficient or disordered students for whom reassignment would be unrealistic. At the beginning of the new school year, the reassigned students attended regular classes. The classroom teachers were told that the educationally handicapped students were being reassessed. They were further told that if a student could not maintain performance in the regular class, special classwork would begin again, but that the student's regular class desk would remain empty, as the teacher could anticipate the student's return to regular class.

Hewett reported results over a two-year period. Twenty percent of students reassigned the first year were never referred again. In addition, there was an error rate of approximately one-third between special and regular class teacher agreement. One-third of the students seen as ready for regular class integration were referred back to special classes, and one-third who were considered not ready for integration were never rereferred.

If teachers are not always in agreement about which behaviors constitute learning and behavior problems, then serious consideration must be given to the use of precise measurement of pupil performance in the regular classroom. Teacher agreement should be reached on the occurrence of behaviors, and initial attempts at remediation should occur in the classroom itself. Careful and cautious thought must be given to the effects special class placement and special education labels may have upon students.

Consideration of these issues can cause impact for change upon existing special education policies. For example, as a result of reports (Barnes, 1974; Mercer, 1970; 1971a, 1971b, 1973; C.E. Meyers, 1973) of cultural and economic disadvantages having an effect on intelligence test scores, some school districts have moved toward decertification of some EMR students. During the years 1969 to 1972, 12 California school districts (Meyers, MacMillan, & Yoshida, 1975) implemented decertification as a result of court orders and legislative movement. In these districts almost half of the EMR students were returned to regular classes.

Meyers et al. (1975) compared Metropolitan Achievement Test scores in reading and math of the following three groups: (1) students remaining in regular classes; (2) decertified EMR students; and (3) low achievers in regular classes who had never been classified as EMR. The low achievers were matched to the decertified students on grade level, sex, and ethnicity. When effects of grade level were equated through analysis of covariance, significant group differences were reported. Special class EMR students scored lower than decertified students on both reading and math achievement. Likewise, decertified students scored lower than low achievers on both measures. There were no differences between decertified and low achieving students in regard to letter grade assignments made by teachers.

SUMMARY

Reports such as those reported in this chapter have led some professionals to wonder whether some deliberate alterations must be executed in current models of service for mildly handicapped students. It seems, at best, that student potential for performance in regular classes must be examined rather than educators moving directly to special class or resource services as the first solution for students referred to special education. Consultation between special and regular educators is one solution to ensuring optimal regular class performance of problem students, with or without special education labels.

Chapter 3

Consultation: An Alternative Approach

CONCEPTS AND THEORIES

Consultation provided as a service to regular classroom teachers has been conceptualized by both educators and psychologists. J. Meyers (1973) proposed a consultation model for school psychologists based on the premise that specific treatments to children be provided indirectly from the consultant through another agent, in this case, the classroom teacher.

Meyers based some of his ideas in the triadic model of consultation (Tharp & Wetzel, 1969; Tharp, 1975). Tharp and Wetzel saw consultation as an extension of the principles of reinforcement to a systems level analysis of behavior change. In such a system, the consultant, the mediator, and the target have reciprocally reinforcing effects on one another. In the case of school consultation, the mediator would be the regular class teacher and the target would be the problematic student(s). Reciprocity is ongoing, as the consultant reinforces the regular class teacher for ideas and strategies that have an effect upon the student. The consultant is reinforced as the classroom teacher accepts and implements child management strategies that the consultant and mediator have prepared.

Effects of these strategies upon the student are reinforcing to the student as well as to the consultant and mediator. This positive effect increases the probability of more collaborative consultation in the future. Tharp (1975) makes an added point that the consultant forms a social contract with the mediator. Agreements are formed between the mediator and the target, but the primary basis for consultation is the social contract between the cooperating adults.

Over a seven-year period in the special education literature, proponents of consultation began to speak of the concept of special education consultative support of classroom teachers (Deno, 1970; Dunn, 1968; Lilly,

1971; Little, 1975; McKenzie, 1972; Meyen, 1969; Parker, 1975; Sabatino, 1972).

Deno (1970) presented a cascade of services that described the hierarchical types of special services that should be ideally available to exceptional students. At the top at the cascade (Level I), Deno described children in regular classes, including those "handicapped" who are able to get along with regular class accommodations with or without medical or counseling support services. Consulting teacher services would fit within this level. Level II is described as regular class attendance plus supplementary instructional services. Resource services would fit here; however, services provided by a resource/consulting teacher would include both Levels I and II. These services would include some resource instruction and some consultative services. Deno further identified these levels of service delivery as being noncategorical in nature. She took the position that the "problem is not in the child but in the mismatch that occurs between children's needs and the opportunities we provide to nurture his self-realization" (Deno, 1970, p. 229). Deno characterized special education as a tool to develop effective instructional approaches for hard-to-teach students in regular education as well as special education.

Some supporters of the concept of consulting teachers (Lilly, 1971; Newcomer, 1977; Reynolds & Birch, 1977) have recommended that consulting teachers or instructional specialists teach skills to classroom teachers so that they can cope with the classroom situation. Lilly maintained that during this period the diagnostic or tutorial work should be accomplished in the classroom itself in order to contribute to preparation of teacher coping skills.

Some advocates of consultation (Christie, McKenzie, & Burdett, 1972; McGlothlin, 1981; McKenzie, 1972; Meyen, 1969) have taken the position that the most effective way to teach these coping skills to classroom teachers is through inservice education programs. From this point of view, the primary role of the consulting teacher is to offer the inservice instruction. In Iowa, Meyen (1969) described a program that offered inservice through revolving consulting teachers. This way each district could disseminate areas of expertise of many individual teachers rather than a few. Consulting teacher appointments rotated from year to year among different special education teachers. These consulting teachers were trained to conduct inservice at the University of Iowa. At the University of Vermont, graduates of the consulting teacher program work as adjunct faculty to the university (Christie et al., 1972; McKenzie, 1972). These consulting teachers train and assist regular classroom teachers.

McGlothlin (1981) has proposed an alternative approach to the teacher consultant model: the school consultation committee. Each committee is made up of one special education teacher, one regular education primary-grade teacher, one regular education upper-grade teacher, and any personnel involved in consultant roles. Teachers selected have demonstrated success in classroom management. The members are selected by the building principal and a special education administrator. This committee screens referrals; pinpoints and assesses discrepancies between teacher expectations and child performance; and designs, implements, monitors, and evaluates intervention programs.

Similar to McGlothlin's school committee approach is an area team approach used in Texas, known as the Houston Plan (Dollar & Klinger, 1975). In this plan, the Houston school district was divided into six areas. Each area was assigned eight to ten supportive personnel, for example, psychologists, diagnosticians, special education counselors, and teacher consultants. An intent of the plan was to change systematically an existing categorical system for special education. The children were described as having behaviorial and/or learning difficulties. The teams gave support to maintain children in or return them to regular classrooms.

In contrast, Sabatino (1972) viewed resource services as those that should be broadened to include that of teacher consultant. This person would deliver methods and materials to regular classrooms. As an example of implementation, methods and materials specialists are used in New Mexico and Kansas. Sabatino described this job as one in which work could be done in the following areas:

- educational diagnosis, that is, rendering instructional objectives and special education curricula to be used primarily by other teachers
- development of curricular units and instructional processes
- team teaching with special or regular educators
- support of work of handicapped children in regular classes
- a front line of defense in establishing priorities for referrals

Some supporters of the concept of consultation would amend the first item in Sabatino's list (Blankenship & Lilly, 1981; Deno & Mirkin, 1977; Idol-Maestas, 1981; Jenkins & Mayhall, 1976). They would be more likely to recommend that remedial instruction should occur in the same curricular materials rather than using special education materials. In making recommendations for the role of school consultants, further support has been given to the idea of curricular assessment and instruction by writers in the field of psychology (Englemann, 1967; Forness, 1970; Valett, 1968). They posited that diagnosis of learning disorders should not be based on norm-referenced tests, but instead on specific academic programs regardless of chronological age in grade level. They encouraged school consultants to assess skills directly related to classroom tasks through task analytic procedures and then to make recommendations to classroom teachers. Procedures for developing CBAs are offered in Blankenship and Lilly (1981).

Jenkins and Mayhall (1976) proposed that two types of services be provided within a resource model: direct service and indirect service. Consultation with classroom teachers by resource specialists is defined as an indirect service. Direct services are those educational programs provided by the resource specialist in physical settings that are separated from the regular classroom. Jenkins and Mayhall are speaking strictly of resource services when they define direct services that are to be provided in concert with indirect services. They define the direct service process as containing six steps:

1. identifying core tasks
2. assessing core task performance
3. planning and implementing an intervention program
4. providing one to one daily instruction
5. instructing from a data base
6. terminating direct services (p. 24)

Some existing types of special settings that could be transformed to meet these direct service processes are all resource rooms, self-contained classrooms, remedial classes, federally funded programs for mathematics and reading instruction for the disadvantaged (that is, Title I programs), and speech and language tutorial programs. Any of these types of services could be modified to provide this type of direct service. Modification would include an indirect, consultative service to facilitate return to the regular classroom for many students. The majority of these types of services probably offer some of the direct service steps or at least partial approximations of them. This is especially true of the first four steps.

ALTERNATIONS IN DIRECT SERVICE PROGRAMS

Many direct service programs identify core tasks for students to work on, especially if these are special education programs and are generating IEPs. Jenkins and Mayhall (1976) recommended that when identifying core tasks, the tasks should be related to the curricula that are used in the regular classroom. In contrast, many special programs use a special set of curricula that is different than those used in the regular classroom. Some supportive data that reflect the academic gains that special children have made when direct instruction is offered in the same curriculum that is used in the regular class are reported by Idol-Maestas, Lloyd, and Lilly (1981). Gains of two and three months per month of instruction were not unusual. It is important to note that these pupil gains were true, regardless of labeled exceptionality or lack of labels, or if the students were labeled LD, cross-categorical, mildly retarded, or EMR, or if they were recipients of Title I instructional services. Related to core task performance in the curriculum, Jenkins and Mayhall also pointed out that the students should be assessed in the curriculum itself.

Planning and implementing intervention programs are factors that characterize most direct service programs. Obviously a change to curricular instruction would necessitate a change in the content of intervention programs. However, the important issue is that the framework already exists within all types of service delivery. Provision of one-to-one daily instruction is also an inherent part of most of these types of service. What may need some revision is the inclusion of data-based instruction. Education programs must move toward documentation of the measured effects of particular strategies of instruction. It is not sufficient to administer pretests and posttests, or group and individual tests as indicators of program success or failure. Direct and daily measures of pupil progress can be successfully collected in direct and indirect service settings.

The final step of the Jenkins and Mayhall model is terminating direct services. Two situations seem to be occurring in returning special students to regular classrooms. One is that there is a small body of research to describe systematic transfer to regular classes. Second is that, based on practical observation, many support service teachers are reconciled to the position that being "learned disabled" or "mildly retarded" is an unchanging situation. They are immersed in developing special programs for students to be offered in special environments. Such thinking may result in recommending continued special program support for the majority of their students. If special teacher interests are directed toward mainstreaming, they are often concerned with altering materials or modes of learning in the regular class. A concerted effort to combine instructional methodology to be used in regular class curriculums with behavioral levels of performance and criterion levels that meet classroom teacher expectations is an effort that is not occurring as often as it might.

The following example of a practical observation made in an elementary school illustrates this lack of systematic planning for eventual reentry into regular classes. A graduate intern in a competency-based teacher education program (Idol-Maestas, 1981) was required to return at least one student to regular education during the course of a year. When the graduate student had the student reading at the grade level that was required in the child's classroom, she began to make plans to transfer reading instruction to the regular classroom. The resource teacher, who served as cooperating teacher, responded that it was great that the student was reading at grade level, but the school district policy was to review the progress of special education students at the end of the school year. This teacher further recommended that the child continue to receive resource services for reading for the remainder of the year. The rationale was that if the student was doing so well, then progress would be even better by the end of the school year. Supportive personnel must begin to plan constructively for returning remediated behaviors to regular class settings, especially when projected performance levels have been reached.

EVALUATION OF CONSULTATION

A pertinent question raised by educators who are contemplating the inclusion of consultation within their existing service delivery models is whether or not consultation is an efficacious alternative. A survey designed to assess current teaching practices (Westland, Koorland, & Rose, 1981) revealed a relationship between consultation and superior teaching in special education. Some teaching practices of special educators who were selected by the directors of special education in 80 percent of the school districts in Florida were compared to a group of average special educators in three of the same districts. The average group were the remaining special educators after the top special educators had been selected. In response to a questionnaire item, 58 percent of the superior teachers consulted with regular class teachers as part of their regular teaching duties. The majority of the average teachers did not consult with classroom teachers as a regular duty.

If superior teachers do consult, then it may benefit school districts to train teachers to work as supportive personnel to classroom teachers. In 1976, Cantrell and Cantrell reported on the results of implementation of the Prevention-Intervention Project, which was designed to solve student problems prior to referral for formalized services. This involved training "support" teachers to work in conjunction with public school teachers. The support teachers were trained in areas found useful by teachers in Re-ED schools. Project Re-ED (Hobbs, 1963) is an educational model used in some programs for emotionally disturbed children. It was originally implemented in short-term residential settings. Some intervention principles were applied by Cantrell and Cantrell in remediation of public school students. Ten support teachers were trained in the following areas: (a) behavioral principles; (b) basic evaluation techniques; (c) program relevant assessment; (d) academic programming; (e) methods of contingency management; (f) group process; and (g) coordinated ecological planning.

Program evaluation consisted of comparing an experimental group of first graders (723 pupils and 37 classroom teachers), who worked with the ten support teachers, to a first-grade control group (355 pupils and 18 classroom teachers) with no supportive assistance. Two elementary experimental schools and two control schools from each of five school systems in Tennessee were included. One-half of the control schools participated in pupil achievement testing and classroom observations for one year. The second half of the control schools were included in the pupil referral data gathered during the project's second year. Achievement was measured by constructing predicted achievement scores. The predicted achievement scores were obtained by regressing students' initial scores on listening, reading, numbers, and IQ scores to predict outcome on the past year scores for the same measures. The residuals of the resulting prediction equation were used as the dependent measures (predicted achievement scores) to compare the academic achievement differences between experimental and control groups. As a group, the children in the first-grade classes with support teachers had significantly higher academic achievement at the end of the first year than did the classes with no consultative support.

The Cantrells (1976) also examined the incidences and types of special education referrals that were made over a two-year period. Over four times more first-grade children and two times more second-grade children were referred by control teachers with no support than were referred by teachers working with support teachers. The types of referrals are reported in Table 3–1. It is interesting to note that the referral types that were most discrepant between the groups were intellectual handicaps, underachieve-

---

Table 3–1 Types of Referrals from Experimental and Control School Teachers for Psychological Services

Groups	Intellectual Handicap	Perceptual Handicap	Under-achievement	Physical Handicap	Emotional Handicap	Other
Experimental	2	8	7	1	5	6
Control	12	9	34	0	10	5

Source: Reprinted from R.P. Cantrell and M.L. Cantrell, "Preventive Mainstreaming: Impact of a Supportive Service Program on Pupils," *Exceptional Children,* 1976, *42* (7), 381–386.

ment, and emotional handicaps. First- and second-grade teachers with support had markedly lower referrals for these areas.

Three reports (Knight, Meyers, Paolucci-Whitcomb, Hasazi, & Nevin, 1981; Miller & Sabatino, 1978; Wixson, 1980) have been published that evaluated program successes of consulting teacher programs compared to more traditional resource programs. Miller and Sabatino (1978) compared effects of a control group to a special education resource model and a model containing teacher consultant and resource services. The control group was not clearly defined, but it was assumed that it was composed of LD and EMR students attending regular classes with no services. The subjects in the study were 504 LD students (IQ<85; ≥ 2 years behind academically; poor performance on perceptual language expression measures) and 43 EMR students (IQ<75; ≥ 2 years behind academically).

In the teacher consultant model, 17 consultant teachers offered supportive service to 153 regular teachers in 29 schools. The consultants served the schools in the following variable schedules depending on the school: full day every day, full day every other day, or full day every third day. All services offered were of an indirect type. In the resource room model, 16 resource teachers served 122 regular teachers in 29 schools. The tests used to measure performance were the Wide Range Achievement Test (WRAT) and the reading comprehension subtest of the Peabody Individual Achievement Test (PIAT).

The duration of the Miller and Sabatino study was six months. During that time, the students in both the teacher consultant model and the resource room model achieved significantly higher posttest scores for WRAT word recognition and arithmetic. There were no significant differences between the resource room and the consultant models. The students in the control group made no changes in measured performance during the six-month period. For these students, placement in a regular classroom served by a consulting teacher was as beneficial as being assigned to a resource room for a portion of the school day.

Miller and Sabatino also observed some specific teacher behavior in order to identify changes or differences in how teachers acted within the two models. The behaviors were observed three days a week for three weeks at the beginning and end of the study. The observation periods were 20 minutes, and there were four observers. Interrater reliabilities calculated during the training session ranged from .88 to .94. Teacher consultants made significantly better gains than resource teachers for the following three behaviors: accepting feelings; praising and encouraging students; and accepting or using ideas of the students.

Wixson (1980) also compared direct and indirect services for learning and behavior disordered (LBD) students. Wixson hypothesized that a two-component resource program offering direct and indirect services could serve more LBD students than one conventional direct service program without appreciable loss in program effectiveness. During the first year of this evaluation, students were served through direct service; for the second year they received direct and/or indirect services. In the direct service component, students were assessed, and a prescriptive program was offered in resource rooms. The students receiving indirect services were evaluated in the same manner, except the prescriptive program was implemented by the classroom teacher. Teacher consultation was provided to each student's classroom teacher.

For the second year the characteristics of students in direct versus indirect services were different. In direct services approximately 130 students previously assigned to self-contained classes for LBD were transferred to regular classrooms and subsequently referred for resource services. These students were described as typically manifesting multiple deficits in academic skills together with motivational problems and/or behavior disorders. The most frequent cause for referral to resource programs was academic difficulty. Behavior disorders were the second most frequent referral problem. The 73 students who received indirect services presented less severe and less persistent learning and/or behavior disorders. In contrast to students in direct services, the most frequent referral cause was behavior disorders; academic difficulty was the second most frequent cause of referral. At least for the students in this report, the classroom teachers more readily accepted students who had academic problems with satisfactory behavior than students with lesser academic problems and persistent behavior disorders.

Program effectiveness was evaluated by measuring the proportion of the total number of direct and indirect service programs that were successful during the academic year. A successful program was one in which a student was returned to full-time participation in the regular class without supportive services from the resource teacher. Academic and/or social adjustment had to be deemed satisfactory by the classroom teacher in order for a program to be rated as satisfactory. During the first year, six resource teachers provided direct service to 156 students. Thirty percent of these students were returned to regular classes, and these programs were classified as successful. The average number of program successes per teacher was 10.1. During the second year, 30 percent of the students in direct services were again classified as program successes. Fifty-seven percent of students in indirect services were program successes. The average number of direct program successes decreased from 10.1 to 7.1 students per resource teacher. However, an average of six students per teacher were program successes in the indirect component. The final result was that the average number of students served with the direct/indirect component was larger than the direct service component alone.

The state of Vermont has used consulting services since 1970. A four-year evaluation of the Vermont consulting teacher program is reported by Knight et al. (1981). This consulting service consists of an integration of inservice teacher education and child instruction. The underlying principles of these services are based on direct measurement, behavior analysis, instructional design, and data-based instruction. Direct observation, review of school documents, and interviews were used to assess the services. Elementary schools that utilized teacher consultation were compared to schools that did not. Specific comparisons were made between service and nonservice groups' reading and mathematics achievement as measured by the Stanford Achievement Test (SAT). Prior to the use of the teacher consultant, there were no significant differences between the two subsets of schools in the spring of grade five (1975). After implementation of teacher consultation in service schools (spring of 1976), there were significant differences between service and nonservice schools for reading and mathematics for grade six. The initial gain made by students in grade six maintained through grades seven and eight. Those gains remained significantly higher than student gains in nonservice schools for the same grade levels.

Equally supportive of consultation is a program evaluation report for consulting teachers in Kentucky (Nelson & Stevens, 1981). Nelson and Stevens have recorded the frequencies of successful and nonsuccessful regular class consultations over a two-year period. These data were provided to assess the efficacy of a consultation model that could be used by public school personnel. The teacher consultants were university personnel (faculty and advanced graduate students). In 1977–1978, twenty-five consultation projects were completed. Fifteen were successful, eight were partially successful, and two were failures. In 1978–1979, consultation cases were divided into formal and informal categories. Thirteen formal cases were evaluated, of which eight were successful, four were partially successful, and one was a failure. The evaluation was collected via questionnaires sent to the regular class teachers. *Successful* was defined as three criteria in the questionnaire being met, *partial success* was defined as two of the three criteria being met, and *failure* meant less than two criteria were met. In summary, approximately 60 percent of the consultations were successful. Of a total of 29 projects, only three were evaluated as failures. As a matter of further reference, Nelson and Stevens have also delineated the exact types of student behaviors involved in the projects and which ones were successfully remediated.

Given that consultation is a relatively recent approach to providing support services for handicapped students, these efficacy reports are encouraging. If consultation is as effective as these accounts indicate, then preparation programs for teachers of the mildly handicapped might do well to consider adding a consultation component to resource training models.

TRAINING PROGRAMS FOR CONSULTATION

University of Northern Iowa

At the University of Northern Iowa, special education consultants and resource strategists complete training modules in consultation skills. Little (1975) asserts that teacher consultation students need training experience in the following:

- change agent skills
- interpersonal relations
- communication techniques
- personal growth techniques
- group process
- educational problem solving
- advanced diagnostic and treatment design techniques

This graduate training program is presented in package form and is used to develop competencies for content and process aspects of consultation. The package was specifically written for categorical consultants, noncategorical consultants, and resource strategists. Little indicates that other professionals (school psychologists, educational diagnosticians, resource teachers, and classroom teachers) who are engaged in consultation may also find the training package useful.

Within this package, the consultation process is viewed as containing five subcomponents: planning; observation; analysis; strategy; and conference. During *planning* the consultant identifies teacher objective(s) and areas of concern related to the objectives. Then, as a result of information exchange between the teacher and the consultant, the objective and/or strategy is reformulated. This reformulation is based on feedback, effect data, and desired changes from the initial teacher/consultant conference or follow-up conferences. *Observation* is the collection of performance data obtained during the planning step. During *analysis,* data patterns are examined, and hypothesized sources and effects of the patterns are considered to determine if a problem exists and the nature of the problem.

During *strategy,* specific patterns of concern and possible alternative steps for remediation are identified and prioritized. A provisional strategy is formulated based on the desired changes. During *conference,* the consultant and teacher convey patterns of concern and possible training steps in the form of a treatment strategy. If a new objective or other substantial changes are appropriate, then the consultation process is returned to the *planning* stage.

University of Minnesota

At the University of Minnesota, special education resource teachers (SERTs) are prepared to work with regular education teachers to maintain handicapped children in mainstream classrooms (Deno & Mirkin, 1977). Special education resource teachers provide direct service with individualized, data-based instruction and indirect service by consulting with or training classroom teachers. For the SERT model, the goal of consultation is to ensure that a client, usually the classroom teacher, implements data-based program modification for individual students who are eligible for special education services. The measure of consultation effectiveness is the extent to which the SERT is successful in helping client teachers use data-based instruction to identify pupil progress and performance problems of mainstream students. Deno and Mirkin have outlined the services that are provided by a school-based SERT, which are listed in Table 3–2.

Note that the central theme of the consultation activity in Table 3–2 is the consultant guiding and assisting the classroom teacher, rather than becoming directly responsible for problem identification, data collection, and program modification and implementation. An important strategy included within this list of activities (item number 7) is the inclusion of a contractual agreement between involved parties. A consultation agreement is written that delineates the targeted behavior; the remediation procedures; and the responsibilities of the student, the teacher, and the SERT. All three persons read and sign the contract. Deno and Mirkin (1977) have provided some excellent referential examples of various forms of such a contractual agreement.

University of Vermont

At the University of Vermont, consulting teachers are prepared to train other teachers primarily through inservice offerings in child management strategies (McKenzie, Egner, Knight, Perelman, Schneider, & Garvin, 1970). Students in this two-year master of education program (McKenzie, 1972) are instructed in behavior modification techniques as a means of

Table 3–2 Consultation and Training Activities

Consultation Activity
1. Teacher identifies the need for assistance from SERT in developing a program modification for a student in his/her class.
2. SERT meets with the teacher to help pinpoint the specific behavior that the teacher wishes to modify.
3. SERT provides teacher with necessary materials and assistance to collect data on the discrepancy between the student's current level of functioning and the desired performance for the pinpointed behavior.
4. SERT helps teacher summarize the data collected and establish importance of the problem.

----

5. SERT meets with the teacher and student (and parent) to develop a program modification.
6. Guidelines are established for implementing and monitoring the program modification, and the responsibilities of all persons involved are defined.
7. Commitments are elicited from persons involved on their willingness to participate in the program plan. The result of this action is usually in the form of a contract.

----

8. Teacher begins to implement plan.
9. SERT assists teacher as specified in contract.

----

10. SERT and teacher meet to evaluate effectiveness of program plan weekly or at least every other week.
11. SERT assists teacher in summarizing data and generating alternative strategies on the basis of data collected by teacher.
12. Teacher implements program changes as agreed upon and continues with program operationalization.

----

13. Teacher meets with student and parent (when appropriate) to evaluate objectives achieved and determine if program should be terminated.

Source: Reprinted from Deno, S.L. and Mirkin, P.K. *Data-Based Program Modification.* Reston Va.: Council for Exceptional Children, *1977, p. 209.*

assisting regular classroom teachers with social and academic behaviors of handicapped children. The following is an itemization of what the consulting teacher learns to do during the course of preparation (Christie, McKenzie, & Burdett, 1972):

- Learns principles of applied behavior analysis.
- Applies these principles to eligible children in regular classrooms.
- Learns to measure and monitor daily performance to ensure that applications are effective.
- Individualizes instruction.
- Adapts materials typically available in elementary classrooms.
- Learns to derive for classrooms and entire elementary schools a minimum set of objectives that every child should achieve in language, arithmetic, and social behaviors.
- Learns procedures for training teachers, parents, aides, and other school personnel in behavior analysis, measurement, individualizing instruction, and deriving minimum objectives.

In the Vermont consulting teacher model (Fox, Egner, Paolucci, Perelman, McKenzie, & Garvin, 1973), the consultation process begins when a student has been referred by a classroom teacher for special educational services. Eligibility for special services is determined when the following criteria are met:

1. The teacher refers the child to the consulting teacher. This referral must include a statement indicating deficits in language, arithmetic, and/or social behavior, and a statement signed by the teacher indicating that the referred child has a profound need for consulting teacher services.
2. *Measured* levels of language, arithmetic, and/or social behaviors, which the referring teacher had indicated are deficient, *must* deviate from minimum objectives (Fox et al., 1973, p. 24).

The consulting teacher then begins to train the referring teacher by developing classroom management systems that will assess referred target behaviors that deviate from minimum objectives. The consulting teacher and the classroom teachers identify target behaviors, entry level behaviors, instructional objectives, teaching/learning procedures, reinforcement procedures, and methods for evaluation.

For the first year of the training program, trainees complete coursework and school practica, which include training of school personnel and consultation with parents of eligible children. During the second year, internships are completed in Vermont school districts. Consulting teachers-in-training are evaluated on the basis of mastery of minimum training objectives.

There has also been cooperation between the university program and the state of Vermont. The Vermont State Department of Education has been directly involved in the development of this approach (McKenzie et al., 1970). The Division of Special Education and Pupil Personnel Services provides 75 percent of consulting teacher and necessary aide salary, which provides incentive to school districts to adopt a consulting teacher model. The division also discourages the use of special classes for moderately handicapped students when consulting teacher services are available or can be made available. Before consulting teachers are hired by districts, representatives from the university describe the objectives of the consulting teacher approach to district administrators. Consulting teachers and those in training offer presentations to school personnel and school board members to facilitate adoption of this model. Upon employment by a district, the consulting teacher becomes an adjunct instructor at the university; thus, teachers taking training courses from the consulting teacher are offered graduate courses.

Simmons College

The generic consulting teacher program at Simmons College in Massachusetts (Lates & Mesch, 1981) is similar to the Vermont program in that it is competency-based, and a major focus in placed upon implementation of the principles of applied behavior analysis to manage problematic students. Teachers who are employed in local districts attend this program on a part-time basis for two years while they continue their school employment. They earn certification as generic teachers and/or complete a master's degree program. This program has provided inservice training to professional educators in school districts in the Boston area since 1975. Upon completion of the master's degree program, graduates are eligible to become inservice trainers for regular educators and to act as adjunct faculty to the college. These graduates also continue to work as consulting teachers in their respective buildings. Five competency areas have been identified as component parts of the generic teacher role:

1. service to special needs learners
2. curriculum development and adaptation
3. training other educational personnel

4. dissemination and communication
5. program development, management, and evaluation.

University of Illinois

The Resource/Consulting Teacher (R/CT) Program at the University of Illinois (Idol-Maestas, 1981; Idol-Maestas, Lloyd, & Lilly, 1981) offers a competency-based training model for consulting teachers that encompasses direct and indirect services. The direct services part of the model has developed from that proposed by Jenkins and Mayhall (1976) and discussed earlier in this chapter. For direct service, the resource/consulting teacher works in a resource-type setting. The direct service is offered in the form of tutorial or small group instruction. As recommended by Jenkins and Mayhall, the instruction is data-based with direct and daily measures of pupil performances. An emphasis is placed upon training students in the curricula used in each regular student classroom. All decisions regarding curricular placement are data-based and depend on criterial performance. Cross-age tutors are used to increase the number of students who receive direct, data-based instruction. A booklet that delineates how peer tutoring can be used with children with learning problems has been written by Jenkins and Jenkins (1981). In essence, the R/CT acts as a monitor over a number of tutor/tutee pairs. The tutor follows an instructional sequence that is an exact replica of that provided by the R/CT in one-to-one instruction. This tutor makes no instructional decisions, but rather follows the prescribed sequence. The teacher-monitor takes reliability measurements on the pupil progress data that the tutor is recording and ensures that the tutor is following the instructional plan using correct methodology and error correction procedures. Use of a tutor model is an expedient solution in order to serve a number of students in direct instruction and yet reserve a sufficient number of hours for the R/CT to work as a consulting teacher.

An integral part of an R/CT's job is to plan and implement systematically the transfer of behaviors acquired in the direct service setting to the regular classroom. This transfer component requires close cooperation and collaboration between the R/CT and the classroom teacher of the student who is being transferred. Identical teacher expectations and reinforcement programs must be agreed upon so that the variable that changes in the student's instructional program is a site change (from resource to regular classroom) and nothing more.

For a portion of the school day, R/CTs offer indirect service through consultation with regular classroom teachers for special students attending

regular classes. The consultative services are provi
tion students, but they are not an inclusive group of
benefits. Other problematic students, without special
benefit from this service. All consultative efforts are
objective evaluation by all members of the consultal
ples of consultations that are reported in this book have been accomplished
by R/CTs while studying in this preparation program. Parents are sometimes included in consultation efforts, as are social workers and other
support personnel who are involved with a student. This work with parents
is one form of child advocacy that R/CTs offer. They also serve as advocates for special children in the school and the community. They complete
coursework pertaining to supportive laws for and rights of handicapped
students. They demonstrate competency in preparing and presenting inservice training sessions. They are prepared to offer inservice for small groups
of classroom teachers, as well as to share information on an individual
basis.

R/CT consultations with classroom teachers are designed to fit the following set of guidelines. These have been established to ensure that R/
CTs provide consultative services, not tutorial services, within the regular
classroom.

- Establish a referral system that ensures that teachers can request
  assistance without formally referring a student for special services.
  This practice eliminates the need to refer some students to special
  education and encourages teachers to solve problems.

- Meet with the classroom teacher to define and prioritize problematic
  social behaviors and/or academic subject areas collectively. Some
  students may have so many problems that teachers are overwhelmed.
  A good practice is to identify a workable number of problems to focus
  on. Other problem areas can be added later. Sometimes targeting on
  a few behaviors eliminates other troublesome behaviors.

- Design and demonstrate a data collection procedure that can be implemented in the classroom by the classroom teacher. If the data collection system is too elaborate, the classroom teacher may become discouraged and terminate collection.

- Obtain behavioral observation data to determine the extent of the
  referred problem(s) (baseline data). If possible, these data should be
  collected by the classroom teacher. The consulting teacher should
  obtain reliability data. Under some circumstances the data collection
  roles must be reversed. If this role reversal is necessary at onset, it is

important to trade roles as soon as the classroom teacher feels comfortable with the measurement procedures.

- For academic subjects, analyze the student's performance skills on CBAs that reflect samples of curricular content. This should be done in collaboration with the classroom teacher. Criterial definitions of acceptable performance must meet classroom teacher expectations.

- Confer with the classroom teacher to summarize performance data and select appropriate remedial interventions. The interventions must be those that the classroom teacher is willing to try. They must be easy to administer.

- Demonstrate or practice the selected intervention with the classroom teacher. What the two collaborating teachers have designed on paper may be difficult to administer. A practice demonstration is a solution to this problem. It also serves as a means for the two collaborators to ensure that they agree upon the procedures.

- Collect direct and daily measures of pupil performance after the method of remediation has been selected. This should be structured so the classroom teacher can easily collect the data. The consulting teacher collects reliability data.

- Examine the performance data regularly to determine whether further modifications are necessary. This is a crucial step. Sometimes novice data collectors become immersed in collection and forget to examine performance trends. It is also important to measure the effects of an intervention for at least five days before dropping or changing it. It may take that long for the intervention to take effect.

- Share the pupil performance data with students and their parents. Accumulated data are useful to illustrate to parents and students the actual progress a student has made. For many students these charted data become powerful reinforcers.

SUMMARY

Some elements of five preparation programs for consulting teachers have been reviewed. All of the programs are competency-based, which illustrates the importance the diagnosis of those programs places upon demonstration of mastery of skills. All of the program philosophies view collection of a data base of pupil performance as an essential and integral part of consultation. One program (Little, 1975) is designed particularly to give consulting teachers preparation in communication skills essential to consultation.

COMMUNICATION EXCHANGE

Exhibit 3–1 Do's and Don'ts for Consultants

DO	DON'T
. . . remember that people *are* capable of solving their own problems.	. . . tell a teacher you will help with a child without spelling out exactly what you think your responsibilities are.
. . . try to accept other's values.	
. . . be fully aware of your own values.	
. . . have a specific way that teachers can get your help.	. . . schedule yourself so tightly that you don't have time to meet with teachers for immediate consultation.
. . . be knowledgeable about all school and community resources available.	. . . act as if you have all the answers to solve a teacher's problem.
. . . save time and help more teachers learn how to use your services; meet with a teaching team or department at meeting times.	. . . become the "middle person" to take teacher's gripes to the principal.
	. . . push when the consultee is not ready to move.
. . . have a wide variety of materials to help teachers.	. . . let your need to help get in the way of the needs of the consultee.
. . . let teachers know you value their knowledge.	. . . expect to see immediate results you'll get discouraged.
. . . try to be involved in school activities.	

Source: Reprinted from Deno, S.L. and Mirkin, P.K. *Data-Based Program Modification.* Reston, Va.: Council for Exceptional Children, 1977, p. 215.

Chapter 4

Laying the Groundwork for Systematic Transfer to the Regular Classroom

Successful mainstreaming of mildly handicapped students into regular classes depends on concentration in two major areas: (1) remediation of academic and social behavior problems in regular classrooms; and (2) systematic transfer of skills remediated in special education settings to regular classrooms.

AN EMPIRICAL BASE FOR SUCCESSFUL TRANSFER?

Special educators, particularly resource teachers, often aim for the ultimate goal of eventual return of mildly handicapped students to regular class instruction with a gradual "phasing out" of special education services. Yet, one follow-up study involving LD resource teachers in 20 school districts that were selected for offering preferred service delivery in North Carolina does not support the premise that resource teachers actively maintain progress data on students returned to regular classes (McKinney & Feagans, 1980). Seventy-five percent of reviewed LD teachers indicated that they had not followed children who were returned to mainstream settings. These were children who no longer received direct special education services. The same teachers indicated that they did their own formative evaluations while children were enrolled in the special programs.

A more pertinent finding than the lack of immediate follow-up strategies was that although LD teachers perceived positive changes on important dimensions of classroom behavior, their perceptions were not consistent with those of classroom teachers. These data were collected in a follow-up study one year after students had received resource services. This report indicates that the improvement seen in the resource setting by the

61

LD teachers did not generalize to regular classroom teacher observations a year later.

Also supporting the report from North Carolina that LD students did not maintain gains made in the resource room are data collected by Ito (1980) in New Mexico. Ito conducted a follow-up study of 62 learning disabled children who had previously received resource services for academic difficulties. At the time of the study, the subjects had been enrolled full-time in elementary grades for one full school year following resource room attendance. The WRAT was used to measure reading, spelling, and arithmetic achievement (1) upon placement in the resource program; (2) upon termination of participation in the resource program; and (3) upon completion of a one year, full-time placement in regular grades. The children made significant gains as a result of receiving resource services, but these increased learning rates were not maintained after the children attended regular programs for a year. The data were also examined by the length of time children received resource services. The shorter the duration (two to six months), the higher the reading gain was; the longer the stay (seven to ten months), the lower the reading gain was. The differential performance regarding program duration may be due to differing abilities upon entrance to the resource program, in that the more seriously disabled students may have spent more time in the program. However, the fact remains that, regardless of degree of handicap, achievement gains were not maintained over time.

A reservation that could be placed on interpretation of these results concerns the adequacy of the test used to measure performance gains (WRAT). It is limited in terms of what is measured (isolated word recognition with no comprehension measure, and isolated word spelling and arithmetic computation on a single trial basis with no arithmetic comprehension on problem-solving tasks). However, the same device was used to measure gain in all three phases, which should reflect gain over time however limited the obtained information might be.

An earlier study (Vacc, 1975) reported the same decrease in achievement gains after return to the regular class for behavior disordered students. Vacc reexamined the subjects of an earlier study (Vacc, 1968) to determine whether gains made in special classes were lasting. Although the number of subjects had decreased from 32 to 21, the special class and regular class groups continued to be homogeneous for social class, grade level, intelligence, age in months, and achievement level. Progress data were examined for children who had experienced special class placement and had then returned to the regular class for at least two years, as compared with the records of those who had always attended the regular class. Over this extended period of time, achievement gains on the WRAT of those students who were once in special classes did not differ from those consistently retained in regular classes, even though five years earlier the gains of the special class students had been superior.

Another study (Glavin, 1974) also documented the lack of generalization of academic and behavioral resource program gains of behavior disordered students once they were returned to regular classes. Half the students in this follow-up study had been attending regular classes on a full-time basis for two to three years and had previously been enrolled as resource students in programs using token economies in which behavior modification procedures were used. The remaining students had always received instruction in regular classes. The majority of students in both groups exhibited conduct-problem behaviors. The initial findings indicated that resource students had significantly improved social behavior and academic gains when compared to controls. Social behavior of the resource students did not improve in regular classes, which was not different than social behavior of controls. Essentially, social behavior improved under the effect of the token economy program, but the desired behaviors did not maintain under the looser structure of child management strategies used in the regular classes.

Even more serious than the lack of immediate transfer of improved social behavior were the findings of the follow-up study itself. Academic gains as measured by the California Achievement Test (CAT) (reading vocabulary, reading comprehension, arithmetic reasoning, and arithmetic fundamentals) failed to sustain over time. The same lack of maintenance of social behavior gains as measured by the Behavior Problem Checklist was reported at follow up. These disappointing results were true for both the second and third years of follow up.

Reported follow-up data on groups of mainstreamed students are clearly lacking in the literature. Four available studies (Glavin, 1974; Ito, 1980; McKinney & Feagans, 1980; Vacc, 1975) contain disappointing results. They infer that special educators cannot depend on the assumption that academic and social behaviors remediated in special settings will generalize to regular classrooms. One study (McKinney & Feagans, 1980) further implies that special teachers do not always systematically follow mainstreamed students to ensure their success. In some instances (Glavin, 1974), the remediated behaviors may not even generalize across settings to regular classes *while* the students are receiving special instruction.

O'Connor, Stuck, and Wyne (1979) established highly structured resource programs for second, third, and sixth grades based on J.B. Carroll's (1963) model of mastery learning and then examined the aftereffects of this intensive programming. The basic finding was that resource room pupils spent significantly more time on-task and achieved at significantly higher levels of reading immediately following the intervention when compared to counterparts in regular classrooms. An added strength of the O'Connor et al. (1979) study is that a follow-up evaluation component was included to examine generalization effects after the resource students were returned to regular classes on a full-time basis. Over a period of four months, improved on-task and reading levels maintained in regular classes. An important trend was observed for on-task behavior for both second/third grades and sixth grades. Three to four weeks after students had returned to regular classes, there was a decrease in desired on-task behaviors. After the older students had been in the regular classes seven to eight weeks, there was a subsequent increase in on-task behavior. (See Figure 4–1.) The younger students maintained the same average level of on-task behavior during the seventh/eighth weeks as they did after the third/fourth weeks. (See Figure 4–2.) A similar phenomenon has been reported by Walker & Hops (1976), who also observed generalization of appropriate behaviors to regular classrooms from an experimental classroom.

These follow-up data not only demonstrate that the remediated behaviors were generalized to regular classes, but that teachers should expect a decrease in desired performance when classroom environments are altered.

Figure 4–1 Mean Percent Time On-Task of Resource-Room and Comparison-Group Sixth Graders

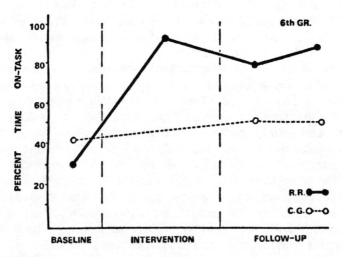

Source: Reprinted from P.D. O'Connor, G.B. Stuck, and M.D. Wyne, "Effects of Short-Term Intervention Resource-Room Program on Task Orientation and Achievement," *Journal of Special Education,* 1979, p. 380.

Figure 4–2 Mean Percent Time On-Task of Resource-Room and Comparison-Group Second and Third Graders

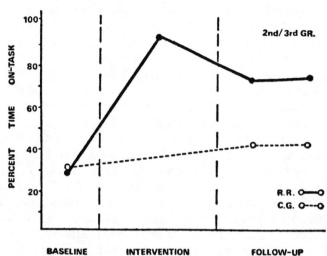

Source: Reprinted from P.D. O'Connor, G.B. Stuck, and M.D. Wyne, "Effects of Short-Term Intervention Resource-Room Program on Task Orientation and Achievement," *Journal of Special Education,* 1979, p. 379.

The data may suggest that special education teachers should set slightly higher criterion levels for performance in direct service settings as a precaution for less efficient performance, which may be a behavioral reaction to a change in classroom settings.

CONCEPTS THAT FACILITATE TRANSFER

While training teachers to work as teacher consultants (Idol-Maestas, 1981), some concepts have been identified that have proved to facilitate transfer of remediated behaviors from direct service settings to regular classrooms. Those concepts are the following: (1) mastery learning; (2) data-based instruction; (3) direct curricular instruction; (4) systematic structuring of learning environments; and (5) programming for behavior generalization.

Mastery Learning

Mastery learning (Bloom, 1971, 1974) is based on the premise that most students can reach a criterion level of achievement if sufficient time, necessary assistance, and student motivation to use allotted worktime are provided. Another basis of mastery learning stemming from the J.B. Carroll (1963) model of learning is that individuals differ in their learning rates, which leads to the hypothesis that individualization of learning rate with a sequenced set of learning materials should result in mastery of materials for most students. In mastery learning, accepted criterion levels of performance are set, and a formative criterion-based test is used to determine student mastery. Performance to criterion is also an integral part of data-based instruction, which is described in a subsequent section.

Mastery learning studies (Bloom, 1974) indicate that if time and assistance are provided as needed, 90 percent or more of students finally attain the set criterion. This predictive percentage is based on group instruction for individual learning units. The special needs students who might be referred to a consulting teacher could fall within this 90 percent or they may fall within the remaining 10 percent. To determine into which percentage group a referred student might fall, the instruction in the regular class could be altered. This could be accomplished through copreparation between the classroom teacher and the teacher consultant. The collaborating teachers could make certain that the lesson materials were sequenced in a hierarchical order, and they could construct criterion-referenced tests for subunits within the materials. They could structure the management system of the classroom so that amount of assistance provided is relative to the needs of individual students. A cross-age or within-class tutoring program (Jenkins & Jenkins, 1981) might be implemented to increase instruction time for students needing the most time for instruction. Advanced students could be given the opportunity to progress at their true aptitude levels rather than advancing at the slower average rate of progression of the entire class.

If a special needs student still fails to master materials under these defined conditions, then direct instruction with a resource teacher is an alternative. If direct resource instruction becomes inevitable, then precautions should be taken to use the same instructional units and criterion levels established for the regular class. A goal should be set at the onset of resource instruction as to when the classroom teacher can expect the student to return to regular class instruction.

Data-Based Instruction

Data-based instruction (DBI) is a means by which behaviors can be remediated and successfully transferred to other settings. Data-based instruction is a scientific way of describing, measuring, and assessing behavior. It has developed from the behavioral theories of B.F. Skinner, who defined the principles of operant conditioning (Skinner, 1938) and continued to experiment with behavior analysis through the 1960s.

Precision Teaching

A predecessor to DBI is precision teaching. Precision teaching is characterized by the application of applied behavior analysis to instructional remediation of academic behaviors. A typical definition of precision teaching is included in a mainstreaming project for mildly handicapped children (Bradfield, Brown, Kaplan, Rickert, & Stannard, 1973) completed in the early 1970s. In that project, precision teaching was defined as the following:

- pinpointing a behavior by selecting and operationally defining the behavior of concern
- recording the frequency of the pinpointed behavior and the number of minutes during which the behavior occurred
- computing the rate of the behavior, based on frequency of behavior per minutes
- charting the behavior rates on a six-cycle logarithmic chart
- intervening to accelerate or decelerate the behavior rate
- repeating and modifying the intervention if the charts indicate less than desirable changes.

From this basic concept of precision teaching, in which behaviors were operationally defined, measured, recorded, and assessed to determine success of instructional programming has evolved the precise and systematic means of instruction known as DBI. Blankenship and Lilly (1981) have listed eight basic steps of the DBI model as being:

1. Statement of problem in behavioral terms.
2. Collection of baseline data.
3. Statement of instructional objectives.
4. Analysis of instructional objectives into teachable components (if necessary due to the complexity of objectives).
5. Determination of teaching-learning procedure and initiation of instruction.
6. Continuous measurement of student progress toward objectives.
7. Charting student progress data.
8. Instructional decision-making concerning adequacy of intervention. (p. 41)

The Efficacy of the DBI Model

Chapter 5 contains child-change projects that focus on returning students to regular classrooms. These projects are based on a data-based instructional model as defined by Blankenship and Lilly (1981).

The effects of using a precise teaching methodology to ensure successful and acceptable mainstreaming of students with behavioral and academic problems have been documented in the earlier mainstreaming literature. A good example is that in which Bradfield et al. (1973) devised an educational treatment that included precision teaching and concrete reinforcement based on the premise that the structure of the regular class must be modified not only to accommodate the special child but to provide individualized instruction. They reasoned that to return children to the precise environments that rejected them would be to ensure mainstreaming failure. For the first year, which began in 1969, three EMR and three educationally handicapped (EH) were placed in a third-grade classroom. All six children had previously attended self-contained classes.

The instructional design for the entire class included a learning center approach to individualized instruction together with behavior modification techniques and inservice training for teachers. Pretests and posttests for academic achievement, self-concept, and behavior ratings were used to measure progress. At the end of their first year, the special children saw themselves more favorably and did as well academically as previous classmates who remained in special classes. However, a more serious result emerged: the overall achievement of the remaining third graders in some subject areas fell below that of another control group of regular class children.

For the second year, Bradfield et al. (1973) made substantial alterations in the instructional designs and examined the differences between third- and fourth-grade integrated and nonintegrated classes. Inservice training and behavior modification were continued, but curricula were modified, and precision teaching was added. Individualized reading instruction was implemented by using sixth-grade tutors.

Three EMR and three educationally handicapped (EH) students were fully integrated into a third-grade experimental class. The same was done for a fourth-grade experimental class. A total of 160 regular class students ranging in age from 8 to 12 years were randomly assigned by third and fourth grade to one of eight groups. There were three control groups for third grade, three for fourth grade, and an experimental group for each grade. As a further means of analysis, two regular students from each of the control classes and two EMR and two EH students from special classes were chosen to represent each of the six control groups. This was done in order to compare performance with EMR and EH students in the experimental classes.

There were no significant differences on WRAT scores over seven months between the experimental third grade and the three third grades with no special children. For the fourth graders, there were no significant differences for arithmetic and reading using the CAT as the performance measure. Arithmetic gains were significantly higher in the integrated fourth grade than in the control fourth grades.

Individual student comparisons were also made. Third-grade EMR and EH students in integrated classes performed the same as control students in special classes for reading and spelling. EH students in the integrated class performed significantly better in arithmetic than did special class controls. There were no arithmetic differences between integrated EMR students and EMR controls. Third-grade integrated special education students performed better in reading and arithmetic, and equally in spelling compared to special class controls. Fourth-grade integrated and nonintegrated EMR and EH children performed equally in reading, language, and arithmetic.

Behavior comparisons indicated that third- and fourth-grade EH students behaved equally in integrated and nonintegrated settings at the end of the study. Behavior of EMR students in integrated classes was superior to that of students in special classes.

The efforts of Bradfield et al. (1973) to integrate mildly handicapped students into regular classes point to the need to use precise teaching methodology and child management systems. During the first year, they effectively documented that special student integration can have adverse effects upon regular class members, even though the special students themselves maintained academic growth as well as special class controls. More important, during the second year they demonstrated that application of precision teaching eliminated the problem of reduced academic achievement of classroom peers. Of course, of most importance is the lack of difference in total group performance between third- and fourth-grade integrated classes and similar nonintegrated classes.

Haring and Krug (1975) also assessed the effects of precision teaching and token reinforcement on 12-year-old EMR students in special classes and then collected follow-up data on their return to regular classrooms without precision teaching. Two special classes using daily performance charts, a highly structured reading program, precision teaching, and a reinforcement program were compared to two control classes, which received teacher-specified programs. Forty-eight students were randomly assigned to one of the four classes with 12 students in each class. The students in the experimental classes made a 13½ months gain in reading and a 16 months gain in math during a school year. Control class gains were 4½ months in reading and almost 5 months in math.

At the end of this project, 8 out of 24 students in the experimental classes were returned to regular classes, based on performance criteria. The following school year, five additional students were returned. None of the students in the traditional special classes had been returned to regular classes. It is doubtful that return procedures were a formal part of these traditional programs. For the second year, a follow-up study was reported (Haring & Krug, 1975) on the progress of the 13 students who were returned to regular classes. Based on WRAT and Gray Oral Reading Test (GORT) scores, the newly integrated students were "matched" (without teachers' knowledge) with students in the same class whose reading scores were most similar. A comparison of the gain scores of the experimental subjects and their matched controls was as follows:

	WRAT Reading	GORT Reading	WRAT Math
Experimental Subjects:	12 months	13 months	9 months
Matched Controls:	9 months	7 months	6 months

The teachers of the children indicated that 10 out of 14 former special class children could remain in the regular class without special help.

Use of precision teaching (or, in its more advanced stage, data-based instruction), is a method by which regular classroom performance can be enhanced. The follow-up data collected by Haring and Krug (1975) on EMR students returned to regular classrooms indicate that the use of precision teaching can result in maintenance of gains once students are integrated into regular classes. The regular classroom intervention project by Bradfield et al. (1973) illustrates that precision teaching is not only an effective tool for increasing special students' skills, but it can also be implemented in regular classes without impeding the progress of regular classroom peers.

Systematic Structuring of Learning Environments

A teacher who uses DBI creates a *learning environment* that is conducive to conducting field-based research. Learning environment means the exact situation or condition under which a student receives instruction. The effect of this environment is evaluated by using precise, observable, measurable behaviors. With precise measurement, teachers can raise research questions and test their own hypotheses. They can measure the effects of particular instructional strategies upon single students or upon many students. The key to this type of evaluative research is to *structure* carefully the learning environment in such a way that the effects of one variable (or factor) are assessed at a time.

Attention to this type of detail is the very principle that educational researchers rigorously adhere to in order to make meaningful statements about the effects of various types of instructional practices used with students. If teachers using DBI adhere to the same principles of precision and control, then they can generate their own research results that are specific to the individual students they serve.

As pointed out, a key factor in creating research-based classrooms is carefully structuring the learning environment. This careful structuring is also a crucial element for successful transfer of remediated behaviors from special to regular education. It may be that one factor affecting the lack of transfer of remediated behaviors from special to regular education is an abrupt shift of the learning environment. In this case, the new learning environment contains several, simultaneous changes in such important factors as teacher, curricula, number of classmates, schedule of reinforcement, and teacher expectations.

In such a situation the logical step is to control as many of these factors as possible. The way to do this is to alter one factor at a time for those that are controllable. For instance, the list of possible factors influencing lack of transfer can be prioritized in the order in which they might be controlled. The list would read:

1. curricula
2. teacher expectation
3. reinforcement schedule
4. number of classmates
5. teacher

Curricula are first controlled by offering remedial instruction in the same curricular series so that by the time students are transferred to regular classes, they will be working in the same book as classmates. (A subsequent section contains more on the topic of curricular instruction.) Second, after the student has been placed at a curricular level at which material can be mastered, the exact performance that is expected from the student is defined to determine individual lesson mastery (criterial performance). These criteria are defined by consulting with the classroom teacher and selecting criteria that will readily transfer to the regular classroom. If criterial performance levels that are different than those in the regular class must be used, plans must be made to alter them gradually until they meet classroom teacher expectations. Third, a schedule of reinforcement is defined that is clear to the student and easily implemented in regular classes. The fourth condition that is altered is to train the student to work under independent study conditions. This is to prepare the student for the regular class, where there are many students, and the teacher has little time for intensive, individualized instruction. Of course, after all of this careful planning, consulting, preparation, and training, the student is transferred back to the regular class.

These examples are a few of many factors that could affect behavior of students returned to the mainstream. Some factors are more easily controlled than others. The primary point is that the more factors that are planned and controlled, the more accurate educators can be in predicting success in the regular class. Another way of saying this is that if the learning environment is structured to reflect gradually the environment in the regular class, the more likely long-term, behavioral changes in students across environments will result. This is not to say that changes in the learning environment of the regular classroom might also result as special educators carefully plan, prepare, and consult with regular classroom teachers.

Direct Curricular Instruction

Direct curricular instruction, as mentioned by example earlier, is one way to control a variable that may impede a student's regular classroom performance. If a student receives remedial instruction in a curricular series or in a set of special teacher-defined curriculum, the content as well as the difficulty level are different than the regular class curriculum. This difference is likely to cause difficulty when the student returns to the regular class. The regular classroom teacher may even wonder what prompted the return from special education if the student is unable to perform in the curriculum.

With direct curricular instruction, a remedial student is placed in the same curriculum as used in the regular class but at a lower grade level in the same series. The student receives special instruction in a resource setting for a period of daily instruction. Determination of appropriate grade level is accomplished by using criterial performance levels (Lovitt & Hansen, 1976a).

For students at elementary levels, remedial curricular instruction is usually offered in reading, spelling, language arts, and mathematics. The content areas are more likely to be used for reading materials that can be used to generalize reading behaviors across curriculum once the student has attained reading at grade level. For students at lower levels of middle school, the same general rule would be applied.

For upper level, middle school and secondary students whose skill levels are low (lower than sixth grade), instruction in the same curricular series is impractical. Secondary curricula do not always include lower levels of the same general theme. For example, it is more likely that an individual could find a hierarchical series based on grade level for mathematics than other areas.

For many mildly handicapped, secondary students, the most deficient subject area is reading. For these students, curricular instruction in a basal reader at low elementary levels seems out of the question. A more workable solution is to offer direct curricular instruction in a remedial reading series that is designed for older readers and is well sequenced for reading difficulty levels. After students advance through these lowered levels of reading materials, they can be promoted to the upper level of a basal reader series (fifth-, sixth-, seventh-, and eighth-grade levels). When these more difficult levels are mastered, students receive curricular instruction in the same content area text that is used in the class that they may eventually attend as a mainstreamed student. Some examples of content area texts that are used for this preparatory instruction are English literature, history, social studies, psychology, health, and driver's education books.

Placement in the Curriculum

Assessment of student performance in a curriculum is accomplished by means of a curriculum-based assessment (CBA) as described by Lovitt and Hansen (1976a), Blankenship and Lilly (1981), Idol-Maestas, Givens-Ogle and Lloyd (1981), and Idol-Maestas, Lloyd and Ritter (1982). The CBA combines aspects of the informal reading inventory with some principles of applied behavior analysis. A good rule to follow is to assess the student on three different days in repeated levels of the same curricular series. For example, a second-grade student with referred reading problems would read 100-word sample passages from each level (preprimer through second grade) of the basal reading series used in the regular classroom. On the second day of testing, this student would read similar passages from the same levels. The same procedure is repeated on the third day.

Testing over three days is a means of ensuring that an accurate sampling of a student's reading ability has been obtained. Three-day testing is especially crucial with students who are known for erratic and variable performance. Extenuating circumstances, such as difficulty at home, in the regular class, on the school bus, or in the play area, or illness, excitement, and apprehension can affect student performance. A measurement over time gives a better picture of the student's most usual performance patterns.

Students are placed in the highest level in which they meet criteria (median scores over three days of 95 percent correct word accuracy, 80 percent correct comprehension, and 40 correct words per minute. Once the appropriate oral reading level is determined, this level is plotted on a "normal progress in curriculum" chart (Deno & Mirkin, 1977, 1980; Jenkins, Deno, & Mirkin, 1980).

Figure 4–3 is an example of a normal progress in curriculum chart designed for use with elementary school students in grades one to six, and it is thus referred to as a six-year chart. The abscissa (horizontal line) of the chart reflects the number of years that an elementary student is in school. Each year is subdivided into the nine months normally used for school instruction. The ordinate (vertical line) of the chart reflects the grades that a student normally progresses through in elementary school (first grade through six grade). These grade levels are indicated by 1.0, 2.0, 3.0, 4.0, 5.0, and 6.0. The ordinate of the six-year chart also contains the book names for each level and the number of stories contained within each level.

By the time a student has completed sixth grade and is ready to continue to seventh grade, all levels of a curricular series theoretically have been completed. Therefore, when a student's reading ability is assessed through the student's current grade level, the testing must extend through the levels the student would have normally completed by the end of the year in which the student was tested. A diagonal line is drawn from the bottom left corner to the top right corner. This line represents the theoretical normal curricular progress of a student from time of school entry at first grade, to exit from elementary school at the end of the sixth grade. To illustrate, at the end of first grade, a student should have completed all of the levels of reading material associated with first grade and so on.

After a three-day curriculum assessment is administered and the performance criteria mentioned earlier are applied to determine appropriate placement, this placement level is recorded on the six-year chart. A large, filled-in circle is placed at the intersection of the beginning of the placement level and the month in which assessment was done. In Figure 4–3, this second-grade student was placed in *Worlds of Wonder,* a primer level for first grade in the MacMillan reading series (1975). A diagonal, broken line is then drawn from the bottom left corner to this placement point. This diagonal represents the theoretical rate of curricular progress that this student would have exhibited if consistent curricular instruction had been given. This "actual" rate of progress serves as a comparative contrast to the expected rate of progress of a "normal" student.

A second diagonal line (solid line) is drawn from the placement point to the point at which the student's grade peers will have finished the grade

Figure 4–3 Six-Year Chart Reflecting Program through the Curriculum for a Second-Grade Student

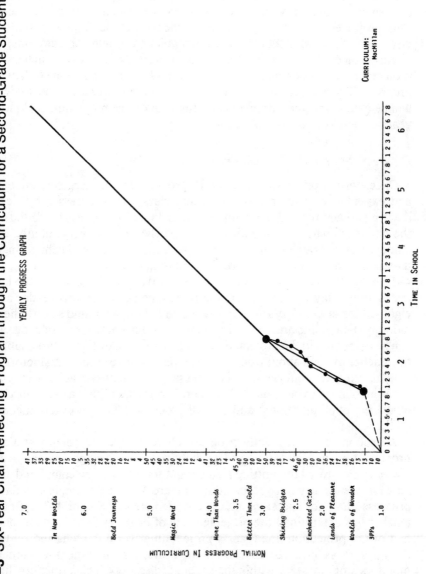

appropriate book level at the year's end. In the illustrated example, this student's grade peers will have finished *Shining Bridges,* the 2^2 reader, by the end of the current school year. This line represents the rate at which the remedial student would have to progress to catch up to grade peers. This projected rate of progress gives teachers, students, and parents a clear idea of how students compare to regular classroom expectations.

This projected rate also serves as a measurement device for teachers to project a rate of progress at which they would like the remedial student to progress. The projection is made as to the number of readers the student will be able to master within a year's time. (Average projection is 1½ to 2 years' progress in one school year.)

Progress through the Curriculum

Once normal progress, past rate of progress for the targeted student, and expected rate for return to normal classroom progress have been determined and plotted, the student's actual rate of progress is plotted on the six-year chart on a monthly basis. At the end of every month, the student's actual rate of progress in the series is plotted by placing a single data point on the intersection of the month and story number. In Figure 4–3, this girl had completed seven stories in *Worlds of Wonder* by the last instructional day of September, the remaining stories in this reader and eight stories in *Lands of Pleasure* by the end of October, and so on. These monthly data points are connected so the student's actual rate of progress can be compared to the projected rate of progress. Use of this chart enables the teacher to think about whether the student is progressing satisfactorily, whether an added intervention is necessary, or whether teacher expectations might need to be revised. The yearly progress graph is a useful device in sharing pupil placement and overall progress data with other teachers and parents.

A second chart, the daily progress chart, is used to record student progress for daily instruction. The daily progress through lessons completed is monitored by plotting a data point for every story completed and. an *x* for every story not yet mastered. Figure 4–4 is an example of a daily progress chart for the same student as depicted in Figure 4–3. After a teacher has determined the projected rate of progress for a student, one-half of the projection line (year's projection growth) is recharted on the daily progress chart. The abscissa of the chart monitors time; the ordinate monitors story mastery within the sequenced readers. This projection line defines the expected progress of the child for the semester. Data plots above the line indicate adequate progress; data points below the line for three consecutive days indicate the need for a different intervention strat-

Figure 4–4 Daily Progress Chart Reflecting Mastery of Stories in
Three Basal Readers

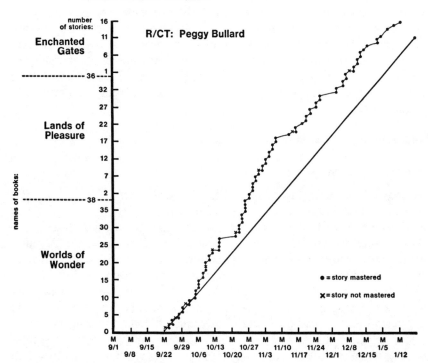

egy. This daily monitoring of progress allows immediate remediation for
students not making adequate progress. Figure 4–4 displays the daily
progress in curriculum semester chart for a second-grade female student.
After administration of a CBA, she was placed in the MacMillan Reading
Series primer, *Worlds of Wonder,* on September 22, 1980. By December
12, 1980, she had completed the eighth story in the 2^1 reader, *Enchanted
Gates.* This demonstrated a 3.5 month gain for every month in the program.
A total of 87 stories had been mastered in a three-month period.

Direct curricular instruction is a viable way in which to control for
curricular materials that may influence eventual classroom performance
of mildly handicapped students. The examples presented illustrate how a
student can receive curricular instruction in the same series used in that
student's classroom yet at a lower level. When students place much lower
than grade peers, it is advisable to offer special instruction through a

resource program rather than in the regular class. This is advisable under the conditions for which most regular classes are structured, where most students are working in the same level of a curricular series. As regular classroom instruction moves toward an individualized small group model, this will certainly make it easier to implement direct curricular instruction at a lowered level within a classroom setting. In Chapter 5 examples are presented illustrating how consulting teachers prepared students who were receiving direct curricular instruction in resource settings to perform in regular classes.

Programming for Behavior Generalization

Stages of Learning

Behavior analysts (Haring, Lovitt, Eaton, & Hansen, 1978; Smith, 1981) have examined five basic stages of learning that are pertinent to the topic of transferring mildly handicapped students back to regular classrooms. Those stages are the following: (1) acquisition; (2) proficiency; (3) maintenance; (4) generalization; and (5) adaption. Consulting teachers must be able to identify readily a student's stage of learning for targeted skill areas. Once this is accomplished, teachers can program the student's instructional program so that ultimate performance is obtained in each stage. The long-term instructional goals are to advance students through the stages of learning until they are able to work independently, to perform similar tasks under a variety of conditions, and to discover new areas to which skills can be applied.

The following section contains definitions and examples of the five basic learning stages with some adaption included to recognize an intermediate step between *acquisition* and *proficiency* called *reversion*.

Acquisition. During this stage, the student is in the process of acquiring a new skill. During initial testing of the targeted skill, the student fails to respond or consistently responds incorrectly, which demonstrates a lack of knowledge about how to perform the skill. This assessment is taken on at least three separate occasions.

- Example 1—A student does not know the basic multiplication facts. The student never responds correctly.
- Example 2—A student fails to call out correctly any number of letter-sound association patterns that are presented on at least three separate testing occasions.

Reversion. A student in this stage has acquired some basic skills, but the skills are not really firm. One cannot predict that the student will consistently respond. Rather, student response is variable and unpredictable. Sometimes the student responds correctly, but the chances are just as likely that the student will revert to exhibiting incorrect responses used before the acquisition stage.

- Example 1—A student has had some exposure to memorization of multiplication facts, but has yet to master them consistently. Responses vary from correct to incorrect when the same stimulus problem is presented over several trials.
- Example 2—When presented with a letter-sound association task, a student responds correctly on some occasions and incorrectly on others for the same letter-sound pattern.

Proficiency. At this stage the student consistently responds correctly, but the response rate is slow and arduous. In order to perform proficiently, the student must combine accuracy of response with speed of response.

- Example 1—A student can complete a worksheet designed to drill response to multiplication facts, but is unable to complete the exercise in the amount of time allotted.
- Example 2—A student meets criterion (correct response on three separate occasions) for acceptable response to letter-sound patterns, but the duration of time between presentation of the symbol and the student's response is more than ten seconds.

Maintenance. By this stage a student demonstrates an ability to maintain acceptable skill performance outside of the confines of direct instruction that occurs during the acquisition stage or during monitoring during the proficiency stage. Blankenship and Lilly (1981) define maintenance as "the lasting effects of a behavioral change once instruction or reinforcement has been withdrawn" (p. 345). Smith (1981) describes maintenance as "retention of learning" (p. 69).

- Example 1—A student demonstrates that he or she can correctly and quickly answer math facts when working independently without reinforcement for acceptable responses.
- Example 2—A student independently decodes letter-sound patterns correctly and quickly without repeated drill or teacher reinforcement.

Generalization. During this stage the desired skill should occur across situations and time (O'Leary & Drabman, 1971).

- Example 1—A student who has learned to call out answers orally to math facts writes the answer correctly and rapidly. This is an example of behavior generalization to other behaviors.
- Example 2—A student who demonstrates proficiency in math facts continues to respond accurately and quickly when the math facts are embedded within calculation problems. This is an example of behavior generalization across situations.
- Example 3—A student who successfully passes through acquisition, proficiency, and maintenance of correct response to math facts continues to respond correctly and use math facts in a variety of problems one year later. This is an example of behavior generalization over time.

Adaption. In this stage a student must apply a learned skill area to a new area of application without direct instruction or guidance, which is otherwise known as problem solving.

- Example 1—A student who is proficient in correctly answering multiplication math facts "discovers" that division is the reverse of multiplication, and can quickly and accurately answer division facts without practice.
- Example 2—A student who decodes letter sounds quickly and accurately for the first ten consonant letters in the alphabet independently decodes the remaining consonant letters without instruction or practice.

The types of instructional strategies to use vary from stage to stage. Three excellent sources for guidelines for selecting optimal strategies are Blankenship and Lilly (1981), Haring et al. (1978), and Smith (1981).

Guidelines for Generalization

The idea of transferring a mildly handicapped student from resource to regular classroom services can be greatly simplified if teachers identify stages of learning, select appropriate teaching strategies, and systematically plan for pupil transition from stage to stage. Generalization is the stage that is of utmost interest when one plans to transfer a student systematically. Two groups of applied behavior analysts (Stokes & Baer, 1977; Wildman & Wildman, 1975) have compiled guidelines and rules to enhance the likelihood of achieving generalization of subject behavior. Although written as guides for behavioral researchers, they can serve as excellent guideposts for consulting teachers who are concerned with returning mildly handicapped learners to regular classrooms.

Wildman and Wildman (1975) have proffered some tentative rules for use when token economy programs have been used to elicit desired behaviors. References to research studies from which the rules were generated can be found in the original source. The rules are as follows:

- Do not instruct the subjects that rewards will be available only at certain times or under certain conditions.
- Do not attempt to achieve generalization among incompatible behaviors by reinforcing or richly reinforcing only one of the behaviors.
- Match attention and social reinforcement with the delivery of tokens and their exchange for backup reinforcers.
- Decrease the number of times per day ratings are given over the course of a token economy program.
- Progressively increase the delay between the earning of tokens and their exchange for tangible reinforcers over the course of a token economy program.
- Decrease the actual amount of reinforcement awarded for each unit of academic work or appropriate behavior.
- Give those individuals who exercise control over the environment to which the student will be returned specific, step-by-step instructions on how to maintain treatment gains.
- Treat the subject in an environment that, as much as possible, approximates the environment to which the child will be returned.
- Attempt to involve the students' parents in the treatment program and in the maintenance of treatment gains.
- Insofar as is possible, focus the token system on the instruction of skills that will be reinforced and maintained by the environment to which the child will be returned.
- Employ small, readily available reinforcers.
- Involve the subjects in the rating of their own behavior, and then fade out the external ratings.

Stokes and Baer (1977) developed the following list of tactics that is useful not only for exit from token economy programs, but for overall programming for generalization of behaviors:

- Look for a response that enters a natural community; in particular, teach subjects to cue their potential natural communities to reinforce their desirable behaviors.
- Keep training more exemplars; in particular, diversify them.

- Loosen experimental control over the stimuli and response involved in training; in particular, train different examples concurrently, and vary instructions, discrimitive stimuli, social reinforcers, and backup reinforcers.
- Make unclear the limits of training contingencies; in particular, conceal, when possible, the point at which those contingencies stop operating, possibly by delayed reinforcement.
- Use stimuli that are likely to be found in generalization settings and in training settings as well; in particular, use peers as tutors.
- Reinforce accurate self-reports of desirable behaviors; apply self-recording and self-reinforcement techniques whenever possible.
- Reinforce at least some of the generalizations sometimes, as if "to generalize" were an operant response class.

FINAL REMARKS

This chapter contains a series of recommendations for laying a sound base for systematically transferring remediated responses from direct service settings to regular classrooms. This is a part of the role of any teacher who is providing remedial instruction outside of the regular classroom. Research studies indicate that remediated behaviors are not always maintained after students are returned to regular classes and that teachers do not always systematically check on students to determine how they have acclimated to new environments. Teachers can expect that most students will react to environmental change in a negative response direction. Therefore, teachers must follow some principles of systematization in order to facilitate transfer. Some concepts which are an integral part of systematic transfer are mastery learning, data-based instruction, systematic structuring of learning environments, direct curricular instruction, and programming for behavior generalization.

COMMUNICATION EXCHANGE

A Consultation Log

Some consulting teachers keep a log in which contacts made with classroom teachers are recorded. A notebook divided into labeled sections for each classroom teacher or for each student consultee is used to record observations and information. Section labeling can be done with indexing tabs so a section can be easily located. If a three-ring notebook is used, actual raw data sheets from behavioral classroom observations can be stored with the written account of teacher contacts. Information kept in the log might include the following:

- a calendar in the front of the log to remind the consulting teacher of future meetings on scheduled classroom visitations
- dates of actual contacts as a heading for each entry
- goal(s) set by the consulting teacher stating the preconceived intention of the contact
- a brief summary of the results of the contact
- any commitments made by either the classroom or consulting teacher
- raw data sheets, if applicable
- information for use in planning for systematic transfer (that is, name of curricular series, agreed-upon performance criterion levels, reinforcement strategies used in regular classroom, potential reinforcers for the student)
- a comment regarding any discrepancy that might have occurred between what the consulting teacher intended to accomplish and what actually happened during the contact

Self-evaluation of discrepancies that might occur between intent and actuality can serve as a mechanism to assist the consulting teacher in determining whether realistic goals are being set. Discrepancy evaluation can also serve as a reinforcer to the consultant if more is accomplished during a contact than had been anticipated.

Types of Consultation Transfer Projects: From Special Education to Regular Education

"We chart because we care."
—*Ogden Lindsley*
(cited in Mowrer [1972])

This chapter contains transfer projects designed and implemented by resource teachers who also work as teacher consultants to regular classroom teachers. Primarily, these projects serve as a mechanism for offering empirical evidence for the efficacy of attempting systematic transfer. Readers may be more readily convinced of the possibility of implementing systematic transfer strategies for transition from special to regular education if they examine these accumulated data demonstrating success in transferring special students to regular educational services.

Second, all of the projects were implemented in public school settings and represent real situations, rather than situations constructed for research purposes. These situations can serve as an impetus to those aspiring to become teacher consultants. The idea of transfer of skills back to regular classes may move closer to actuality if an individual has, as a guide, projects completed by professional peers.

Third, each project contains a series of precise instructional and consultation strategies that were used to achieve success in remediating academic behaviors. This collection of strategies could become a useful model for readers to implement similar strategies and serve as impetus for readers to create improved strategies for direct instruction and consultation.

All of the projects were based on the following set of ten basic guidelines for transfer that the reader will see reflected within the individual projects:

1. Select a curriculum that is appropriate for the student's instructional needs, is relevant for regular classroom use, and is preferably already used in the regular classrooms of the targeted student.
2. Place the student at a level within the curriculum based on a criterion performance across curricular levels (curricular-based assessment).

85

3. Plan the transfer in collaboration with the regular classroom teachers and parents, if applicable.
4. Collect normative population data reflecting average performance of the student's regular classroom peers in the problematic skill area. Use these data as a guide for establishing mastery levels for performance.
5. Plan the classroom transfer in advance using a task analytic approach. This means to break a large task into a hierarchical series of smaller components, with the ultimate goal being to combine all components into a mastered task.
6. Use a changing criterion approach to alter the student's performance systematically in a positive direction.
7. Collect direct and daily measures of pupil progress in both special and regular classroom settings.
8. Use systematic monitoring to record and observe pupil progress.
9. Examine the pupil performance data carefully in order to determine when changes are needed in all student programs.
10. Continue to check with the classroom teacher on pupil performance *after* the transfer has been accomplished.

The following projects are presented in order of the academic subjects for which transfer was achieved. (See Table 5–1.)

Reading

Project 1: Transfer of Increased Reading Rate

R/CT: Jill Cunningham

R. was a second-grade boy who was receiving direct instruction in reading for 30 minutes daily in the resource room. R. was initially placed in the second preprimer *(Sun Tree)* in the Economy basal series (1975) in September 15, 1980. At first, he worked with a resource teacher and then with the R/CT. *Sun Tree* was the highest level in this series, where he read orally with 95 percent accuracy, 80 percent correct oral comprehension, and at least 30 correct words per minute (CWPM). These were the *placement criteria.*

Each day, R. orally read a story to the resource teacher and then answered comprehension questions. Daily measurement of the three behaviors used for criteria placement was obtained during a 100-word, timed reading sample for each story. In order to progress to each subsequent story in the series, R. had to meet the aforementioned criteria for the story he was currently reading. Failure to meet criteria resulted in rereading the story until criteria were met.

Table 5–1 Overview of Projects Contained in Chapter 5

Project	Task
1	Improving silent reading rate of a second-grade boy
2	Improving oral reading of a first-grade boy
3	Improving the reading comprehension of a fifth-grade boy
4	Transferring newly acquired letter formation in D'Nealian handwriting to a first-grade class
5	Monitoring the effect of resource room drill of spelling words in a sixth-grade class
6	Teaching a fifth-grade boy to subtract and transferring the skill to regular class
7	Training a third-grade girl to complete and self-correct math assignments
8	Teaching a fifth-grade girl multiplication facts and multidigit multiplication problems

In March, when R. was reading in grade-level materials, the R/CT and the classroom teacher met to determine the skills R. would need to acquire before being transferred to the regular classroom for reading instruction. R.'s problems in the regular classroom were his rate of silent reading and his rate of completion on comprehension questions and workbook pages. The classroom teacher said that R. was often off-task and inferred that this accounted for his lack of completion of assignments. The R/CT observed R. during the 30-minute reading session in the classroom, and recorded attending and nonattending behavior at 60-second intervals. *Attending* was defined as eyes on book, not talking unless to teacher, writing in book with pencil, eyes open, and hands not covering eyes. Over three days of observation, R. was attending during 75 percent of the observed intervals. As the time spent attending was fairly high, the collaborating teachers decided to concentrate on improving R.'s silent reading rate rather than on-task behavior. Silent reading rate was chosen over workbook completion rate because, in the classroom, silent reading was the first in a series of tasks to complete. Once R. got behind in this area, all subsequent areas of study were then disrupted.

Silent reading rate was computed by determining the number of words in a story (or pages read) and the amount of time taken to read the story or passages. Thus,

$$\text{rate} = \frac{\text{\# of words in story} \times 60}{\text{time needed to read story (seconds)}}.$$

In order to establish a goal for optimal silent reading rate, the rate of an average student in the second-grade classroom was measured. The classroom teacher selected the student. The average normal rate for that student was 100 words per minute.

At the time the consultation for transfer began, R. was reading an entire story silently, but he had started to reread stories due to failure to meet criteria for oral comprehension. This indicated that R. was not reading as carefully as he might. As a result, the R/CT had R. read two pages silently, rather than the entire story. She planned to increase the number of pages for silent reading as the silent reading rate increased.

Phase A (Baseline)

R. read each story orally with the R/CT in the resource room with the exception of two pages that were read silently.

Results. During the five days of baseline, R.'s median rate for silent reading was 40. The mean was 49 silent words per minute. (See Figure 5–1.)

Phase B

During the silent reading of two to three pages (approximately 250 words), if R.'s rate was 50 or above, he would receive a point. When he

---

Figure 5–1 Transfer of Increased Silent Reading Rate from Resource to Regular Classroom

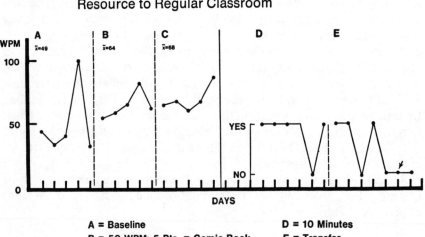

A = Baseline
B = 50 WPM; 5 Pts. = Comic Book
C = 65 WPM; Same

D = 10 Minutes
E = Transfer

earned five points, he was allowed to read a comic book of his choice in the resource room. This phase lasted five days.

Results. R.'s median rate was 65, with a mean rate of 64. A glance at the charted data in Figure 5–1 will confirm that his rate was improving over time.

Phase C

During the silent reading of three to four pages (approximately 300 to 350 words), R. earned a point if his rate was 65 or over. Five points equaled the reading of a comic book. This phase lasted five days.

Results. R.'s median rate was 64 with a mean rate of 68. The rate continued to improve over time.

Phase D

The R/CT changed the method of measuring silent reading rate to one that would be easy for a classroom teacher to implement. R. was given ten minutes to complete a silent reading assignment. The length of the time period was selected by examining peer performance and estimating that about four pages of work were completed in approximately ten minutes. Data were recorded as "Yes/No" depending on whether R. did or did not finish the assignment during the allotted time. This phase lasted five days.

Results. For four out of five days, R. completed the silent reading assignment in ten minutes and passed the stories on all criterion measures including acceptable comprehension performances.

Phase E

R. was returned to the second-grade classroom for reading instruction. He was given a daily silent reading assignment to complete during a ten-minute period. This phase lasted for seven days.

Results. For three days, R. completed the assignment during the allotted time period. On four days, he did not complete the assignment.

Discussion

When R. had silent reading instruction in the resource room, the R/CT increased his average silent reading rate from an average of 49 to 68 words per minute. The R/CT used a changing criterion design during phases B and C where R. had to read at an increasingly faster rate in order to receive a reinforcer. The reinforcer was assignment of five points that could be exchanged for time to read a comic book. The student selected comic book reading as a desired reinforcer. Allowing students to self-select reinforcers can be an important technique for effective student management.

An important feature of this project is that the R/CT altered the method for recording behavior to one that was less precise but easier for a classroom teacher to implement during group instruction. Simplifying data collection is sometimes crucial to successful classroom consultation. When the measurement technique was changed and R. was given ten minutes to complete an assignment, he successfully completed it 80 percent of the time while in the resource room. When he was moved to the regular classroom, he completed the assignments 43 percent of the time. At the end of phase E, the R/CT discovered one reason why R.'s performance dropped upon transfer. On the sixth day of instruction, the classroom teacher reduced the time to complete the silent reading assignment to six minutes. (See arrow marking the sixth day of phase E in Figure 5–1.) This decision was not made in consultation with the R/CT.

Over the first five days of phase E, when the allotted time period was 10 minutes, R. completed the assignment 60 percent of the time. This is still a reduction compared to performance in the resource room, but it is not as severe. As discussed in Chapter 4, teachers must be prepared for reduction in desired behaviors as a result of changing learning environments.

Two important principles for consulting teachers to use are embedded in this consultation project. They are the following: (1) teachers working in collaboration must agree to check with one another before making changes in the student's program; and (2) consulting teachers must check the performance data frequently upon immediate transfer of students to classroom instruction.

As a result of these data, the R/CT and the classroom teacher agreed to reinstate the ten-minute time allottment. A suggested next step would be to reduce the ten-minute period gradually until the six-minute period was reached, rather than initiating an abrupt time change. The first gradual change might be to set the time period at 9½ minutes and announce to the students that they were doing so well that the teacher would like to see if they could work even faster. Then the second step might be to reduce the time to eight minutes, and so on. Obviously a changing time span should not be implemented until targeted students are successfully completing all assignments during the ten-minute time period.

Another factor must be taken into consideration when examining the data in Figure 5–1. Reading passages in basal readers may vary in complexity. For example, the isolated, high data point during baseline was due to an unusually easy story. Regardless of some variation in story complexity, the R/CT increased R.'s silent reading rate by approximately 20 words per minute over a period of 15 instructional days.

Project 2: Transfer of Oral Reading Instruction from the Resource Room to the Regular Classroom

R/CT: Peggy Bullard

T. was a first-grade boy seen by the R/CT for 30 minutes a day for direct instruction in reading. T. was initially referred because he had spent the previous year in a self-contained class for mildly mentally retarded students. He was reading at least one story per day in the resource room at grade level and had repeated only four stories (not read to criterion the first time) during the previous month of instruction.

The R/CT met with the classroom teacher to discuss T.'s progress in reading. According to the classroom teacher, T. was reading successfully in the top reading group in her class. When the R/CT asked if she thought T. needed to continue receiving special services, the teacher suggested services could be discontinued, but she immediately expressed a concern that there might not be an opening for him later on should he begin to have trouble. The R/CT explained that she would rather not stop serving him altogether without some means of monitoring his progress. The classroom teacher then suggested sending T. to the resource room fewer days per week, gradually fading him out.

Four days later, the R/CT and the teacher met more formally to develop a system for taking some data on oral reading accuracy and comprehension in the regular class. The R/CT did not suggest a measurement for reading rate because this was not a variable measured in the class, even though rate had been an integral part of direct reading instruction. The R/CT felt that the process of collecting data in itself in a regular classroom was enough to introduce at one time, without introducing another behavior to measure. The R/CT suggested that she and the teacher needed some way to keep track of how T. was doing, especially to measure what would happen as they decreased the amount of time T. would spend in the resource room.

The only modification made by the teacher was to mark T.'s passage ahead of time so that she would be sure to have a 25-word sample each day. The R/CT explained how to calculate accuracy based on a 25-word time sample embedded within a story. If, for example, T. read 26 words and missed one, the number correct (25) would be divided by the total number (26), to yield the percent correct (96.1 percent). But if T. read 25 words each day, each error would be worth exactly four points, and the four points could easily be subtracted from 100 percent to determine the percentage of words read accurately.

Phase A

The classroom teacher agreed to take a week of baseline data measuring T.'s oral reading accuracy and comprehension during group instruction. The R/CT continued to see T. every day for individual reading instruction. This phase lasted five days.

Results. T. was reading with an average accuracy of 97 percent ranging from 90 to 100 percent. The most common score was 100 percent. His reading comprehension ranged from 67 to 100 percent, with a mean of 92 percent. Again, the most common score was 100 percent.

Phase B

The R/CT saw T. three days each week instead of every day. For a portion of this phase, group instruction was given by the student teacher. This phase lasted seven days.

Results. When seen for three days a week by the R/CT, T.'s accuracy improved to an average of 99.6 percent. On one day, he read with 96 percent accuracy. On all other days, he did not make any errors in the 25-word sample. His comprehension dropped during this phase to a mean of 78 percent, but the trend was rising.

Phase C

The R/CT stopped seeing T. in the resource room. Monitoring in the regular class continued as before. The classroom teacher resumed instruction of T.'s group.

The results were the following: When the R/CT discontinued direct instruction with T., he averaged 95 percent accuracy over the next two weeks. On the first two days recorded by his teacher, T. missed four words and then three words. No other data were collected for this week. During the next week, T. again scored 100 percent on all but one day. The mean for comprehension was 95 percent, with 100 percent on every day except one, on which he scored 67 percent.

Reliability

A reliability check between the classroom teacher and the R/CT showed 100 percent agreement on length of time sample (25 words), accuracy, and comprehension. (See Figure 5–2.)

Figure 5–2 Rate of Oral Reading Accuracy and Comprehension Across Transitional Phases from Resource to Classroom Instruction

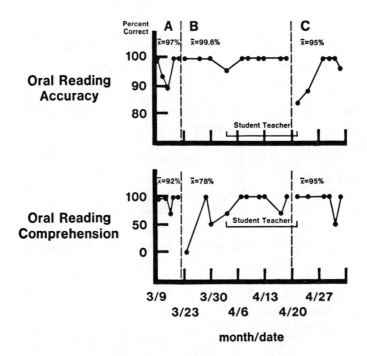

A = Baseline in regular class during group instruction, with daily resource instruction

B = Reduction of frequency of resource instruction

C = Termination of resource instruction

Discussion

This transfer to the regular class was successful, since T. was averaging 95 percent on both accuracy and comprehension in the top reading group in the class. The daily monitoring system provided valuable feedback to the teachers during the transition, so that appropriate decisions about T.'s schedule with the R/CT could be made. T. continued to see the R/CT three days per week slightly longer than either the teacher or the R/CT expected because of the initial drop in comprehension. This may have been totally unrelated to the change in services, but it did indicate that it was not a good time to discontinue resource services altogether. By continuing to collect either daily performance data or periodic spot-checks on T.'s reading accuracy and comprehension in the group, the classroom teacher had an excellent means of identifying any changes in T.'s needs.

In this transfer project, the R/CT used an important technique to facilitate return of a special student to classroom instruction. When the classroom teacher saw the progress that T. had made during direct reading instruction with the resource teacher, she was reluctant to discontinue the special service program. She was concerned that the student's progress would be disrupted if special services were discontinued. The R/CT's response to this was to assure the teacher that T.'s progress would be closely monitored and that if progress were disrupted, T. could return to special services. This was an excellent strategy for reassuring the teacher that support services would continue indirectly in the form of continuing to measure student progress. It was also an excellent strategy for implementing data-based instruction in a regular classroom.

A second consultative strategy that this R/CT used was to establish a way in which the classroom teacher could collect pupil progress data on a special student during group instruction. Even though the R/CT routinely measured accuracy, rate, and comprehension of oral reading during resource instruction, she simplified this for use in a regular classroom. She eliminated use of rate data because the teacher was not accustomed to using this information and would have had to learn to use a stopwatch. This is not a difficult task, but the R/CT was concerned that the classroom teacher might not cooperate if too many new techniques were introduced at one time. The R/CT did ask the classroom teacher to count the number of errors the student made on a 25-word sample for ease of calculation. She also asked the teacher to count the number of correct and incorrect responses to comprehension questions. The R/CT provided a raw data sheet, which is exhibited in Figure 5–3, that was easy and reminded the teacher to collect all necessary information.

The final important strategy that the R/CT used was to decrease gradually the time spent in resource instruction. It was a good strategy because a clear message was sent to the classroom teacher that the R/CT would continue to provide assistance. Consultative services also provide assistance. However, from the perspective of a teacher who is accustomed to direct resource services and unaccustomed to consultative services, the former may be viewed as assistance, but the latter, because it is unknown, may be thought of as returning a problem student to the regular class with no further assistance. By gradually reducing resource instruction, the R/CT also used a form of systematic transfer where the student was

Figure 5–3 Raw Data Sheet for Use in Recording Oral Reading
Behaviors in a Regular Classroom

Student's Name _____

	Number of Words Read	Number of Mistakes	% Correct	Number of Questions	Number Correct	% Correct	Comments
Monday							
Tuesday							
Wednesday							
Thursday							
Friday							

gradually shifted from resource to classroom instruction, rather than initiating an abrupt environmental change.

Project 3: Reading Comprehension Transfer

R/CT: Mary Pilosof

A. was a fifth-grade student who was receiving direct instruction in reading for 30 minutes daily in a resource room. A. was initially placed in the 3^2 reader in the Laidlaw series (1976–1978). Since A.'s progress was good, the R/CT and the classroom teacher defined the following skills that A. would need to acquire before being transferred to the regular class for reading instruction:

• Reading in the middle of the fifth-grade reader with 95 percent accuracy

- Comprehension questions with the correct written answer in a complete sentence, with legible handwriting and correct spelling.

Baseline A_1

The student answered five to six questions from each story in the fifth-grade reader after reading the story orally with the lowest reading group in the fifth-grade class.

Phase I

After orally reading in the resource room in the appropriately placed reader, A. answered five factual questions orally. In addition, A. wrote two of the five answers after the oral responses. These two questions were randomly selected from the five questions. The student was given immediate feedback for written responses.

Criteria. The correct answer had to be given for both questions (100 percent).

Results. A. averaged 100 percent correct.

Phase II

Silent reading was introduced. A. had to read part of the story silently and part orally. A. still had to write the answers for two of the five factual questions. The majority of the questions were from the silent reading; a few were from oral reading. When A. responded incorrectly, the correct response was modeled.

Criteria. The correct answer had to be contained within a complete, punctuated sentence for each question.

Results. A. had difficulty the first two days. The remaining responses were 100 percent correct.

Phase III

A. first began answering five comprehension questions from the silent reading without giving oral answers. The type of comprehension questions were branched out gradually to include sequential and inferential questions, as well as factual questions. A. continued to read orally and answer different questions orally as well.

Criteria. The questions had to be answered 80 percent correctly with complete, punctuated sentences.

Results. Over 12 days, A.'s mode response (n = 8) was 80 percent.

Phase IV

The silent reading and the written comprehension questions were transferred to the regular classroom. A. completed this assignment instead of the regular classroom assignment. The classroom teacher and the R/CT praised A. each time he met criteria.

Criteria. This was the same as phase III with the addition of legible handwriting.

Results. Over seven days, A.'s mode response (n = 5) completed to include eight written comprehension questions.

Phase V

This condition was the same as phase IV except A. completed eight written comprehension questions.

Criteria. This was the same as phase IV except the criteria were raised to 90 percent correct for comprehension.

Results. A. always met criteria at 90 percent or above.

Baseline A$_2$

Again, A. read orally with the lowest reading group in the fifth-grade reader and answered the written questions. This is the same condition as the initial baseline measurement.

Criteria. This was the same as phase III with the addition of correct spelling. (Percentage for comprehension was again lowered to 80 percent correct.)

Results. A. met criteria eight out of nine days. The mode response was 80 percent correct. The slightly lowered response was probably due to the inclusion of correct spelling. (See Figure 5–4.)

Discussion

A. progressed through three books in five months. He learned to answer comprehension questions with a written response. The R/CT trained him to do this in the regular classroom, as well as in the resource room. An added generalization effect was that at the onset of this project, A. failed to complete book report assignments. During the first semester, he com-

Figure 5–4 Transfer of Reading Comprehension to a Regular Classroom

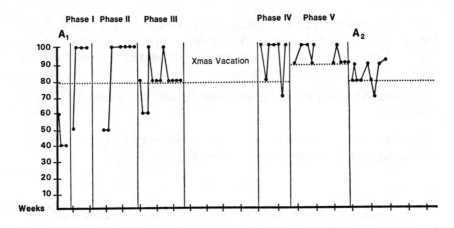

Source: L. Idol-Maestas, "A Teacher Training Model: The Resource/Consulting Teacher," *Behavioral Disorders*, 1981, p. 114–115.

pleted 8 book reports. For the second semester, he completed 15. The expected criterion was 16 per semester.

This R/CT used four important transfer strategies. First, she planned this project well in advance, in collaboration with the fifth-grade teacher. (At the end of this chapter in the Communication Exchange, the reader will find an example of a progress report memo that this R/CT used as a device to inform parents and professionals of this student's progress as well as involving them in the planning stages of the transitions.) Second, she used a changing criterion plan where she gradually, yet systematically increased the number of questions for which A. had to write answers. Third, she used a task analytic approach where she gradually built together the complete skill this student would need, that is, writing correct answers to comprehension questions in complete sentences with legible handwriting and correct spelling. Fourth, she purposefully set the criterion for comprehension at 90 percent correct in the last phase prior to actual transfer. Before and after this phase, the criterion was set at 80 percent correct. She was making an accommodation for an expected decrease in behavior (O'Connor et al., 1979) upon transfer to a new setting. Fortunately, this criterion change provided a cushion for the impact of adding correct spelling as part of the requirement for acceptable performance in the classroom. As can be seen in phase A_2 of Figure 5–4, the correct percentage for comprehension did drop slightly during this phase. The lowered differential performance was due to spelling errors in the written responses.

The R/CT did encounter two major obstacles in the course of this project. When she initially assessed A.'s reading ability, she used the Laidlaw basal reading series as the source of assessment. This was the series that was most widely used in the school. However, when A.'s progress indicated that the R/CT should begin to plan for transfer of reading instruction, she discovered that the Scott, Foresman basal series (1978) was being used in A.'s fifth-grade class for the low reading group. She compensated for this by giving a second placement test in the Scott, Foresman fifth-grade reader to ensure that A. was reading as well in this series as he was in the Laidlaw series. There was no difference in A.'s reading performance between the two series. (The exact assessment results are reported in the Memo for Academic Progress displayed in the Communication Exchange at the end of this chapter.)

The second obstacle was that the R/CT and the teacher did have a discrepancy in the criterial performance for A. in the regular class. The classroom teacher did not define correct spelling as a part of criterial performance until A. was actually transferred to the regular class. Had the R/CT known that spelling would be part of acceptable performance, she would have systematically included spelling as a part of the performance before the classroom transfer.

Handwriting

Project 4: Transfer of Handwriting Skills

R/CT: Julie Keller

J. was a first-grade boy who was having difficulty with writing skills, having mastered only 13 lower case letters in the resource room at the beginning of this project. Mastery was defined as the letter being written from memory using the following criteria for three consecutive days:

- D'Nealian method is used.
- Top part of letter starts on the top or center line or in the upper quarter of the space.
- Lower part of letter stays on or slightly above the lower line (lower quarter of the space).

- The letter that goes below the line (for example, j or g), reaches into the lower quarter of the space.
- The sweep upward does not go into upper half of the space.
- All lines are connected where appropriate.

J.'s teacher and the R/CT decided that in order to give J. more practice and to see if the letters mastered in the resource room would transfer into the classroom setting, a daily assignment would be given in the resource room to complete in the classroom. The assignment consisted of J. writing his first and last name, copying the letter he was currently trying to master in the resource room ten times, and copying two phrases in which that letter and other letters mastered were used. This was later changed to copying a sentence.

Phase A (Baseline)

Data were taken on the percent of the total letters written that were formed according to the above criteria and the percent of the words copied correctly. A word copied correctly was defined as all the letters written in the right order and in the D'Nealian style. Percent of the mechanics that was done correctly, such as spaces left between words and periods at the end of sentences, was also charted. This phase lasted three days.

Results. J. averaged 81 percent of the letters written correctly, 83 percent of the words, and 100 percent of the mechanics were correctly mastered.

Phase B

J. took a writing assignment to the classroom to complete. He still completed his writing assignment in the resource room. This phase lasted four days.

Results. J. averaged 89 percent of the letters, 100 percent of the words, and 80 percent of the mechanics correct in the resource room. His classroom work averaged 83 percent of the letters, 100 percent of the words, and 100 percent of mechanics correct.

Phase C

The R/CT asked the classroom teacher if J. had any classroom writing that could be monitored. The class had almost completed a handwriting book, but J. had done little of the work. Both teachers agreed that the

R/CT would give J. assignments in the handwriting book to complete in the classroom along with his other writing assignment.

Results. J. averaged 91 percent of the letters, 87 percent of the words, and 100 percent of the mechanics correctly in the resource room. His classroom writing was never completed during this phase. He was absent four out of seven days. Two pages were completed in the handwriting book with an average of 50 percent of the letters written correctly.

Phase D

As J. was having trouble completing the assigned writing work, he was given a sticker each day his classroom writing was completed. The arrow in this phase indicates that by this time J. had progressed to writing sentences. (See Figure 5–5.)

Results. J. completed his daily assignments seven out of nine days. The days of noncompliance were at the beginning of the phase. He was absent three days. In the resource room, letters written correctly averaged 96 percent, words 100 percent, and mechanics 100 percent. Correct writing in the classroom averaged 98 percent of the letters, 98 percent of the words, and 100 percent of the mechanics. Correct letter formation in the writing book averaged 89 percent.

Discussion

J.'s average performance for letter and word formation remained high (above 80 percent) throughout the project in the resource room and in the classroom. Letter writing did show improvement over the course of the project, going from an average of 81 percent of the letters formed correctly during baseline in the resource room to 96 percent in the last phase. Likewise, in the classroom, the average of correctly formed letters rose from 83 percent to 98 percent. When J.'s handwriting task previously completed in the resource room was assigned for completion in the regular classroom, copying of letters and words generalized well. However, when the assignment was expanded to include completion of pages in a handwriting book, J. failed to do the usual assignment and only completed two book pages, one-half of which were incorrect.

When the R/CT selected a contingent reinforcer for completion of assignments, J. took two days to adjust to the new condition and then completed all assignments for the remainder of the phase, averaging high percentages of correctness in letter formation. J.'s initial failure to complete the additional handwriting assignment is an example of being in the proficiency stage. J. could master the tasks, but he apparently was not sufficiently

Figure 5–5 Transfer of Handwriting Skills Reflecting Comparative Data for Performance in Resource Room and Regular Classroom

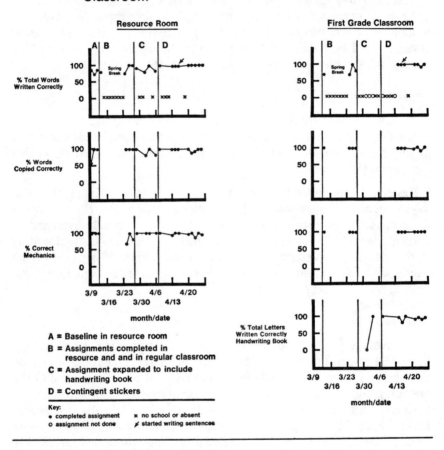

motivated to do so. It is important to reiterate that when the "sticker" condition was implemented, J. did not immediately respond to treatment. Sometimes teachers who select reinforcers become discouraged and give them up because there is no impact the first occasion they are used. Some individuals take time to respond to a new environmental change. With contingency changes, students may need time to test the conditions to see if they are consistent and meaningful. J. is probably an example of this type of responder.

Spelling

Project 5: Monitoring the Effect of Direct Spelling Instruction on Regular Classroom Work

R/CT: Chris Bedford

B. was a sixth-grade student receiving direct instruction in reading and math in the resource room. He was required to answer written comprehension questions after reading each story orally. The R/CT noticed that many of the words that he consistently missed were basic sight words. B.'s parents and teacher were contacted by the R/CT with the intent of starting a sight word training program in the resource room. Approval was obtained, and B. was told to come to the resource room ten minutes prior to his regular time for daily spelling instruction.

Baseline

Baseline data were obtained by looking at B.'s written response to his daily comprehension questions. A percentage was computed as follows:

$$\% = \frac{\text{number of Dolch words spelled correctly}}{\text{number of Dolch words attempted}}$$

Words that had a Dolch sight word (Dolch, 1936) as the root were included in the figures. They were counted as incorrect if the error occurred in the root, and as correct if the error occurred in the suffix. B. was allowed to use his reading book and dictionary to look up any words. When he asked the R/CT how to spell a word, it was given to him only when he had tried his book and dictionary, and he could not produce the correct spelling on his own. At no time did the R/CT give him the spelling for a Dolch word. B. never used the dictionary for Dolch words because he thought he always spelled them correctly. Baseline lasted for six days.

Intervention

A five-day training program was instituted consisting of the following steps:

- *Day 1:* Dolch words were read from a random list for the student to write. Examples of the words' used were given as necessary (for example, their/there). Each word was checked immediately, and incorrect spellings were noted. This continued until five words were missed. All words missed were recorded on the recording form.

- *Day 2:* The same list was given as on the previous day, stopping at the same place, regardless of the words missed. Incorrect words were recorded.
- *Day 3:* All words missed on days 1 and 2 were written on index cards. The cards were shown to B. one at a time. He was instructed to pronounce the word and give a sentence using it correctly when indicated by the R/CT. The card was then turned face down, and B. was instructed to write the word. The words were then recorded as being either correct or incorrect on the recording form.
- *Day 4:* Same as day 3.
- *Day 5:* B. was tested on the group of words he had drilled on during days 3 and 4 in the following manner: Each word was read to him; he was given a sentence as an example when necessary; and he was told to write the word. This was checked immediately, and any words misspelled were automatically added to the list for the next set to be drilled and tested.

Beginning the third week, the drill words from the previous two sets were involved in the day 1 and 2 list, serving as a postcheck. Any words missed were drilled and tested along with the set three words.

All spelling errors in written comprehension work done in the resource room were checked. Any misspelled words that had been previously drilled and passed on the test were automatically included in the next set to be drilled and tested. In addition to the written work done in the resource room, random samples of written work done in the regular classroom were also analyzed, and the percentages were plotted on the same graph for comparison.

Results. During baseline, the percentage of correctly spelled Dolch words ranged from 86 percent to 100 percent with a mean of 92 percent. Only one sample was obtained from the regular classroom, which had a 70 percent accuracy. This phase lasted for six school days. During the drill phase of the program, which lasted for 26 school days, the scores ranged from 76 percent to 100 percent, with a mean score of 93 percent. Due to the construction of the program, it seemed logical that the scores would show gradual improvement. Thus, the last ten days were isolated and showed a range of 90 percent to 100 percent with a mean of 96 percent. The papers from the regular classwork showed a range of 69 percent to 100 percent with the mean being 87 percent. Again, the scores from the last ten days were isolated and were found to range from 71 percent to 100 percent with a mean of 91 percent. (See Figure 5–6.)

Figure 5–6 Comparison of Dolch Word Spelling in Resource Room and a Sixth-Grade Classroom

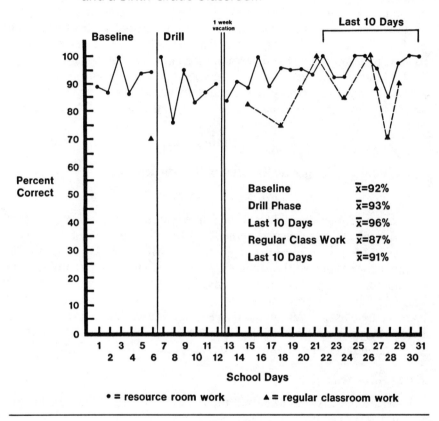

Discussion

This daily procedure was simple to implement and required no more than ten minutes for administration and scoring. Because of its cumulative effect, the most recent scores were the best indicators of the success of the program. It was noted by the classroom teacher, parents, and the R/CT that B.'s overall spelling improved as well, possibly because he was more aware of spelling the words correctly.

This project can serve as a good model to a teacher consultant as a means of monitoring performance in the regular classroom. This R/CT devised a system of intermittently checking spelling of Dolch words on written classroom assignments. The system was simple and required little time to implement. The method of calculating number of correct occurrences over total number of occurrences is one that could be applied to many areas of regular class academic performance. Resource teachers could devise similar tracking strategies for cross-classroom performance as they implement direct instruction programs. Use of such a system can remind resource teachers to ascertain that instruction offered in the resource room is relevant to expected performance in the regular classroom.

The degree to which the R/CT involved the classroom teacher and parents at the onset of this project is another strategy important to resource teachers who expect to expand their duties to that of teacher consultant.

Mathematics

Project 6: Transfer of Subtraction Skills

R/CT: Anita Andrews

P. was a fifth-grade student receiving resource instruction in math four days a week. P. was referred to the R/CT by his math teacher and a Title I teacher because he was having problems with subtraction facts. The math teacher expected the students to write the answer to 80 problems in five minutes with 80 percent accuracy. This is a rate of approximately 13 correct problems per minute (CPPM). Since this task was to be transferred back to the class, it was agreed that P. would reach the following criteria before being transferred back: (1) accuracy of 95 percent or better on subtraction facts when doing 80 problems; and (2) a rate of 20 CPPM.

Phase A (Baseline)

P. wrote the answers to 80 subtraction problems daily (facts 0–20). He was timed for accuracy and rate. (See Figure 5–7).

Results. Average accuracy was 73 percent, and average rate was 11 CPPM.

Phase B

P. completed subtraction problems (0–10). Every incorrect problem was circled, and P. had to rework those problems the following day. The R/CT modeled the correct answer and procedure, helped P. complete the problem, and then left the corrected completed problem on the page. P. then took a new timed test.

Criteria. The criteria were 100 percent and 25 CPPM for four days.

Results. Average accuracy was 99 percent, and average rate was 27 CPPM.

Figure 5–7 Direct Instruction and Transfer of Subtraction Skills

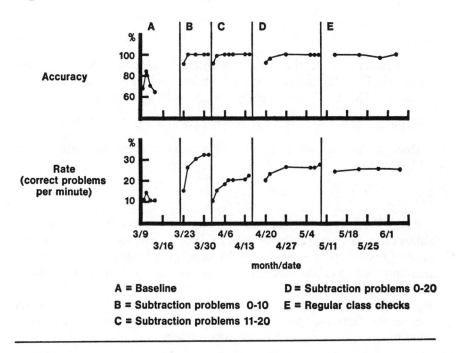

month/date

A = Baseline   D = Subtraction problems 0-20

B = Subtraction problems 0-10   E = Regular class checks

C = Subtraction problems 11-20

Phase C

P. completed 80 subtraction problems (11–20). The same error correction procedure used as in phase B.

Criteria. The criteria were 100 percent accuracy and 20 CPPM for four days.

Results. Average accuracy was 99 percent, and average rate was 18 CPPM.

Phase D

P. completed 80 subtraction problems (0–20), which were a combination of problems from phases B and C. The error correction procedure from phase B was used. (P. had been absent because of problems related to asthma.)

Criteria. The criteria were 100 percent accuracy and 25 CPPM for four days.

Results. Average accuracy was 99 percent, and average rate was 25 CPPM.

Phase E

P. was returned to the regular math class. Weekly timed tests were given, and P. had to meet criteria in order to pass each set of 80 subtraction problems. The R/CT made weekly checks on P.'s progress.

Criteria. The criteria were 95 percent accuracy and 20 CPPM.

Results. Average accuracy was 99 percent, and average rate was 25 CPPM.

Discussion

The R/CT successfully improved a student's ability to answer written subtraction facts correctly by direct resource instruction. For incorrect student responses, she used a Model-Lead-Test strategy as an error correction procedure. She modeled the correct answer, assisted the student in making the correction, and then retested the student. She used a changing criterion strategy that set the rate criterion at a slightly lower level for subtraction facts 1–20 than she used for facts 0–10. When all facts (0–20) were practiced, she again raised the rate criterion.

When the student was transferred to regular math class, she lowered rate and accuracy criteria slightly. She based her criterion strategy for transfer on the reported observations of O'Connor et al. (1979), who found that desired behaviors initially decreased upon return to regular class. (See Figures 4–1 and 4–2 in Chapter 4.) The accommodation for expected decrease in performance upon transfer was included by setting both rate and accuracy and rate criterion higher in phase D than in phase E. A glance at Figure 5–7 will reiterate the fact that for this student the expected decline in desired behavior occurred only slightly during the third-week check for accuracy and during the first-week check for rate. A steady average performance was maintained for both behaviors.

Another strength of the project was the close cooperation that occurred between the math teacher and the R/CT. The R/CT was careful to ascertain a criterion performance level that was acceptable to the math teacher. This was completion of 80 math facts at a rate of approximately 13 correct problems per minute with 80 percent accuracy. The R/CT then purposefully set the minimal levels of performance criterion at levels that were higher than this. Again, this was done to ensure that the student would succeed upon changing learning environments and teachers.

A final comment for this project is that P. had asthma and missed school frequently as indicated by the spaces with missing data in phases A, D, and E. Yet, in spite of this complication, P. still mastered the math facts and performed above criteria in the regular math class.

Project 7: Transfer of Independent Math Assignments to a Regular Classroom

R/CT: Polly Petry-Hill

M. was a third-grade student who attended a learning disabilities resource room primarily for reading difficulties. The school principal approached the R/CT to discuss the possibility of expanding direct services to include math instruction. M. was scheduled for entry the following year into an option C class where no particular curricular series was used, and emphasis was placed on working independently. The principal wanted M.'s math problems to be cleared up before the class change. The principal described M.'s math difficulties as a confusion over when to borrow or regroup in subtraction problems.

Administration of a criterion-referenced math test, which included borrowing across one to three digits, confirmed that this was indeed a problem skill area for M. The difficulty levels on this assessment tool contained two levels that pertained to subtraction facts and eleven levels with subtraction problems with regrouping in ascending order of difficulty. For instruction, M. was placed at the beginning of the first level for math facts. The R/CT established three major objectives for M. The first was to set up an independent study task where M. would practice computing correct written responses to subtraction problems that included regrouping. The second objective was to transfer this independent work to M.'s regular classroom as soon as possible. It was expected that M. would complete at least 80 percent of the problems correctly in the regular class. The third objective was that the R/CT projected that M. would progress through ten levels of subtraction with borrowing.

Independent Work in the Resource Room

The following particular set of five strategies was devised to aid M. in successfully completing independent math work:

1. M. completed two sample problems placed on the top of each work-page.
2. M. checked these two completed sample problems by re-solving them on a calculator.

3a. If both of M.'s answers were correct, she completed the remainder of the worksheet that contained 15 problems.

3b. If one or both answers were incorrect, she reworked the incorrect sample problems and checked the corrected answers with the calculator. Upon attaining 100 percent mastery on the two sample problems, M. then completed the entire worksheet.

The worksheet containing 15 problems was subdivided into two parts. The first five problems were modeled after the sample problems. The last 10 problems were a review of problems previously mastered.

4. M. then checked the completed worksheet with the calculator. She calculated her own score reflecting the percent correct. The criterion for passing a level was to attain 100 percent mastery of three separate worksheets on three separate days, excluding the sample problems.

5a. When criterion was met, M. progressed to the next level of problems.

5b. On days when 100 percent was not attained, M. had to correct the worksheet at the same level on the following day.

Independent Work in the Classroom

When M. had completed five consecutive days of assignments with 100 percent mastery, she was transferred back to the regular classroom. The same set of self-corrective strategies to facilitate independent work in the resource room was used in the regular classroom. An alternation was made in the criteria for mastery. M. now needed to achieve only 80 percent correct for the first five problems representing new material on the worksheet. Criterion for review, which comprised the last 10 problems on the worksheet, remained at 100 percent.

Results. M. completed worksheets in the resource room for 33 instructional days. By this time she had mastered three levels, and for the past 5 days she had achieved 100 percent mastery, which were the criteria for transfer to the regular class. After the transfer she reached 100 percent mastery on 11 out of 15 days for new problems (the first five problems on each worksheet). She met the 80 percent criterion level on 14 out of the 15 days. For review problems she attained 100 percent mastery on 12 out of the 15 days. The R/CT originally projected that M. would complete ten levels of materials by the time this project had ended. M. had, in fact, completed 12 levels of problems, which was two more than initially projected.

Discussion

The most important consultative strategy contained within this transfer project was the plan the R/CT used to provide the requested service for this student. To reiterate, the principal requested additional services. The R/CT already had a heavy caseload, which included reading instruction for this student. From onset, the R/CT made this an independent study project. This fit well within the tight instructional schedule in the resource room. It also provided an excellent opportunity for M. to practice working and learning independently. Ability to work independently was a desired skill in the classroom that M. would enter the following year. From onset, the R/CT also planned to transfer this study task to the regular classroom as soon as possible. In advance, she defined a performance level that the student had to reach in order to be transferred.

This R/CT also employed some other useful consultative strategies. She trained the student to use a calculator and to score her own worksheet. She conducted reliability checks to ensure that the student's scoring was accurate. The student had no difficulty with the use of the calculator or with self-scoring. She did, however, have considerable difficulty charting her own progress data on a performance graph. The R/CT always assisted M. with the charting. When M. was returned to the regular class for independent math work, the R/CT continued to assist with the charting.

Given that M. was unable to master charting, the R/CT's visits to the classroom for charting assistance were beneficial. These visits allowed the R/CT a few moments to view M.'s performance in a regular class and provided more opportunity for interaction between the classroom teacher and the R/CT. Toward the end of this project, the classroom teacher took over the responsibility of assisting M. with the charting. This turned out to be a subtle way for the R/CT to share some charting techniques with the classroom teacher without immediately imposing on the teacher's time. Instead, the R/CT moved slowly toward classroom teacher assistance after she had frequently visited the classroom.

It is important to point out that the R/CT was working when she visited this classroom. She did not appear only as a visitor to observe the classroom. Nor did she send a message that said, "The assistance I'm providing is so specialized that only a special educator could do it." The R/CT also demonstrated through practice that charting the student's performance data took a small amount of time.

The R/CT kept the calculator in a separate location. In this way, the student could make certain that she completed the problems before checking them. Keeping the calculator (or stopwatch) in a separate and special place can encourage students to think of this equipment as being special and valuable. It is also a good idea to implement a rule stating that equipment is always used at the same table where it is stored and that it is returned to the *center* of the table when the student is finished. This practice decreases the chances of equipment being misplaced, dropped, or inadvertently knocked off a table's edge.

In summary, deficient math skills of this student were efficiently remediated across a resource room and a classroom setting. It is essential to note that, in this case, all skills levels for this math area were *not* mastered prior to transfer. Instead, ability to work and self-correct independently were mastered prior to transfer to the regular classroom.

Project 8: Acquisition of Multiplication Skills in Direct Service with Generalization Across Settings

R/CT: Mary Petry-Cooper

F., a fifth grader, was referred to the resource room by her classroom teacher, primarily because she had not mastered basic multiplication and division facts. She was unable to perform multidigit multiplication problems consistently and accurately. The classroom teacher had presented the textbook lessons in these areas to F. and others in her math group, and the classroom teacher felt she needed to move on, even though F. had not mastered the skills.

Multiplication and Division Facts

The multiplication and division facts were broken down into 12 sets of 24 to 26 facts each for practice and mastery. Flashcards and daily timed tests were constructed to coincide with these fact sets. Six review problems were included on each daily test (except for the first set of facts) to ensure maintenance of facts previously learned.

Performance Criteria

The R/CT obtained rate and accuracy data from three average students in F.'s classroom over three days to use for setting mastery criteria for the facts. A minimum rate of 20 correct problems per minute (CPPM) was established using these data. Mean accuracy for these average students was 84 percent. The R/CT raised this to 96 to 100 percent to ensure fact mastery. Criteria were ≥ 96 percent correct for accuracy with 20 CPPM for three consecutive days.

After baseline data were collected, F. came to the resource room daily for flashcard practice and a written timed test of the flashcards practiced.

After three consecutive days of meeting mastery criteria on one set of facts, F. proceeded to the following fact set.

For practice on math facts, the R/CT used a specific error correction procedure, which utilized a Model-Lead-Test strategy. This strategy was based on principles of direct instruction utilized in Direct Instruction for the Teaching of Arithmetic and Reading (DISTAR) (Englemann & Bruner, 1974). The R/CT called her procedure Flashcard Drill. This procedure is presented in Figure 5–8.

Baseline Results

The student was tested on four of the twelve fact sets, which were selected randomly. F. could compute these basic facts with accuracy scores ranging from 69 percent to 96 percent ($\overline{X}$ = 87.75%) and with rate scores ranging from seven to ten correct problems per minute ($\overline{X}$ = 8.25 CPPM).

Results of Instruction

Three to five days of flashcard practice were required for F. to reach mastery criteria for each fact set for three consecutive days. All facts were mastered in 9½ weeks of instruction.

Figure 5–8 Flashcard Drill Used as an Error Correction Procedure in Project 8

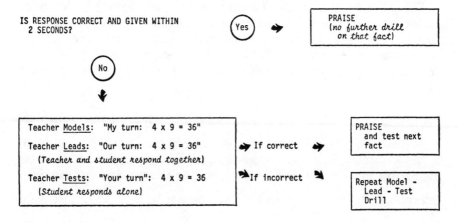

Multidigit Multiplication

A pretest was given over three days consisting of different kinds of one-, two-, and three-digit multiplication problems with and without regrouping. This showed that F. was already able to calculate correctly problems of the types

$$
\begin{array}{llll}
\text{nn} & \text{nnn} & \text{nnc} & \text{ccc} \\
\underline{\text{x n}} & \underline{\text{x n}} & \underline{\text{x n}} & \underline{\text{x n}}
\end{array}
\text{, but not}
$$

$$
\begin{array}{llllll}
\text{nc} & \text{cc} & \text{ncc} & \text{nn} & \text{nc} & \text{cc} & \text{nn} & \text{ncc} \\
\underline{\text{x n}} & \underline{\text{x n}} & \underline{\text{x n}} & \underline{\text{xnn}} & \underline{\text{xnn}} & \underline{\text{xnn}} & \underline{\text{xnnn}} & \underline{\text{xnnn}}
\end{array}
$$

(where n = any number without carrying, and c = any number requiring carrying).

For placement, problem types were introduced one at a time in the above sequence until 100 percent mastery in the resource room was demonstrated (three consecutive days of at least nine out of ten problems calculated correctly).

Criterion for Instruction

The criterion for instruction was greater or equal to 90 percent correct for accuracy for three consecutive days.

Baseline Results

The student computed an average of 43.5 percent of the multiplication problems correctly. (The range was 41 percent to 46 percent.)

Results of Instruction

The student was given daily instruction and practice with each type of multiplication problem that she had not computed correctly during baseline. Upon project completion, she mastered four additional types of problems requiring an average of five days of instruction for each (range three to seven days). At this time she was working on the fifth new problem type area.

Generalization Skills

Since not all possible types of multiplication problems were pretested, a test for generalization was constructed. This consisted of problems similar to, but not identical to, problems on the pretest. For example, generalization for $\frac{\text{cn}}{\text{xn}}$ was tested since only nc and $\frac{\text{cc}}{\text{xn}}$ were tested for placement. Generalization was tested after the student had shown mastery of similar problems of the same type. If the student mastered these problems by calculating three out of three problems correctly for at least two out of the three days, then generalization was assumed to have occurred. If mastery was not shown, then direct instruction was given.

Results. In all cases tested (1 digit × 2 digit; 1 digit × 3 digit), generalization was shown to have occurred.

Transfer to the Classroom

The student was given a daily assignment to be completed in her classroom to ensure that she would be able to perform skills learned in the resource room in her usual classroom setting. Assignments consisted of ten multiplication problems that the student had mastered in the resource room. Mastery could have occurred on the placement test, after instruction, or on the generalization test. Some worksheets contained a single problem type; others contained a mixture of problem types. If the student could perform multidigit multiplication problems successfully in the classroom, then transfer of basic facts mastered was also assumed.

The R/CT questioned the student to make sure she actually did work the problems by herself in her classroom. Her classroom teacher also confirmed that she did. These assignments were considered to be part of daily math assignments in the classroom, although F. also continued to receive instruction in her usual classroom group.

Results. The student was able to perform all types of multiplication problems assigned with 80 percent to 100 percent accuracy ($\overline{X}=95.5$ percent) in her classroom.

Table 5–2 contains a summarization of criteria, baseline performance, and results for each of the above areas of instruction. These included direct instruction in multiplication facts, multidigit problems, and transfer and generalization of these skills.

Discussion

During a 2½ month time, F. mastered multiplication facts with a response rate that increased by more than twice the original rate. Over the next 14 days, F. mastered four new problem types using multiple digits. F. also mastered all problems that were of a similar type as the mastered multidigit problems (generalization). All correct responses to mastered problems transferred successfully to the regular math class.

The R/CT found this Model-Lead-Test error correction procedure to be so successful that she used the same procedure for several students. She

Table 5–2 Performance Criteria and Results for Direct Instruction, Generalization, and Transfer of Multiplication Skills

Area	Criteria	Baseline	Results
DIRECT INSTRUCTION Multiplication Facts	96–100% correct 20 CPPM for three consecutive days	$\overline{X}=87.75\%$ correct $\overline{X}=8.25\%$ CPPM	All facts mastered at criteria in 9½ weeks
Multidigit Problems	90% correct for three consecutive days	4 correct problem types 8 incorrect problem types $\overline{X}=43.5\%$ correct	8 correct problem types 4 nonmastered problem types
GENERALIZATION	100% correct for 2 of 3 days		All measured problems transferred
TRANSFER	≥80% accuracy for three consecutive days		$\overline{X}=95.5\%$ for problems assigned

incorporated this type of instruction into a tutor program for math mastery. She also taught this procedure to the parents of some students to facilitate home practice of math facts. A detailed report of a home project using this strategy is contained in Chapter 9.

Aside from use of an effective error correction procedure, a teacher consultant might also be interested in some other strategies that this R/CT used. The R/CT obtained normative data for average performance of F.'s classmates. She used these data to establish a criterion performance level for direct instruction. Mastery learning was used, as F. was expected to master each set before proceeding to the next. Performance was measured daily so that both F. and the R/CT were certain of student progress. After math fact mastery, the R/CT assessed F.'s ability to answer multidigit problems correctly by use of a criterion-referenced test that included each problem type. The R/CT made certain that F.'s correct responses generalized to similar problem types. The method that the R/CT used to measure performance was one that could be easily implemented in a regular classroom so that performance could continue to be monitored after the student was transferred to regular math class.

SUMMARY

This chapter contains eight projects that typify transfer consultation projects that have been accomplished by special education teachers who work as direct instruction resource teachers and as consulting teachers. These projects represent a variety of individual interpretations of the guidelines for transfer presented at the beginning of this chapter, as well as those offered by Wildman and Wildman (1975) and Stokes and Baer (1977). Within these transfer projects, the reader can also observe examples of practical application of five concepts recommended by this author as useful for facilitating transfer of special students from resource to classroom instruction. These concepts, which are reviewed in Chapter 4, are mastery learning, data-based instruction, direct curricular instruction, systematic structuring of learning environments, and programming for behavior generalization.

COMMUNICATION EXCHANGE

When a student's deficient skills are assessed within the normal school curriculum, it is important to share the information with others who are involved and concerned with that student's progress. By having access to curricular placement and pupil progress information, these concerned individuals may form more realistic perceptions of the student's ability. For example, to describe a student as dyslexic with auditory processing problems may cause parents serious concern about something they do not understand. This approach may serve to convince parents that their child has such serious learning deficits that many special adaptations must be made within that child's school experiences. This approach may also serve as a strong signal to classroom teachers that the student will be unable to learn in a regular class setting and can only learn in a special education classroom.

In contrast, when curriculum-based assessments are used to describe student's skill levels, the result is a clear, behavioral description of performance. There is no implication that the student needs highly differential instruction. A behaviorally-oriented description of performance in curricula also gives everyone concerned a clear, intelligible picture of the skills that that student has acquired and those that are deficient.

A memo written by the consulting teacher to all concerned individuals is one way in which assessment and progress information can be communicated. The following is an example of a memo designed to report on the academic progress of student A. This student initially received direct reading instruction in a resource room with a resource/consulting teacher, Mary Pilosof. As reported in Project 3 of this chapter, A.'s reading program was transferred back to a fifth-grade classroom. This memo is a form of an academic progress report and contains curricular placement information, pupil progress information, and an indication that a transfer to regular classroom has been planned.

Sample Memo for Academic Progress

DATE: March 6
TO: Ms. Morgan (fifth-grade teacher)
         Mr. and Mrs. J. Williamson (parents)
         Mr. Barclay (building principal)
FROM: Mary Pilosof (resource/consulting teacher)
RE: Academic progress report for A. Williamson

I) *Oral Reading:*
   a) Initial Placement: As you will recall, A. was placed in the 3^2 Laidlaw reader (Laidlaw, 1976–1978) in September.
      Placement Criteria: 95 percent accuracy or more on a 100-word sample, and 80 percent correct comprehension or better (four correct answers out of five) for scores read at each grade level on three separate days.
   b) Current Progress: A. started the fifth-grade Laidlaw reader on February 6.
The reading group that A. would most likely fit into in Ms. Morgan's class is currently reading in the fifth-grade reader in the Scott, Foresman series. A.'s performance in that series was as follows:
New Placement: A placement test was given on March 4, 5, and 6. A. was tested in the Scott, Foresman fifth-grade reader.
Results: Average of three testing days: 97 percent accuracy, 100 percent comprehension, and 83 correct words per minute.
Criteria for placement: 94 percent accuracy or more; 80 percent comprehension or more than three days in a row for each level.

II) *Silent Reading:*
   a) Intervention: On November 5, A. started silent reading and written comprehension in the resource room in the Laidlaw curriculum used for oral reading.
      Criterion: For comprehension, the student's average for this period was 80 percent correct.
   b) Intervention for written comprehension started in November 1979. The written comprehension was gradually increased from two written answers to eight written answers.
Criteria: 80 percent for two to five written questions and 90 percent for six to eight questions. A.'s average for the last month was 90 percent correct.

III) *Handwriting:*
  a) A placement test was given on December 5, 6, and 7. The student was tested on all the letters in the alphabet (lower and upper case) in isolation and in connective.

Results: The following letters were found incorrect *in isolation:* (1) lower case a,c,d,f,g,l,o,p,q,s,t,x, and y; and (2) upper case C,I,J,L,P,S,U,X,Z, and Y. The following letters were incorrect *in connective:* o,b,k,y,c,g,h,p,s,t,x, and z.
  b) Intervention started on December 10. A. had to write three to four letters from the list presented earlier—ten times for each letter per day.

Criteria: 100 percent correct three days in a row for each new letter.

IV) *Spelling:*
  a) A placement test was given on February 18, 19, and 20. A. was tested in the Scott, Foresman Spelling Book, levels 2, 3, and 4.

Results: A. was placed in grade level 2.

Comments: Since the beginning of the school year A. has made significant progress in oral reading. He started at grade level 3.2 and reached his grade level in February 1980. He reads well in both the Laidlaw and the Scott, Foresman series. A. will be transferred to his regular classroom for oral reading. He will still come to the resource room on a daily basis for spelling instruction.

Final Note: Please remember to share your enthusiasm for his progress with A.

Chapter 6

Consultation: Academic Problems in the Regular Classroom

Mildly handicapped students experience many problems in regular classes, but probably the most outstanding is poor academic skills in, reading, arithmetic calculation and problem solving, spelling, handwriting, and working independently. A usual response to students with these difficulties is to refer them for special education services. A separate and special approach has been the norm in public education. Naturally, as special services are made available, the number of students in need of such services increases. As more and more students are identified who need academic assistance, alternative forms of service delivery must also be considered. Through a teacher consultation model, not only can more students be served, but more can be helped in the regular classrooms. An added bonus is that classroom and consulting teachers working together can form remedial solutions that can be applied to many students with learning problems, not just to those students who happen to carry a special education label.

REFERRAL TO SPECIAL EDUCATION

As school districts begin to adopt teacher consultant models, the traditional system in which students are referred to special education must be altered. Provision must be made for classroom teachers and teacher consultants to get together prior to a formal referral to special education. Classroom teachers should be able to contact a teacher consultant when they identify a student who is having problems. The teacher consultant should be available to visit that teacher's classroom to observe the student and to discuss the problem. The collaborating teachers should experiment with a variety of solutions to determine if they can remediate or at least alleviate the student's problem in the classroom setting.

Resource/consulting teachers at the University of Illinois have designed referral forms for classroom teachers to use for informing teacher consultants of classroom problems. These forms are designed to provide the teacher consultant with information such as the curricula used in the classroom, the teacher's expectations for classroom performance, the specific areas in which the student has problems, and the times that the classroom teacher will be available for consultation. Figure 6–1 contains an illustration of such a referral form. Other good examples can be found in Deno and Mirkin (1977).

ANALYSIS OF LEARNING STAGES

Academic problems can vary across levels of severity as well as across subject areas. A primary rule for consulting teachers is that the stage in which the student is performing must be considered. Following is a review of six stages of learning: *acquisition, reversion, proficiency, maintenance, generalization,* and *adaption.*

A teacher consultant must carefully consider which stage a student is in when selecting the best method of remediation or intervention. If a student is in the *acquisition* stage, some method of direct instruction may be the best solution. In the *reversion* stage, practice and intensive drill may be preferable. If a student demonstrates *proficiency,* but at the characteristic slow pace, the consultant will probably select some type of changing criterion or reinforcer to increase speed. Once a student is *maintaining* performance, the consultant may want to reduce reinforcement gradually, reinforce intermittently, or check on the student less frequently. For *generalization,* the consultant may spend time planning for new situations and settings in which the desired behavior can occur. For *adaption,* teacher consultants may spend more time examining curricular materials to determine whether sufficient opportunities are provided for students to apply a skill to a new area of application.

TYPES OF PROBLEMS

This chapter contains some illustrations of various types of academic problems that consulting teachers and classroom teachers have solved. (See Table 6-1.)

Figure 6–1 A Referral Form to Facilitate Communication between Classroom and Consulting Teachers (Developed by R/CT Trainees, Spring 1980)

REFERRAL FORM FOR THE RESOURCE/CONSULTING TEACHER

Directions: Please complete all items on this form. Additional comments are welcomed but not required. Please leave this form with the Resource/Consulting Teacher. A conference will be scheduled within five days of receipt of request.

Request for Program Modification

To: Special Education Resource Team

From: _____ Date: _____

Name of student: _____ Grade: _____ Age: _____ Room #: _____

Name of parent: _____ Home phone: _____

Parent's address: _____

Reason for referral: (describe student's problem in brief but specific terms)

Provide the requested information in the appropriate spaces below:

Areas of difficulty	Level of present performance	end of year level for non-problematic performance	series and/ or book being used	optional additional teacher's comments
READING	with 90% accuracy			
SPELLING				
MATH				
OTHER AREA (be specific)				

Figure 6–1 continued

SOCIAL DIFFICULTY—Please list below, specific things the student does that sets the student apart from other classmates. (feel free to use extra paper)

_____

_____

_____

To make a conference for us possible, could you please list three alternative days and/or hours during the next school week that are convenient for you. Would you also rate the student in terms of how soon assessment is needed by circling either 1, 2, or 3. (with 1 being a student in need of *immediate* assessment)

	Time	*Rate the need for assessment:*		
Monday	_____ _____	1	2	3
Tuesday	_____ _____			
Wednesday	_____ _____			
Thursday	_____ _____			
Friday	_____ _____			

*All referrals will be assessed; the only reason for the rating is so that I will know which students are top priority in terms of assessment.

Table 6–1 Overview of Projects Contained in Chapter 6.

Project	Task
9	Improving writing skills
10	Helping students with assignments in workbooks that accompany basal readers.
11	Helping students with assignments in workbooks that accompany basal readers
12	Increasing the number of classroom assignments a student completes
13	Improving mathematics skills
14	Improving mathematics skills
15	Improving spelling ability
16	Improving spelling ability
17	Providing consultation in a content area

OBTAINING A NORMATIVE SAMPLE OF STUDENT PERFORMANCE

An important strategy for consultation in regular classrooms is to collect samples of average student performances. This normative sample can be used to:

- give teachers a specific, behavioral description of how an average student performs a skill;
- give teachers a clear idea of whether average students are meeting teacher expectations;
- determine any discrepancy between how a poor student performs and how the teacher(s) would like the student to perform;
- give teachers a guide for setting goals, objectives, and criterial performance levels for students.

Project 9: Generating Goals, Objectives, and Criterion Levels from a Classroom Sample

R/CT: Margie Heintz

This R/CT was working with a fifth-grade teacher to improve the writing skills of M., a boy who had been labeled as learning disabled. She identified four writing behaviors that she used to measure performance in the classroom: (1) number of words written; (2) percent of words spelled correctly; (3) number of thoughts; and (4) number of complete sentences. A thought was defined as a phrase containing at least a subject and a verb. A complete sentence included correct syntactical word order with all words necessary to form a grammatically correct sentence with correct punctuation and capitalization. After instruction, the R/CT obtained a daily, three-minute sample. Three stimulus words were supplied to M. to help him write the words that changed from day to day. M. was instructed to write a sentence using those three words. After the sentence was formed, he was given one minute to think and three minutes to write as much as he could about the topic sentence. He was encouraged to write complete sentences.

After a three-week period of instruction, the R/CT questioned how realistic her goals were for this student. To solve the problem, she selected four students from the targeted student's classroom and tested the frequency of these same four behaviors in their writing. These were students who finished their classroom work on time. These students were given a three-minute writing test on three separate days. Identical procedures to those used with M. were used.

Table 6–2 contains the comparative data for all four behaviors. M.'s scores reflect an average performance over three weeks of instruction. The classroom peers' scores reflect measurement over three days. M.'s mean and median scores were lower than any of his peers for number of words and percentage of correctly spelled words. For number of thoughts and number of complete sentences, M.'s mean scores were equal to or better than at least one of the four classroom peers. His median score for number of thoughts was equal to those of two of his peers. M.'s median number of complete sentences was lower than any of the other students.

These normative data proved useful to the R/CT. For instance, the mean number of words written by the classroom peers was 27.6; this was considerably lower than what the R/CT had thought average fifth graders would produce in three minutes. Consequently, she reduced the ultimate goal for number of words for M. to produce. She decided to continue to focus direct instruction on number of words written and percent of words spelled correctly, and she eliminated number of thoughts and number of complete sentences. Knowing the range of responses across the four peers for number of words written and percent of correctly spelled words also gave the R/CT direction in establishing increments for changing criteria for M.'s performance on these two behaviors. For example, the range of words written by peers varied from a mean of 26 to 34 and was at least seven words higher than the average number produced by M. An ultimate goal for number of written words might be set at about 30 and with increments for change at about two to three words. This would mean that

Table 6–2 Comparison of Four Writing Behaviors of a Special Student to That of Four Classroom Peers

Behaviors	Target Student	Peer A	Peer B	Peer C	Peer D
Number of Words Written	$\bar{X}=19$ Mdn = 20	$\bar{X}=29$ Mdn = 24	$\bar{X}=26$ Mdn = 28	$\bar{X}=30$ Mdn = 30	$\bar{X}=34$ Mdn = 37
Percent of Words Spelled Correctly	$\bar{X}=73$ Mdn = 65	$\bar{X}=89$ Mdn = 88	$\bar{X}=94$ Mdn = 94	$\bar{X}=100$ Mdn = 100	$\bar{X}=98$ Mdn = 98
Number of Thoughts	$\bar{X}=3$ Mdn = 3	$\bar{X}=4$ Mdn = 3	$\bar{X}=2.7$ Mdn = 3	$\bar{X}=4.3$ Mdn = 4	$\bar{X}=5$ Mdn = 5
Number of Complete Sentences	$\bar{X}=1.3$ Mdn = 1	$\bar{X}=2.3$ Mdn = 3	$\bar{X}=1.3$ Mdn = 2	$\bar{X}=2.7$ Mdn = 3	$\bar{X}=3.6$ Mdn = 4

$\bar{X}$ = mean (average score)
Mdn = median (absolute middle score)

the first criterion might be set at 19 or 20 words, which were M.'s average scores. Then the first criterion change might be set at about 22 words, then 25, and so on, until M. was producing about 30 words in a three-minute timed sample. The same type of strategy could be used to improve spelling performance.

Some other consultation projects in which normative peer data have been collected are reported elsewhere in this book. In Project 1 in Chapter 5, the R/CT obtained a measure of the average silent reading rate in a second-grade class. In Project 8 in Chapter 5, the R/CT measured the average rate and accuracy of math fact completion by fifth graders in order to establish criterion levels. In this chapter's Project 13, the R/CT measured average time spent on-task by classroom peers in a second grade.

Project 10: Completion of Reading Workbook Assignments

R/CT: Anita Andrews

G. was a fourth grader who received resource services for oral reading and mathematics. He had progressed at an excellent rate in reading. At the time this project was initiated, he was reading at a level higher than the lowest group in his class.

In spite of this progress, G.'s teacher reported that he was not completing his work in the regular classroom. The teacher described him as having problems in all subjects. She said he did not concentrate, always hurried through his work, and constantly came to her desk asking questions. She reported that she had told G. that he was "going to give her grey hair." When asked to specify G.'s behavior, she offered this example. When she asked the group to take out their books or gave instructions to the group, she almost always had to repeat everything for G. In fact, she said she could not think of a time when G. had not asked her to repeat directions. She said that G. had passed through the school years not listening closely, and previous teachers had always repeated everything for him.

The consulting teacher and this classroom teacher also talked about G. having language and vocabulary problems. The classroom teacher said that he had a limited vocabulary and lacked language training. The consulting teacher noted that remembering what he had read was sometimes a problem for G.

As a result of these conversations, the teachers agreed that the R/CT would take a baseline measurement on percentage of assigned work that G. had completed by noon for five days. During this time, G. completed all of his work. The conferring teachers then decided that G.'s primary problem was that he did not understand written directions.

Baseline (A)

The classroom teacher recorded the number of pages that she assigned daily in the reading workbook. At the top of each of G.'s workpages, she marked the number of times G. asked for help during the assigned work period. The R/CT figured and charted accuracy percentage for each page and the frequency of teacher assistance. Baseline condition lasted for five days.

Results. The average accuracy was 72 percent. The average number of teacher assists equaled 3.

Phase B

G. came to the resource room early each morning, and the R/CT read him the directions for the day's reading workbooks assignments. She then talked with G. about the directions, asked him questions about what he was to do, and went over any new or different words in the directions with him. G. worked all exercises on the workpages in the classroom. Phase B lasted for seven days.

Criteria. The criterion was accuracy of 85 percent or better for four days.

Results. Average accuracy equaled 90 percent. The average number of teacher assists equaled .9.

Phase C

G. continued to come to the resource room for assistance with directions. He read the directions to the R/CT and then explained what he was to do. The R/CT prompted him to ask questions on anything he did not understand or any words he did not know. Phase C lasted for six days.

Criteria. The criterion was accuracy of 85 percent or better for four days.

Results. Average accuracy equaled 87 percent. The average number of teacher assists equaled .3.

Phase D

This condition was the same as in phase B, except G. only came to the resource room to read directions three days each week. This phase lasted six days.

Criteria. The criterion was accuracy of 85 percent or better at least 80 percent of the time.

Results. Average accuracy equaled 93 percent. The average number of teacher assists equaled 0.

Phase E

G. received no assistance in the resource room. Phase E lasted for ten days.

Criteria. The criteria were average weekly grade of at least 80 percent correct for accuracy with no more than three teacher assists a week.

Results. Average accuracy equaled 85 percent. The average number of teacher assists equaled .3.

Discussion

Reading the directions to G. increased the accuracy of his responses and decreased the number of teacher assists. This can be noted by comparing the performance data of baseline and phase B in Figure 6-2. The R/CT used a fading technique where she gradually decreased G.'s dependence on her for assistance with directions. When G. read the directions to the R/CT, there was only a three percent reduction in the accuracy of his responses as compared to the R/CT reading the directions. The number of teacher assists decreased slightly more when G. read the directions. When the number of visits to the resource room was decreased from five to three per week, G.'s accuracy improved slightly, and he needed no teacher assistance in class. When resource support was completely eliminated, accuracy decreased by 8 percent but this was still 13 percent higher than during baseline conditions. The number of teacher assists remained considerably lower than baseline, with one teacher assist per week for three weeks. During one week of baseline, there were a total of 17 teacher assists.

One strategy that this consulting teacher used was to set the expected criterion higher during the phases of resource assistance than during the final phase when no R/CT assistance was offered. The two collaborating teachers agreed that 80 percent for accuracy was an acceptable level of performance, even though they set it at 85 percent for phases B, C, and D.

Another important consultative strategy was encouraging the classroom teacher to be more specific in describing G.'s unacceptable behavior. The R/CT obtained an initial baseline measurement on completed assignments

Figure 6–2 Effects of Teaching a Student To Respond
Independently to Written Directions

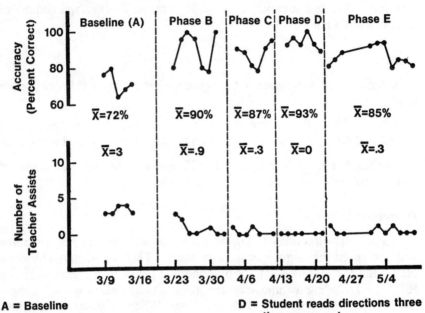

A = Baseline

B = R/CT reads directions every day

C = Student reads directions every day

D = Student reads directions three
times per week

E = No assistance with directions

and found that this was not the problem. It is not unusual for this to occur. Sometimes two teachers working together may have different perceptions of the student's problem. Attending closely to what the classroom teacher said about repeating the assignments may have eliminated the first inaccurate measurement of G's performance. However, the important point is that, when the first baseline measurement showed that assignment completion was not a problem, the R/CT did not conclude that the classroom teacher was inaccurate. Instead, the R/CT redefined the baseline measurement to focus on a behavior that would more precisely illustrate the problem.

A third important strategy occurred when the teachers agreed that G. seemed to have a language problem. They did not resort to requesting special services for language instruction. Instead, they selected a target behavior (following directions) that was a specific example of a language skill and was related to independent work completion. The teachers demonstrated that this particular language skill could be improved in a regular classroom setting with temporary resource assistance.

For practical purposes, this entire project could have been accomplished in the regular classroom. The consulting teacher could have done the training for following directions within sight of the classroom teacher. This method could have helped demonstrate the training procedures to the teacher. An even more practical intervention might have been to demonstrate the procedure to the teacher without the child present. The teacher or the classroom aide could have then initiated and been responsible for the behavior training. Three different teams of educational researchers (Fisher, Berliner, Filby, Marliave, Cahen, & Dishaw, 1980; Stallings, Gory, Fairweather, & Needles, 1977; Stallings & Kaskowitz, 1974) have reported that students in the average classroom spend two-thirds of their time working independently. Thus, the ability to perform workbook exercises adequately is an important area for consulting teachers to consider. A student who fails to meet teacher expectations for these assignments is certain to be perceived as experiencing learning difficulties. The student may not be performing well because certain skills are lacking (*acquisition stage*), or the student may have been conditioned to perform independent work in a resource setting but not in a regular classroom (*generalization across settings*).

The consulting teacher must carefully assess the entire situation, including student skill level, difficulty level of materials, clarity of instructions, and student motivation in order to select the best form of remediation.

Student Skill Level. As illustrated in Chapter 4, a student's skill level should be assessed within the curriculum used in the regular classroom. Samples of the content area work are extracted to construct a curriculum-based assessment. A criterion level of performance is defined, and students are then tested to determine whether they can perform at this specified level. It is often useful to obtain samples of how well average students in the class perform in the same materials. A good discussion of normative pupil performance sampling is available in an article by Epstein and Cullinan (1979).

Difficulty Level of Materials. Sometimes the materials are simply too difficult for a student to master in an independent work situation. It may then be necessary to: (1) place the student at a lower level in the same curriculum; or (2) modify the more difficult components of the materials so they are less complex.

Of interest to consulting teachers are the findings of a study by Moyer (1979) in which difficulty levels of reading materials used in elementary schools were assessed. Moyer compared the readability levels of basal readers to those of the accompanying workbooks. She used the *Fry Readability Graph* (Fry, 1968; 1977) to estimate the grade levels for each book and workbook. Number of sentences and number of syllables within a 100-word passage are the variables measured with the Fry graph. Samples were obtained from the beginning, middle, and end of each book/workbook. The series included in the study were: Allyn & Bacon (1978); American Book Co. (1977); Economy Co. (1975); Ginn & Co. (1976); Harcourt, Brace (1974); Harper & Row (1977); Holt, Rinehart & Winston (1977); MacMillan (1975); and Scott, Foresman (1978).

The workbooks were consistently more difficult than the basal readers for the overall Fry readability level, for the number of syllables per 100 words, and for the number of sentences per 100 words. Figure 6–3 illustrates these overall differences for all ten basal series and workbooks. Out of the possible 55 textbook pairs, only six instances occurred where the readability level of the workbooks was lower than that of the reader.

Moyer's comparative work clearly illustrates that teachers cannot form presumptions about the difficulty levels of materials. If students are having difficulty working independently, one of the first steps should be to examine the task carefully.

Clarity of Instructions. In Project 10, the student was not having difficulty with the materials, but with the accompanying directions. The consulting teacher effectively demonstrated the impact of using a fading procedure to teach a student to follow directions gradually. This is certainly a recommended first alternative in training students to read directions.

Unfortunately for some materials, being able to read directions is not sufficient. The reader must also decipher the meaning of directions that are vaguely written or confusing. Osborn (1981) did an excellent job of analyzing workbooks designed to accompany reading materials at the elementary level. She examined hundreds of tasks in about 20 workbooks. She cited numerous instances in which the workbooks' tasks were confusing, vague, and irrelevant to the lesson in the accompanying basal reader. As a result of this examination, Osborn compiled a list of the following 20 guidelines that were offered to publishers of basal reading programs as a means of improving the quality of workbook exercises and accompanying instructions:

1. A sufficient proportion of workbook tasks should be relevant to the instruction that is going on in the rest of the unit or lesson.
2. Another portion of workbook tasks should provide for a systematic and cumulative review of what has already been taught.

Figure 6–3 Comparison of Basal Readers and Basal Workbooks: Fry Readability, Syllable Counts, and Sentence Counts.

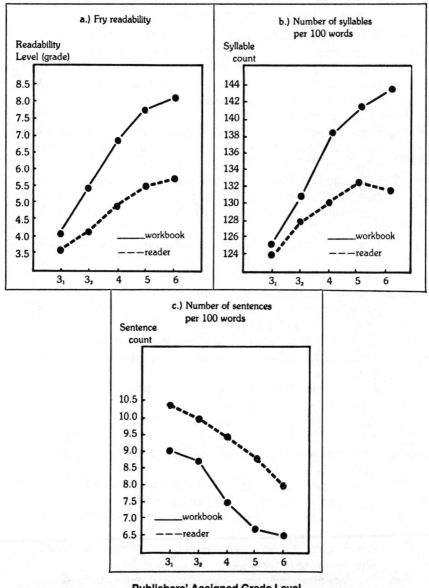

Publishers' Assigned Grade Level

Source: Reprinted from Moyer, S.B. "Readability of Basal Readers and Workbooks: A Comparison," *Learning Disability Quarterly,* 1979, p. 26.

3. Workbooks should reflect the most important (and work-book-appropriate) aspects of what is being taught in the reading program. Less important aspects should remain in the teacher's guide as voluntary activities.

4. Workbooks should contain, in a form that is readily accessible to students and teachers, extra tasks for students who need extra practice.

5. The vocabulary and concept level of workbook tasks should relate to that of the rest of the program and to the students using the program.

6. The language used in workbook tasks must be consistent with that used in the rest of the lesson and in the rest of the workbook.

7. Instructions to students should be clear, unambiguous, and easy to follow; brevity is a virtue.

8. The layout of pages should combine attractiveness with utility.

9. Workbook tasks should contain enough content so that there is a chance a student doing the task will *learn* something and not simply be *exposed* to something.

10. Tasks that require students to make discriminations must be preceded by a sufficient number of tasks that provide practice on components of the discriminations.

11. The content of workbook tasks must be accurate and precise; workbook tasks must not present wrong information or perpetuate misrules.

12. At least some workbook tasks should be fun and have an obvious payoff to them.

13. Most student response modes should be consistent from task to task.

14. Student response modes should be the closest possible to reading and writing.

15. The instructional design of individual tasks and of task sequences should be carefully planned.

16. Workbooks should contain a finite number of task types and forms.

17. The art that appears on workbook pages must be consistent with the prose of the task.

18. Cute, nonfunctional, space-, and time-consuming tasks should be avoided.

19. When appropriate, tasks should be accompanied by brief explanations of purpose for both teachers and students.

20. English-major humor should be avoided. (Some workbook exercises contain jokes and puzzles that only a person majoring in English would understand.)

The Osborn references contain several illustrative examples for each of these guidelines. These guidelines can also be used by consulting and classroom teachers to examine the likelihood of a given workbook task being completed in an independent work situation. As a result, consulting teachers can assist classroom teachers in modifying exercises and directions, eliminating exercises that are irrelevant, and determining which exercises need to offer more practice for the slower learner. In the latter case, the teacher consultant can construct and collect more practice exercises of the same type. Once this task has been demonstrated, a teacher's aide could easily accomplish it. Osborn's guidelines should also serve as a resource to teachers when they select new instructional materials and provide feedback to publishing companies on existing materials.

Student Motivation. Some students may not complete independent work tasks because of lack of motivation, not because they lack the skills. Teacher consultants must remember this when they are working with students who do not complete assignments. They must not introduce an elaborate remedial process or time-consuming material alteration when a reinforcer that is appropriate for the student can be used.

Project 11: Consultation for Independent Study Skills

R/CT: Chris Bedford

The subject in this study was a fifth-grade girl, T., who received daily, direct instruction in reading and math in the resource room. Identification of the problem occurred during a bimonthly meeting between T.'s teacher and the R/CT. A discrepancy was noted between T.'s reading level in the resource room (fifth grade in the Laidlaw series) and her placement in the regular class reading groups (fourth grade in the Ginn series). Through an analysis of the tasks required in the regular class, it became apparent that T.'s main problem was that she only produced one story with the accompanying workbook assignment per week, which was the minimum requirement, and that she needed to be working faster in order to advance to the next higher level. A problem was also noted in her ability to follow the workbook directions independently.

The purpose of this consultation project was to decrease the number of days T. needed to complete each story and the accompanying workbook pages and quiz, thereby increasing her rate of story completion. The final objective was to advance T. to the next highest reading group in her classroom.

Baseline

The data used for baseline had been previously collected by the classroom teacher over a four-week period. During this time, the students read the assigned story silently, took a written comprehension quiz consisting of approximately five questions, and did the accompanying workbook pages with teacher help available as needed.

Intervention

T. was given an index card marked in the following manner:

STORY	Date BEGAN	Date FINISHED	Classroom Teacher	Consulting Teacher	DAYS

T. was told that this was part of a plan to help her increase her story completion rate. T. was instructed to write the name of the story, the date she began it, and the date she finished it in the appropriate spaces on the card. The classroom teacher agreed to verify this by initialing in her column. Then T. was to bring the card to the resource room, where she received a foil star in the column marked "Consulting Teacher." The total number of days for completion was calculated and then transferred to a graph. This intervention was chosen because T. had previously expressed interest and proficiency in charting.

Results. During baseline conditions, T. used the full five days allowed for each of four stories, as did all other members in her reading group. By using self-recording and charting, T. reduced the time spent on each story from five days to two days for four out of five different stories. It took her four days to complete the remaining story.

Discussion

These teachers effectively used a simple motivation system to increase T.'s rate of production. This rate remained quite constant at two days for each assignment, with the exception of the vacation week. During this time, T. took four days to complete one story. T. was scheduled to take a family trip, and the excitement seemed to affect all of her schoolwork. T.'s mother was kept informed of and was pleased with T.'s progress. Parental approval may have had an effect on T.'s productivity.

At the time this intervention was selected, the other members of T.'s reading group took five days to complete each story assignment. As T.

started working faster, several other members of the low group started working faster as well. The classroom teacher's record book indicated that this was the case, yet she was reluctant to attribute the overall increased productivity to any example set by T. The teacher's expectation of work productivity may have been altered by T.'s progress. An additional consultation strategy might have been to offer the reinforcement system to other group members, one at a time, while monitoring the production rate of the entire group.

Project 12: Finding the Right Reinforcer To Increase Completed Assignments

R/CT: Mary Petry-Cooper

Project 12 is an example of using reinforcement to increase the number of completed assignments by a first-grade child. It illustrates how a teacher consultant had to search for the right combination of reinforcers to produce optimal performance for a student who had lower skill levels than his classroom peers.

M. was a first-grade boy in a classroom of first and second graders. He received Title I resource assistance in reading, but he simultaneously received reading instruction in the lowest classroom group. At a workshop for parents of Title I reading students, M.'s mother expressed concern about her son getting Title I tutorial help, because she felt that he would then be unable to work independently in the regular classroom.

The R/CT approached the classroom teacher with the mother's concerns and discovered that she, too, was concerned about M.'s inability to complete independent work. The classroom teacher felt that resource room reading assistance was the key that allowed him to function as well as he did in the classroom reading group, and she was reluctant to curtail his special services for this reason. She was willing to work with the R/CT in devising a system to help M. complete his classroom assignments.

M.'s teacher tried to give M. assignments she felt he could complete independently. She often gave him different assignments than she gave the other children in the class, reduced the workload, copied boardwork for him to complete (other children copied their own work from the board), and gave him 10 to 15 minutes of individual directions each day on how to start and complete the assignments. M. still approached the teacher for frequent help and usually did not complete the assignments. Although the teacher did provide extra help for this student, she did not feel she should have to do this, and she felt the boy should be retained in first grade because of immaturity in working independently. Although M. was slightly behind the other students, he was working on grade level in reading and math.

Baseline

The R/CT provided the teacher with a recording form. The classroom teacher agreed to record the type of assignment given and the percentage completed each day.

Results. The student completed an average of 59.6 percent of his daily assignments (ranging from 33 percent to 100 percent). He received extra teacher help on three of the five days of baseline.

Phase B

The R/CT instructed M. in how to start and stop a stopwatch. Since the teacher was most interested in teaching the student to copy work from the blackboard, this area was targeted for intervention. M. was told to start the stopwatch when he started copying from the board and to stop it when he finished the assignment. After copying the assignment, he was scheduled to go to the resource room for reading instruction with the R/CT. He carried the stopwatch with him, and the R/CT would record the amount of time required to complete the assignment. Unfortunately, the teacher gave him a copying assignment only on the first day of this phase and then stopped assigning this task. The student was then instructed to use the stopwatch to time how long it took him to complete all of his morning assignments.

The teacher continued to record assignments and percentage of work completed; in addition, she agreed to send home a "happy face" note each day if all of the assignments were completed. If assignments were not completed, the teacher agreed to send home unfinished work to be done. M.'s mother agreed to praise happy face notes and to ensure that M. would finish incomplete assignments and return them to school the following day.

Results. M. completed an average of 74.5 percent of the work assigned daily (ranging from 50 percent to 100 percent). He received extra teacher help on two of the six days of this phase. The teacher did not record data for the last three days of this phase because of added work involved with parent/teacher conferences.

Return to Baseline

Baseline was again reinstated. The teacher recorded assignments and percentage completed, but the use of the stopwatch and notes home was discontinued.

Results. M. completed an average of 54.2 percent of his assignments with no extra teacher help (percent completed ranged from 25 percent to 100 percent). This was slightly lower than the original baseline condition when extra teacher help was provided, but the range was more variable.

Phase C

The R/CT provided a daily index card and stars for the student. As the teacher gave him directions each day, she wrote the name of each assignment on the card. The R/CT showed the boy how to award himself a star on the card after he completed an assignment. He then brought the card and his assignments to the R/CT when he came for reading instruction at the end of his morning work period. A sticker was awarded if M. completed all of his assignments. The teacher assumed the responsibility for awarding the stars after M. started giving stars to his friends in the classroom.

Results. Average assignments completed were 51.6 percent (ranging from 25 percent to 67 percent) with no extra teacher help given. The teacher and the R/CT were in 100 percent agreement on the awarding of stars.

Phase D

In addition to procedures in phase C, M. was allowed to leave the resource room five minutes early if he had completed all of his morning work. It had been reported that M. would throw his lunch away so he could go outside to play rather than to take the time to eat it if he was dismissed from the resource room a few minutes late. (Lunchtime followed resource room help.) If morning seatwork was not finished, M. spent the last five minutes of resource room time (and a few extra minutes if needed) completing the assignments independently before he was dismissed.

Results. The first day of this phase represented a turning point. M. completed 100 percent of his assigned work without help, and, in addition, completed six workbook pages on his own that had not been assigned. The mean percent completed for this phase was 90.4 percent (ranging from 75 percent to 100 percent). For the last two days of this phase, the classroom teacher gave M. new assignments (that is, cursive handwriting and copying a dictated letter). Again, the teacher and R/CT were in agreement for work completed. (See Figure 6–4.)

Discussion

This project contains some good examples of difficulties encountered when consulting. By initiating contact with a consulting teacher, a class-

Figure 6–4 Percent of Completed Assignments by a First-Grade Student Illustrating Effects of Various Reinforcers

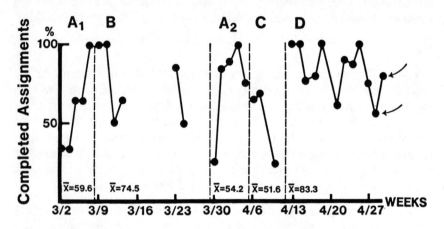

A = Baseline
B = Stopwatch & Notes Home
C = Stars
D = Stars plus Early Dismissal
╱ = New Assignment Type

room teacher is indirectly stating that he or she is willing to make changes in the classroom routine to help the child.

Since the mother initially expressed concern for M., the R/CT approached the classroom teacher about the problem. This may have made the classroom teacher feel that she had to collaborate with the teacher consultant. This teacher, although willing to work with the R/CT and record data, was not willing to alter many areas. The R/CT was concerned that not all of M.'s assignments were tasks he could be expected to complete successfully by himself. For example, some assignments involved counting money or had four-step directions to write words, color the picture, cut it out, and paste or fold. The student was not always able to perform these more complicated tasks without direct supervision. Yet the classroom teacher felt they were reasonable assignments since she provided individual directions for completing the tasks.

An additional consultative strategy might have been to break down complicated tasks into four distinct steps. The student could have been given the first set of directions and completed the first step. He then could be given the instructions for the second step, and so on.

The R/CT also tried to convince the teacher that fewer directions would be needed and expectations for M. would be more routine if she systematized his daily assignments. The R/CT offered to preview the assignments with M. on a daily basis or to provide additional instruction in problem areas (counting money, writing sentences, and so on) if the assignments could be arranged in advance. Instead, the teacher varied the assignments daily, so that M. might cut and paste one day, do workbook pages the next, and count money or write words in sentences the following day. The R/CT stopped exploring these areas with the classroom teacher when the teacher began to express discomfort about these topics.

Teacher consultants must be careful about suggesting alterations in the classroom structure or teaching techniques and when to approach the problem as if it belonged entirely to the student. At times the teacher consultant may be certain that the classroom teacher must make changes, and the teacher may not be ready to do so. The consultant must decide whether it is better to risk antagonizing the teacher to the point of no further collaborative work or whether it would be preferable to view the problem as belonging completely to the student. If the latter choice becomes the only alternative, then the consultant can plan for suggesting student-focused changes that may have an impact upon the entire classroom structure. Project 11 is an example of a case where the student's changed behavior may alter teacher expectations for a group of students.

Contact with M.'s mother was also problematic. Although she was concerned and willing to help, M.'s mother did not always follow through on what had been agreed upon. In one telephone conversation, the R/CT explained three times that the mother should expect a happy face note *or* unfinished work to complete every school night. The mother repeated the agreement back to the R/CT. When the R/CT checked back with the mother one week later, she did not remember what had been discussed. Although she reported that she often had M. complete assignments at home, the assignments were returned to school sporadically. In addition, the mother often blamed the classroom teacher for problems her son was having. The R/CT tried to skirt the issue of blame to help the mother confront the problem more realistically. One positive outcome of contact with M.'s mother was that she became less hostile over time, and some contact with school personnel was reestablished. In this case the R/CT often served as a communication link between mother and teacher.

It became obvious during the final phase of the project that M. was capable of performing most of the tasks assigned to him. This is an example of a student who could master the assignments but would not until the right reinforcer was selected. For M., contingent stars plus early dismissal produced a reinforcement environment that was best. Contingent stars alone failed to produce performance that was better than during baseline conditions. For M., early dismissal from the resource room was the reinforcer that resulted in an approximate 25 percent increase in completion of assignments. The R/CT's overall evaluation of this project was that a combination of appropriate reinforcement and more consistency in the type of work assignments could produce the most optimal environment for this student to complete all assignments every day.

In implementing this project, the R/CT was careful to involve both the classroom teacher and the parent in the project. This is an important consultation strategy, but in this particular case it was crucial because the mother requested the consultative support. The classroom teacher, the mother, and the R/CT met to decide what they would do initially. As a follow up to that planning meeting, the R/CT sent letters to both the mother and the classroom teacher reminding them of everyone's responsibilities. Copies of those letters are displayed in the Communication Exchange at the end of this chapter.

Project 13: Increasing the Number of Math Work Pages Completed Each Day

R/CT: Julie Keller

C. was a second-grade boy who attended a resource room 30 minutes each day for reading. His classroom teacher was concerned about his independent work habits and thought he could progress at a faster rate. During an initial meeting, the classroom teacher and the R/CT selected math period as the one in which to concentrate consultative services. In this classroom, math instruction was individualized, with students progressing at their own rate through the math book. The teacher and a classroom aide helped individual students with difficulties they were having during the 30-minute work period. The teacher also wanted C. to take responsibility for completing work on his own without the need for assigned pages.

Baseline

C. was observed each day, and data were taken on attending behavior using a 15-second interval time sample. *On-task* was defined as C. sitting in his chair with both feet on the floor while looking at or writing in the math book, or counting on his fingers to find the answer to a problem. For three days data were also taken on three other students in the classroom—one each day—to determine an average rate of on-task behavior for that classroom.

Results. C. was shown to be on-task an average of 42 percent of the time sampled as compared to a mean of 75 percent for the average worker. During this time, C. finished from two to three pages in his math book each day. On two days, one extra page was completed. The average worker completed three to four pages each day. The average number of extra pages per day was .29.

Phase B

The classroom teacher continued to assign the number of required pages each day. C. was told by the teacher that in order to earn the privilege of taking artwork to the lunchroom he needed to complete one page more than that assigned. The classroom teacher kept data on pages assigned and completed. The R/CT observed on-task behavior twice during this phase.

Results. C. completed no extra work the first two days of this phase. On the third and fourth days, the extra page was completed, and C. was reinforced. For the last two days, he again completed only the assigned work. The average extra work completed was .33 pages each day. C. was observed to be working 73 percent of the time on the second day of this phase and 43 percent of the time on the sixth day.

Phase C

In addition to doing artwork in the lunchroom for completion of extra work, C. brought his work to the resource room for praise from the R/CT. A star was then marked on a wall chart indicating completion of extra work. The classroom teacher continued extra work and continued to collect data on work completed. Data for on-task behavior were no longer measured, as the teachers agreed that work completion was the primary area of concern.

Results. During the first two days of this phase, C. completed no extra work. On the third day, two extra pages were completed, on the fourth day one extra page was completed, and on the fifth day, no extra work was completed. Average extra work completed was .60 pages each day.

Phase D

It was decided that C. needed more powerful reinforcement to motivate him to work during math period. The collaborating teachers agreed to draw up a contract with C., allowing him to name what he would work for from a choice of the following reinforcement menu:

1 star = a *Star Wars* rub-on sticker.
2 stars = the opportunity to use markers to color in part of a poster of his choice.
3 stars = a "Good Work" note to take home.
3 stars = the opportunity to decorate an Easter egg.
10 stars = a paperback book in an area of interest to C.

The R/CT explained the contract to C. on the first day of this phase. The contract stated that C. would still earn stars on the chart for any extra work completed. These stars could then be traded for one of the reinforcers. After the reinforcer was earned, the R/CT and C. would then contract for another reinforcer. The classroom teacher reminded C. of the contract at the beginning of the math period by saying, "You've agreed to complete your work today. You can earn a star towards __(reinforcer)__ if you do an extra page. You need __(amount)__ stars to earn it."

The reinforcement was delivered in the classroom. The classroom teacher again recorded amount of work assigned and completed. C. still came to the resource room to mark the stars on his chart.

Results. C.'s extra work completed increased. The first day of this phase he completed two extra pages, and he completed one page for each of the next three days. The average was 1.25 pages completed each day.

Reliability. Reliability checks on the number of pages completed were conducted at least once during each phase. The teachers agreed 100 percent of the time.

Discussion

As reflected in Table 6–3, C. completed extra work every day only during phase D when a contract with a reinforcement menu was used. For all preceding pages, his work production was sporadic; some days he completed extra work, and other days he did not. During phase C (reinforcement in the resource room), production increased as compared to that in baseline and in phase B. Baseline consisted of artwork in the lunchroom; during phase B the lunchroom art activity was made contingent upon work completion.

Table 6–3 Summary Data for Completion of Extra Workpages in Math

Phases	A	B	C	D
Days extra work completed	2/7 days	2/6 days	2/5 days	4/4 days
Total number of extra pages	2	2	3	5
Average number of extra pages completed per day	.29	.33	.60	1.25

Finally, at the project's end, the classroom teacher took over responsibility for discussing the daily contract with C. This was an important strategic decision, because if the R/CT had initially requested the classroom teacher to take this responsibility two adverse reactions could have occurred. First, the classroom teacher might have felt that the R/CT was shirking responsibility. The R/CT provided reinforcement in the resource room in the previous phase, which had failed to produce consistently positive results. Second, the classroom teacher had never used a reinforcement menu or a contingency contract. It is crucial that teacher consultants make sure that classroom teachers feel comfortable directing a new management strategy before asking them to take responsibility for the strategy.

The R/CT did a good job of listening to a teacher's complaint that a student was not responsible and then redirecting that complaint into a concrete behavior. Initially the R/CT thought that the amount of time spent on-task would be a good way to measure C.'s responsible behavior. She obtained a normative sample of on-task behavior of three other students in the classroom and determined that C. was, in fact, off-task more than they were.

Two problems arose in using this type of measurement in this classroom with this particular student. First, the effect of the contingent reinforcement had a variable effect on on-task behavior. If this had been the only difficulty, the R/CT should have probably continued to measure on-task behavior. However, the second difficulty was that this was a measurement device that was time consuming for the classroom teacher to use. It also was not possible for the R/CT to be available during this time to collect on-task data. Therefore, the classroom teacher continued to record the number of pages the student completed each day, which was an easy monitoring device for this classroom teacher to use.

Consulting teachers must also note that for this student accuracy of work was not a problem. The student was proficient at the required tasks: he just was not motivated to complete them. Therefore, when the teachers selected the right combination of reinforcers, his work production consistently increased. Had his skill levels been deficient, use of contingent reinforcement would have probably proven to be a useless strategy. Instead, the teachers might have selected a direct instruction technique, placed him in lower materials, redefined the work tasks, altered the directions, or assigned him to a cross-age tutor.

Project 14: DISTAR Math in a Third-Grade Classroom: Increasing Daily Progress

R/CT: Peggy Bullard

J. was a third-grade boy who received individual instruction in math for 30 minutes daily, Monday through Thursday, in the DISTAR math program. Based on the DISTAR placement test, J. began with *Book A* of the first level in the program. Because this was so far below grade level and so far removed from the skills being taught in his classroom, J.'s teacher came to the R/CT for consultation. Her major concern was that J. was not moving quickly enough toward the skills that he needed and that this would prevent him from ever approaching grade level.

Baseline

The teacher continued to work through each lesson as given in the teacher presentation booklet. The number of lessons completed each day were charted for the first two days by the R/CT and from then until the end of the study by the teacher. The teacher projected that at the present rate, 44 lessons could be completed by April 23, bringing J. to lesson 76. Using the DISTAR error correction procedure, each error that J. made was immediately corrected, and the task was repeated. The number of different errors per day was charted, as well as the actual number of lessons mastered. Lesson progress is reflected in Figure 6–5. A different error was defined as any incorrect response that had not already been made on that day. For example, if J. incorrectly named the minus sign three times on one day, this was corrected and repeated each time, but was only counted the first time.

Results. During four days of baseline, J. completed five lessons, averaging 1.25 lessons/day. He did not make any errors.

Figure 6–5 Daily Progress through DISTAR Math by a Third Grader Illustrating a Comparison between Baseline and Intervention Conditions

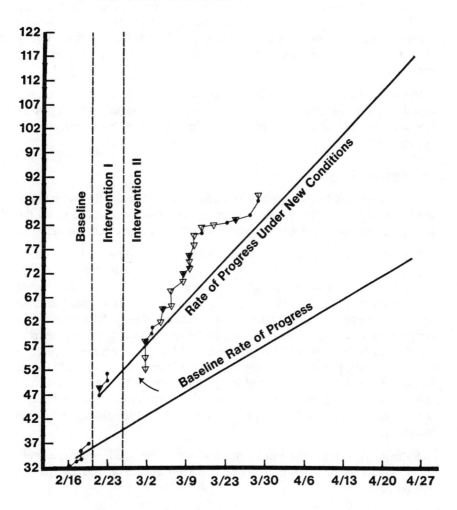

↖ = Field trip - no school

• = Lesson Mastery Test

▽ = Test Mastery

Intervention I

Based on low error rate during baseline, a new schedule for presenting the lessons was developed. Instead of progressing through the book by teaching every lesson, the teacher now skipped the next nine lessons and presented only key parts of the first few lessons that dealt with each new skill. Periodic mastery tests accompanying the lessons taught were also presented.

Results. The number of daily errors increased from zero to one on the first day of the intervention and fell back to zero on the next day. J. passed two lessons and one mastery test on the first day, and two lessons on the second day.

Intervention II

In order to monitor J.'s progress more carefully through the curriculum, the R/CT suggested that every mastery test be presented, even when the lesson accompanying it was skipped. No other changes were made.

Results. By presenting only what she considered to be the key parts of the lesson, the teacher was able to increase the daily rate from 1.25 (baseline) to two lessons per day. On one day during this phase, J. made two errors, and on three days, he made one error. However, the most common number of daily errors was still zero (six days). After four weeks on the new schedule, J. was working on lesson 87, which was a gain from baseline of 50 lessons. The average was 12.5 lessons per week, compared to five lessons per week during baseline. Continuing at the initial rate would have resulted in a gain of only 20 lessons in the same amount of time. A new line of expected progress was drawn, which projected that J. would reach lesson 117 by April 23, rather than the initially projected lesson 76.

Reliability. During the intervention phases, the R/CT made one reliability check for number of errors and charting accuracy. Agreement was 100 percent.

Discussion

Even though the math skills of this student were much lower than those of most of his classroom peers, these two teachers discovered that they could more than double the number of DISTAR lessons he mastered over a seven-week period. The R/CT devised two simple means of monitoring student progress: (1) the number of daily errors made; and (2) the number of lessons mastered. These were used to verify that the student was not progressing too rapidly through the materials but had actually mastered the content. Use of a projected line of progress, depicted in Figure 6–5, was a useful device for teachers and the student. The teachers systematically projected how many lessons they wanted the student to complete by a given point in time. Use of a projected line of progress serves as a means of transforming an educational goal into a concrete monitoring device. The student was also interested in the line of progress and was pleased that he was moving faster through the lessons than his teachers had anticipated. This can be seen in Figure 6–5 where the plotted data consistently fall above the projected line of progress.

The R/CT pointed out that implementation of the second intervention came as a result of faulty communication between the two teachers when the first intervention had been selected. The R/CT had planned that the student would be given a mastery test on all lessons, but she had not clarified this point with the classroom teacher. After two days of instruction under the first intervention, the R/CT realized the communication error and included mastery testing on all lessons from then on.

Project 15: Improving Group Spelling Performance

R/CT: Ray Celentano

A classroom teacher expressed concern over the low scores that some of the students in her classes were getting on their weekly spelling tests. These were remedial classes for high school students. After some discussion between the teacher and the R/CT, it was decided that a new system for learning the spelling words would be introduced.

The method was used in three classes. The total number of students studying spelling for the three classes was 12. The following was the procedure usually used for spelling instruction:

- *Monday:* Students were given 20 new spelling words. They had ten minutes to study them before a pretest was given. The teacher dictated the words to the students by using them in a sentence. If students got a score of 100, they did not have to take the test on Friday.
- *Wednesday:* All students turned in sentences that contained the week's spelling words.
- *Friday:* The students had ten minutes to study the words before the test was given. The teacher dictated the words to the students. The words were again used in a sentence. The students graded their own papers.

The collaborating teachers set a goal for the student group. They projected that the students' spelling scores would improve by an average of ten points for the total group.

Baseline

Baseline data were obtained by averaging the scores the students had received for first and second marking periods, under the conditions described earlier.

Intervention

The intervention consisted of changing the way that the students in the three classes reviewed their spelling words. The Fitzgerald method of studying spelling words was used (Graham and Miller, 1979). The method includes the following six steps for studying each spelling word:

1. Look at the word.
2. Say the word.
3. With eyes closed, visualize the word.
4. Cover the word, and then write it.
5. Check the spelling.
6. If the word is misspelled, repeat steps 1–5.

Changes were also made in the instructional format for the week as follows:

- *Monday:* The students received their spelling words for the week. They had ten minutes to study them. They used the Fitzgerald method to study the words. They took the pretest. They used the method after the test had been given to correct the words they had misspelled. All students took the final test on Friday.
- *Wednesday:* The students turned in their spelling sentences.
- *Friday:* The students had ten minutes to study their 20 spelling words. The Fitzgerald method was used to study them. The test was given. After the test, the students used the method to study the words they had misspelled.

Results. The overall average for the 12 participants for baseline was 78. After the intervention, the average for the new marking period was 86 percent, which is an increase of eight points for the group. The projected goal had been ten points for the group. The percentage of correctly spelled words and the degree of increase or decrease for each of the 12 students before and after intervention were:

Period	Student	Baseline	Intervention	Degree of increase or decrease
First hour	1	68	82	+14
	2	79	90	+11
	3	90	95	+ 5
	4	70	90	+20
Second hour	5	60	60	0
	6	84	84	0
	7	97	98	+ 1
	8	86	90	+ 4
Third hour	9	63	83	+20
	10	87	91	+ 4
	11	84	80	− 4
	12	93	94	+ 1

Discussion

The overall average performance of these students was increased by teaching them to use the Fitzgerald study method. The projected aim for increase was ten points; the actual group increase was eight points. Seven out of twelve of the students increased their average spelling performance. Four of these students increased performance by more than 10 points. Five students appear not to have benefited at all from the program (students 5, 6, 7, 11, and 12); however, student 12 was performing well before the intervention was introduced. The students in first period made the best gains, and those in second period made the least. In total, approximately 58 percent of the students found this intervention useful.

The Fitzgerald method is reported in a review of best practices for spelling instruction. The reported practices are those supported by empirical research (Graham & Miller, 1979). These authors reviewed several approaches to teaching spelling, and they presented seven methods in detail. The Fitzgerald method and the two Horn methods (Horn, 1919; 1954) were those recommended for use by Graham and Miller's literature review. A reproduction of the seven methods appears in Table 6–4.

The results of this consultation project indicate that for slightly more than half of these high school students, the Fitzgerald method proved to be beneficial. Of the five who did not progress, one student needed no assistance. The teachers noted that the remaining four students who failed to improve also felt uncomfortable using the method. They felt silly closing their eyes to visualize the word. As a consequence, they did not faithfully use the method. Three of these four students were in the same class.

Table 6–4 Word Study Techniques for Learning to Spell

Fitzgerald Method (Fitzgerald, 1951)

1. Look at the word carefully.
2. Say the word.
3. With eyes closed, visualize the word.
4. Cover the word, and then write it.
5. Check the spelling.
6. If the word is misspelled, repeat steps 1–5.

Horn Method 1 (Horn, 1919)

1. Look at the word, and say it to yourself.
2. Close your eyes, and visualize the word.
3. Check to see if you were right. (If not, begin at step 1.)
4. Cover the word, and write it.
5. Check to see if you were right. (If not, begin at step 1.)
6. Repeat steps 4 and 5 two more times.

Horn Method 2 (Horn, 1954)

1. Pronounce each word carefully.
2. Look carefully at each part of the word as you pronounce it.
3. Say the letters in sequence.
4. Attempt to recall how the word looks, then spell the word.
5. Check this attempt to recall.
6. Write the word.
7. Check this spelling attempt.
8. Repeat the above steps if necessary.

Visual-Vocal Method (Westerman, 1971)

1. Say word.
2. Spell word orally.
3. Say word again.
4. Spell word from memory four times correctly.

Gilstrap Method (Gilstrap, 1962)

1. Look at the word, and say it softly. If it has more than one part, say it again, part by part, looking at each part as you say it.
2. Look at the letters, and say each one. If the word has more than one part, say the letters part by part.
3. Write the word without looking at the book.

Fernald Method Modified

1. Make a model of the word with a crayon, grease pencil, or magic marker, saying the word as you write it.
2. Check the accuracy of the model.
3. Trace over the model with your index finger, saying the word at the same time.
4. Repeat step 3 five times.
5. Copy the word three times correctly.
6. Copy the word three times from memory correctly.

Cover-and-Write Method

1. Look at word. Say it.
2. Write word two times.
3. Cover, and write one time.
4. Check work.
5. Write word two times.
6. Cover, and write one time.
7. Check work.
8. Write word three times.
9. Cover, and write one time.
10. Check work.

References to Other Techniques

Aho, 1967	Hill & Martinis, 1973
Bartholome, 1977	Phillips, 1975
Clanton, 1977	Stowitschek &
Glusker, 1967	Jobes, 1977

Source: S. Graham and L. Miller, "Spelling Research and Practice: A Unified Approach," *Focus on Exceptional Children,* 1979, p. 11.

The important issue is that not all students respond in the same manner. The information in Table 6–4 indicates that more than one method reported in the literature has proved to be useful, at least for average group performance. The preferred next step in this consultation project would be to experiment with some of the other recommended methods with the students who failed to respond well to the Fitzgerald method.

Project 16: Improved Spelling Performance in a Fifth-Grade Classroom

R/CT: Jill Cunningham

A fifth-grade teacher referred N. to the R/CT because of low spelling grades. Although N. was seeing a resource teacher for 30 minutes of direct spelling instruction per day, he was still having problems in the classroom. He did not complete spelling work, and he failed to write sentences in response to oral dictation. Spelling grades were based on performance on the following four types of assignments: (1) spelling workbook; (2) dictation corrections from a practice test; (3) the final dictation test; and (4) a word test with ten words.

Baseline

A baseline measurement on N.'s weekly spelling grades was taken over a five-week period.

Results. During this time, N.'s grades in the four spelling areas were:

1. *workbook exercises*—two F grades
   —three assignments not turned in
2. *dictation corrections*—two B grades
   —one F grade
   —two assignments not turned in
3. *dictation tests*—three F grades
   —one D grade
   —one C grade
4. *spelling test*—an average of 7.2 words spelled correctly on a ten-word test

Intervention

A home reinforcement system was established with M.'s parents. M.'s parents agreed to allow M. to attend weekly athletic practice for track if his grades met a weekly standard. For each week that he met the standard, he was allowed to attend practices the following week. The R/CT called the parents to report performance on Friday of each week.

Criteria. The weekly standards were the following:

- grade of C or better on workbook exercises
- grade of A on dictation corrections
- grade of D or better on dictation tests
- eight correctly spelled words on each ten-word test

Results.

	first week	*second week*
1) workbook exercises	grade B	grade C
2) dictation exercises	grade A	grade D*
3) dictation test	grade D	grade C
4) spelling test	8 correct words	7 correct words*

---

*failed to meet the standard

Discussion

This consulting teacher chose a home reinforcement system to improve a student's spelling performance in a fifth-grade classroom. This method improved N.'s spelling grades, although performance during the first week of reinforcement was superior to the second week.

Upon follow up, the consulting teacher discovered that the parents allowed N. to attend track during the third week, even though performance on dictation exercises and spelling tests did not meet the expected standard. This student could have been testing whether the contingency would remain firm or whether it could be changed. The student learned that the stated contingency was indeed open to manipulation. During the fourth week, the classroom teacher and parents agreed that the home reinforcement program was not working, and N. was allowed to attend track sessions with no attached expectation for performance. This agreement was reached without the knowledge of the consulting teacher.

Upon reflection, the consulting teacher decided that she would attempt to establish a policy stating that any changes in the student's program must be agreed upon by all three authoritative parties: (1) parents, (2) classroom teacher; and (3) consulting teacher. This is a highly recommended policy, even though situations certainly occur when someone makes a program alteration without consultation. Another way that a teacher consultant can avoid this problem is to involve the other authority figures and the student actively in analysis of the student performance data. In this particular project, the teachers might have sent home a weekly report card with the spelling grades rather than just a phone call. The report card might have included a note reminding the parents whether or not to reinforce.

The consultant might have also had the teacher plot the data so she could see that the home reinforcement was an effective intervention. For some teachers and parents, seeing the plotted, visual display of a student's progress is more convincing than a verbal report. It is also easier to see whether or not an intervention is having an impact.

INSTRUCTION IN THE CONTENT AREAS

Thus far, the consultation projects in this chapter have focused on improving written language, reading and language assignments, and spelling performance. Although most students who have academic problems in regular classrooms lack skills in the basic skill areas, performance in the content areas also poses a problem. The best procedure to follow is to remediate basic skills first and then work on content area performance. With some students, it cannot be assumed that they will perform well in content area instruction once they have become proficient in the basic skills. They may still require instruction and guidance in establishing skills such as studying, taking notes, completing assignments, participating in class, and taking examinations. Some other students in regular classes may have mastered the basic skills yet still lack proficiency in the content area skills. Techniques that consulting teachers develop to enhance performance in these areas can be readily used with many other members of a class, not just with the student who has been referred for services.

Project 17: Improved Grades in a Black American History Class: Direct Instruction in a Content Area

R/CT: Ray Celentano

S. was an eleventh-grade girl enrolled in a Black American History class. Her teacher contacted this R/CT because S. was failing. The teacher knew that the R/CT was giving direct reading instruction to S. and hoped that the R/CT would also help with the difficulties S. was having in history class.

Originally, the teacher suggested that the R/CT and S. go over each test S. had previously taken and have S. correct her responses. The teacher proposed that S. could be graded on the corrected tests, and the grades would be used for additional credit. The R/CT thought that it would be better to provide S. with a set of comprehension questions for each chapter to help her prepare for tests rather than to correct poor responses. The R/CT agreed to write the questions, and the history teacher approved the arrangement.

Assessment in the Content Area

In retrospect, the R/CT decided to obtain a more accurate measurement of how well S. could actually read the history book before asking her to work with the study questions. The R/CT randomly selected nine passages from the history book that were each 100 words in length. He tested S.'s ability to read orally and comprehend these passages. S. was tested on three separate days reading three passages on each day. Her mean performance was 79 percent correct for accuracy of word recognition at a rate of 80 correct words per minute with 20 percent correct comprehension.

A Second Meeting

After examining these performance data the teachers agreed that comprehension was poor, but accuracy of word recognition was a problem as well. The R/CT suggested that S. read each chapter orally during direct reading instruction. S. had previously been reading in a graded reader for upper level students. The oral reading was followed by oral comprehension questions. S. would also be expected to write out notes for each chapter she read and turn these in to the R/CT. The history teacher agreed to this strategy.

Baseline

Baseline data consisted of grades collected from the history teacher's grade book. As indicated in Figure 6–6, S. had failed six out of seven tests.

Intervention

S. received direct instruction, which consisted of orally reading each chapter, answering oral comprehension questions, and writing study notes for each chapter. She earned grades of C on the three history tests given over a three-week period. (See Figure 6–6.)

Discussion

This R/CT successfully altered student performance on history tests by giving direct instruction in the content area. This student did not read or comprehend well enough to pass history tests. The history teacher could have refused to let S. continue in the class. The special educator could

Figure 6–6 Grades Earned by a High School Student in a Black
American History Class before and after Direct
Instruction in a Content Area

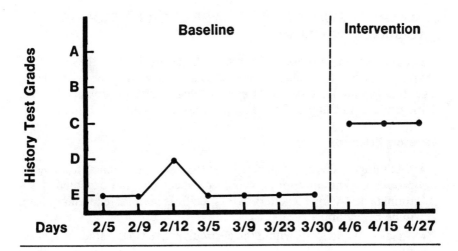

have agreed to increased instructional time in special education giving this student a different curriculum or enrolling her in a work study program. These possible outcomes are not unusual courses of action that are taken by public school personnel when secondary students are failing. Instead, these two teachers worked together to reach a solution that would best meet this student's needs in a least restrictive environment. The R/CT noted that the history teacher was cooperative and willing to try any of the R/CT's suggestions. An important strategy that this R/CT used was to consult with the student regarding selection of the best possible intervention. The R/CT asked the student what would be most helpful to her success in history class. The student suggested that the notetaking strategy would be useful. This is a skill that will be useful to this student in other classes as well. This also illustrates the importance of listening to what students have to say about their own needs.

Although remediation of content area skills is a relatively recent development, there is certainly a need for consulting teachers to develop expertise in this area. Although recourses to date are limited, five resources may be useful to a teacher consultant. One is section 4.6 on training study skills in Carnine and Silbert (1979). A second source is a booklet on reading skills in the content areas (Kaufman, 1980). A third is another booklet that presents a discussion of types of independent study skills (Lock, 1981). A fourth source is a discussion of developing curriculum for independent work skills by Brown (1978). Finally, a fifth source is Piercey (1982), which offers suggested activities for work in the content areas.

SUMMARY OF STRATEGIES USED FOR CONSULTATION OF ACADEMIC PROBLEMS

The following is a review of some of the strategies that these teacher consultants used to facilitate their consultative work. For more detail regarding the implementation of each strategy, refer to projects 9 to 17. Some projects in Chapter 5 are also referred to as well.

Assessing Problems

- Encourage classroom teachers to be specific when defining a student's problems. The description should be specific to the expected classroom task. (Asking teachers to be specific is preferable to asking them to be behavioral.)
- Assess student skills within the curriculum used in the student's classroom.
- Obtain a normative sample of average student performance in the skill area in which the problem student is having difficulty. These data can be used to set specific goals, objectives, and criterion performance levels for the problem student.
- Determine the learning stage the student is in to select the most appropriate intervention strategy. (See Chapter 4.)

Establishing Goals

- Make certain that students master one skill level before progressing to the next.
- Make certain what the classroom teacher's expectations are.
- Make certain that goals as teacher consultant coincide with those of the classroom teachers.
- Set the criterion levels for performance higher when the student still receives resource assistance than when that student is performing in a regular classroom.

Structuring a Data Base

- Select behaviors to measure that are simple to observe and record, but still reflect the true problem.

- Use charting systems that are easy to monitor and easy for others to read.
- Teach students to chart or record their own pupil progress data.
- Provide classroom teachers with all necessary forms and charts for recording student behavior.

Identifying Reinforcers

- Determine whether the students are experiencing difficulty because they lack skills or because they are unmotivated.
- Be flexible in selection of reinforcers. Remember that what is reinforcing to you may not be to the student.
- Remember to ask students what might be most useful or reinforcing for them.
- Select reinforcers that are simple, easy to use in regular classroom, and as close to social and intrinsic reinforcement as possible.

Selecting Remediation Programs

- Select remediation programs that are directly related to what is expected of a student in that student's regular classroom.
- Select a remediation solution that can be used in the regular classroom, or, at least, in the least restrictive environment.
- Select remediation programs for which sufficient time can be provided in the classroom.
- Select remedial solutions that teachers could easily use with other class members who are having problems.
- Remember that the same remedial solution will not work for every student *or* for every teacher.

Managing Classrooms

- Help teachers set up classroom routines that are consistent and well planned.
- Use the fading and chaining principles of behavior modification to increase difficulty of tasks gradually, to reduce extrinsic reinforcement, to reduce teacher assistance, and so on.
- Select solutions that encourage students to work well independently.
- Alter independent work tasks and materials so that students can perform well independently. However, only alter them if it is necessary. Do not select this as a first alternative.

- Help classroom teachers examine classroom materials to ascertain (1) whether all necessary components are included; (2) whether the tasks are too easy or too difficult; and (3) whether the tasks are related to the lesson goals.
- Utilize professional aides and cross-age tutors to increase the amount of instruction that will be offered to problem students.

Facilitating of Communication

- Involve parents in the education of their child by reporting pupil progress.
- Send home notes and daily report cards to keep parents informed of pupil progress.
- Make certain that behavior is consistent and predictable, especially when communicating with parents for home reinforcement programs.
- Meet regularly with teachers and/or parents to discuss progress.
- Write memos to other involved persons reminding them of what has been decided, their responsibilities, and the student's progress.
- Make certain that all involved parties (student, teachers, parents) clearly understand the parameters of the consultation project.
- Make certain that once a reinforcement program has been selected all parties are actually carrying out the program in its original form. If a discrepancy occurs, remember that placing blame does not solve the problem. Take responsibility for suggesting another solution or modification.
- Encourage classroom teachers to take responsibility for program interventions. Be careful not to send a message that says, "What I do is *so* special that no one else can do it."
- Make certain that classroom teachers feel comfortable with a new strategy before expecting them to use it.
- Be willing to give up some immediate strategic plans if the working relationship with the classroom teacher is in potential jeopardy.
- Determine whether it would be better to approach a consultation problem with an alteration in the classroom structure or whether it would be better to focus on the problem as if it belonged solely to the student.
- Be willing to try solutions suggested by others.
- Listen carefully to what the teacher is saying, being careful not to cloud information with personal attitudes and perceptions.

- Read the results of intervention studies conducted in education to increase the repertoire from which ideas and solutions can be selected.
- Remember to reinforce teachers and parents positively as well as students.

COMMUNICATION EXCHANGE

Once classroom teachers, consulting teachers, and parents have agreed upon a possible solution to a classroom problem, consulting teachers should not assume that the final step in the consultative process has been reached. It is essential that the consulting teacher conduct consistent follow-up work to ensure that the proposed consultative plan will be implemented. One way to do this is to write memos to all concerned parties reminding them of the responsibilities to be assumed by each participant in the consultative solution. In Project 12, the teacher consultant worked with a first-grade teacher and the child's parent to increase the number of assignments that this child completed in class. The teacher consultant wrote memos to both the classroom teacher and the parent reiterating the agreed-upon strategy. The consultant was careful to list the responsibilities of *each* person. She reinforced both the teacher and the parent for the willingness to cooperate. Finally, she reminded them that she was available should they need to contact her. The memos are as follows:

Dear (Classroom Teacher),

   I thought it might be helpful if I summarized what we agreed to do in helping M learn how to finish his work independently. If I've forgotten anything, or you see changes that need to be made, please let me know.

You agreed to:

1. Continue to give M directions about how to do this work.
2. Send home 😊 or work to finish with M each day.
3. Send assignments home for M when he is sick if someone stops by to pick them up (his mother, sister, etc.).
4. Keep a daily record of work assigned and work completed for M.
5. Continue to praise work well done and completed.

M's Mother will:

1. Look for M to bring home either 😊 or work to finish each school night.
2. Praise 😊!
3. Continue to see that M finishes work brought home that he didn't finish at school.
4. Ask M's sister (or someone else) to stop by M's classroom to pick up his work if he is sick.

The R/CT will:

1. Help M learn how to time himself when completing seatwork assignments.
2. Record amount of time required and praise progress.

3.   Keep a graph of work M finishes based on your record.
4.   Discuss M's progress with you and together decide if any changes in our system need to be made.
5.   Keep M's mother informed of M's progress in completing work at least weekly.
6.   Provide you with ☺'s and weekly recording forms.

I really appreciate your thoroughness in following through! Let's hope M continues to improve.

Thank you,

Teacher Consultant

Dear (Parent),

I enjoyed talking with you last night! I thought I would try to summarize what we agreed to over the phone so that we can all try to work together in helping M learn to finish his work independently.

You will:

1.   Look for M to being you either   ☺   (all work finished) or papers to finish each school night.
2.   Praise ☺ .
3.   Continue to see that M finishes work at home that he didn't finish at school.
4.   Ask his sister (or someone else) to stop by M's classroom to pick up his work if he is sick.

M's Teacher Will:

1.   Continue to give M directions about how to do his work.
2.   Send home ☺ or work to finish with M each day.
3.   Send assignments home for M when he is sick if someone stops by to pick them up.
4.   Keep a record of work M finishes.

I will:

1.   Help M learn how to time himself when copying work from the board. (I will also record amount of time.)
2.   Keep a chart of work M finishes.
3.   Keep you informed of his progress by note or by phone (about once a week).

Please feel free to call me any evening.

Sincerely,

Teacher Consultant
(telephone number)

Chapter 7

Data-Based, Group Reading: Dissemination through Consultation

A prevalent problem among mildly handicapped students is an inability to read grade level materials. Successful performance in mainstream American education is heavily influenced by a person's ability to read and perform independent work study tasks based on what has been read. For this reason, R/CTs at the University of Illinois learn to implement a reading instruction model that has proved to be successful with mildly handicapped students, regardless of categorical label (Idol-Maestas, Lloyd, & Lilly, 1981). Public school students who have received reading instruction from R/CTs-in-training average at least two years gain for every month of instruction. Some students have gained as much as three and four years in a year's time by using contingent skipping of reading passages based on good performance. This chapter presents the instructional model that R/CTs use for the teaching of reading and demonstrates how R/CTs have disseminated their instructional skills to classroom teachers and to other special educators through teacher consultation.

A MODEL FOR DIRECT, DATA-BASED READING INSTRUCTION

This model for instruction has been developed over the past eight years at the University of Illinois. It has been heavily influenced by Joseph Jenkins, former coordinator of the Resource/Consulting Teacher Program and current director of the Experimental Education Unit at the University of Washington. Program graduates, doctoral students, and cooperating teachers have also influenced the development and implementation of this model (that is, Idol-Maestas, Givens-Ogle, & Lloyd, 1981). This model is based on three crucial elements: curricular assessment; placement in an appropriate curriculum level; and data-based instruction.

Curricular Assessment

First, a reading curriculum is selected that will form the base for assessment and instruction. Preferably this curricular series is the same that is used in the student's regular classroom, although the student is usually placed at a lower level. The assessment procedure is referred to as a curriculum-based assessment (CBA).

The procedures for constructing a reading CBA are outlined in Appendix 7-A. A sample passage of 100 words from each level (book) in a series is given to the student to read. An arrow marks the beginning of the selected passage, a slash marks the end of the 100-word timed sample, and a bracket marks the end of the entire passage the student will read in order to obtain sufficient information for answering comprehension questions. A stopwatch is used to time the student's speed of reading for the 100-word section. Figure 7–1 contains an example of what one passage for one level of a reading CBA might look like. The text was copied from a basal reader, and the comprehension questions were inserted. The questions marked "F" represent factual questions, "S" represents sequential questions, and "I" represents inferential questions. Directions for writing comprehension questions are also contained in Appendix 7-A.

Placement

Three random samples are selected for each level of the series. Testing extends over a three-day period. The student is tested over all levels on the first day. A second set of sample passages representing all levels is used on the second day, and the same procedure is followed on the third day. Testing over several days gives the teacher a clearer picture of the student's reading ability. Resource/consulting teachers affiliated with the University of Illinois have found that student performance does fluctuate from day to day. This may be partially due to inconsistency of sequenced reading difficulty in basal readers and to erratic student performance.

Data-Based Curricular Instruction

After a student has been placed at a level within the curriculum, instruction is begun. Every day the student reads an entire story aloud. The student begins at the beginning of the book in which placement was assigned.

Error Correction Procedure

The teacher uses a specific and consistent error correction procedure. Errors are defined the same way as during assessment. (See Appendix

Figure 7–1 Sample of a Curriculum-Based Assessment for One
Level of a Basal Reading Series

→   Mr. deVarona hurried to her and wrapped his arms around her. "What's the matter, honey?" he asked.
  The answer burst out. "I don't want to dive, Daddy. It scares me."
  Her father rocked her back and forth, just as he had done when she was a baby. "There, there," he said. "You don't have to dive if you don't want to. You don't have to do anything you are afraid of."
  Finally, her sobbing stopped. Her father dried her face and sat beside her on the bed.
  "I didn't know you felt that way about diving," he told her. "I/$_{100}$ certainly wouldn't have encouraged you to do it if I had known. But you see, Donna, you have a certain gift. I recognized it, and so did Coach McGuigan. It's something that very few people have. Do you understand what I'm talking about?"]
  "No," Donna admitted.
  "I'm talking about the natural gift that you have of a fine body and the ability to make it move easily and gracefully. Those who have that gift can become great athletes. Those who don't, can't, no matter how hard they train."
  Donna thought about what her father was saying, not understanding all of it.
  "That's all I have to say to you," he continued. "We will stop the diving lessons for now."

F   Why was Donna crying? (afraid to dive)
F   Who was Mr. deVarona? (her father)
S   After Mr. deVarona rocked Donna back and forth, what did he tell her? (She didn't have to dive if she didn't want to.)
I   Donna's father said that she had a natural gift. What did he mean? (good coordination, good athlete, ability to dive)
I   Another person thought Donna was a good diver. Who was it? (Coach McGuigan)

Source: Reprinted from *Rhymes and Reasons* by B. Thomas with permission of MacMillan, Series r, © 1980.

7-A.) The error correction procedure is displayed in Figure 7–2. Every time the student makes an error, the teacher uses the correction procedure that is appropriate for the word type. Step A is used if the student names the word correctly after the teacher has called attention to the error. Step B is used when the word is phonetically irregular or is a sight word that cannot be logically sounded out. Step C is used if the word is a phonetically regular word that can be sounded out. The student always rereads the sentence in which the error word is embedded. If the sentence is long, then a phrase containing the word is reread. This procedure is continued until the reader reaches the last section of the story.

Figure 7–2 Sample Error Correction Procedure
Used for Oral Reading Instruction

Teacher: "What word?"

A. If correct: Praise!

B. If incorrect and *not* a sound-out word:
   Teacher: tell word
             "What word?" _____.
             "Yes, _____."

C. If incorrect *and* a sound-out word:
   Teacher: "Sound it out."

   If response is incorrect:
   Teacher: "My turn."
       say it slow → m-a-n
       say it fast → man

   Teacher: "Our turn."
       say it slow → m-a-n
       say it fast → man

   Teacher: "Your turn."
       say it slow → m-a-n
       say it fast → man

The student always rereads the entire sentence containing the error word after the correction has been made.

Source: Reprinted, with modification, from Englemann, S. & Bruner, E., *DISTAR Reading Level 1,* Chicago, Il., Science Research Associates, Inc., 1974.

Measurement from a Timed Sample

Somewhere in the final section of the story a 100-word passage is selected that is used as a timed sample to measure the accuracy and speed at which the student is reading. The procedure is identical to that used during assessment. The teacher makes no comment regarding errors unless the student loses the place. The student is redirected to the correct place. During this timed reading, the teacher records the number of errors made and uses a stopwatch to measure the amount of time taken to read the timed sample. After the student finishes the timed sample, oral reading continues until the story is finished. The error correction procedure is used for any remaining words in the story.

Comprehension

The book is then closed, and the teacher asks the student ten comprehension questions based on the entire story. The question types are factual, sequential, and inferential, as they are on the curriculum-based assessment. The usual distribution of question types is five to six factual, two sequential, and two to three inferential. These may vary depending on the complexity of the story. However, as the student progresses to upper level stories, more and more emphasis should be placed upon ability to infer.

Charting Daily Measures

Teachers keep a daily record of the three daily measures for accuracy, rate, and comprehension. Figure 7–3 illustrates a typical multiband chart with daily measurement data for oral reading accuracy, oral reading rate, and oral comprehension. This student read first in *Worlds of Wonder,* second in *Lands of Pleasure,* and finally in *Enchanted Gates* of the MacMillan basal reading series. Criterion levels for passing performance were set at 94 percent correct for accuracy, 30 correct words per minute (CWPM) for rate, and 80 percent correct for comprehension. A differential marking system has been used so that a teacher can tell the difference between stories passed in the first reading versus those that required a second reading.

Instructional Format Sheet

For every student who receives direct instruction, an instructional format sheet is kept that serves as the intervention plan for that student. This sheet contains information describing the instructional task and the instructional intervention selected to teach the task. It also contains information pertaining to criterion, consequences, error correction procedure, amount of time to be spent on the task, and the manner in which the task will be measured. Figure 7–4 is an example of an instructional format sheet for the student whose progress is reported in Figures 4–3, 4–4, and 7–3. It describes the precise conditions that were in effect when the student was reading in three MacMillan readers. This plan corresponds to the multiband chart and reflects any alterations that might have been made in the student's program.

COMMONLY USED INTERVENTIONS

Reading Accuracy

To increase oral reading accuracy, teachers affiliated with the R/CT program have found two basic strategies to be useful. The first is designed

Figure 7–3 Sample of a Multiband Chart Indicating Daily Measures for Oral Reading Accuracy, Oral Reading Rate, and Oral Comprehension

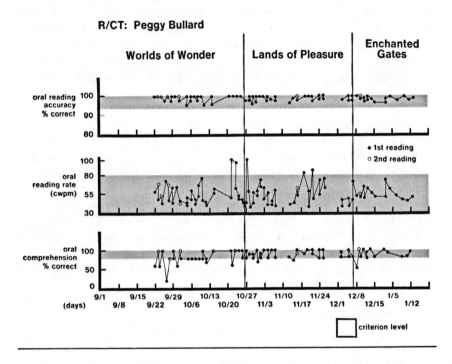

to improve phonetic decoding and involves *soundsheet* practice. The second focuses on improving ability to read phonetically irregular words by use of *daily drill*. Of course, various other strategies are used with different students, but these are the most commonly used. As the consultative projects reported later in this chapter indicate, these two strategies can be easily implemented in regular classrooms.

Soundsheets

Students who do not know phonetically regular letter sound relationships are required to practice daily on these letters/sounds. Rather than arbitrarily selecting sounds, a more systematic procedure is used. Phonetically regular sounds are drawn in order of occurrence from the readers themselves. Sheets of not more than 30 phonetically regular sounds per sheet are constructed. Figure 7–5 is an example of a soundsheet constructed from *Blue Bananas,* the first preprimer in the Laidlaw basal reader

Figure 7–4 Sample of an Instructional Format Sheet for the Student Whose Daily Progress Is Displayed in Figure 7–3

INSTRUCTIONAL FORMAT SHEET

Task	Instructional Intervention	Criterion	Consequences	Error Correction Proc.	Time	Measure
Oral Reading Accuracy	Student reads story orally and is timed for accuracy on 100-word sample near story end 9/22/80	94% accuracy	Reread until criterion is reached	1. What word? Sound it out 2. My turn our turn your turn 3. Say whole word 4. Repeat sentence	20 minutes	% correct
Oral Reading Rate	Same. Timed for rate also. 9/22/80	30 CWPM	Same		Same	% CWPM
Comprehension	At the end of story, student will orally respond to 10 questions asked by teacher 9/22/80	80% accuracy	Reread story until criterion is reached Prize received when book is finished	Correct by referring to context. Teacher gives cues to find answers: Remember? → yes answer → No → Who is question about? →	5 minutes	% accurate

Figure 7–4 continued

INSTRUCTIONAL FORMAT SHEET

Task	Instructional Intervention	Criterion	Consequences	Error Correction Proc.	Time	Measure
				What is happening? → Find page → Find passage → Read passage → Find sentence/words which answer question → Student answers question		

Figure 7–5 Sample Soundsheet Representing 20 Sounds from *Blue Bananas* in the Laidlaw Series

Name_____   Blue Bananas A - 20 Sounds

wh	nt	ere	R	i	s	r	a	a	u
l	H	er	L	t	o	th	an	m	n
u	m	a	a	th	s	t	R	er	nt
H	wh	l	ere	L	i	o	r	an	n
l	wh	H	nt	er	ere	L	R	t	i
o	s	th	r	an	n	a	a	u	m
m	i	u	t	R	a	a	L	n	ere
an	er	r	nt	th	H	s	wh	o	l
ere	l	n	o	L	wh	a	a	s	H
R	th	t	nt	u	r	i	er	m	an

series. This particular soundsheet contains 20 sounds that are represented in the first two rows. The subsequent eight rows contain randomly distributed repetitions of the same 20 sounds. Eight rows are provided for practicing and two more for testing. Explicit directions for construction of soundsheets can be found in Appendix 7-B.

Practice on the soundsheets is done for three to five minutes daily prior to oral reading. The first soundsheet usually represents the first stories in the first preprimer, and subsequent soundsheets represent the remaining readers up through the second grade. Most basal series have presented all sounds by this level. However, soundsheets could be used for any reading materials, not just basal readers.

A standard and consistent technique is used for practicing the sounds. It has been adapted from the sound presentation technique used in DISTAR instructional materials (that is, Englemann & Bruner, 1974). This technique is presented in Figure 7–6.

The student progresses through all levels of the soundsheets. Each soundsheet must be mastered with 100 percent accuracy on three consecutive days before the student progresses to the subsequent sheet.

Word Drill

Phonetically irregular words that cannot be logically decoded and that are difficult for individual students are practiced in isolation. The words are usually written on index cards. These words are practiced for three to five minutes prior to oral reading. Mastery is achieved when a student reads all cards currently being worked on with 100 percent accuracy three times in succession on the same day.

Reading Speed

When a student is reading too slowly, the teacher sets the criterion for words read per minute at a level that the student can achieve. Then the criterion is gradually increased to a faster speed. Caution must be taken not to make criterion changes that are too large, especially at the beginning. As an example, a student may be reading on the average of 25 CWPM. Initially, the student would be allowed to pass stories that were read at this speed provided that criteria for accuracy and comprehension were met. Then the rate criterion might be adjusted to 30 CWPM, then to 35 and 45, and so on. As the student improves, the increments for change are increased.

Figure 7–6 Sample Sound Presentation Technique

SOUNDS

A. Point to the sounds.
Teacher says: "Tell me these sounds."

B. Point to each sound.
Teacher says: "Get ready."

C. Touch the sound.
The students say the sound.

D. Repeat problem sounds until the students can correctly identify all sounds in order.

E. Test on a new row(s) representing all sounds.

Two other techniques used to increase reading rate are:

- *Prompt*—A simple statement during the timing, such as, "Okay, read a little faster now," may be all that is needed to increase a slow rate.
- *Repeated readings*—Self-timed repeated readings practiced before the official timed sample reading has worked effectively with some students. This procedure would be faded once success is indicated by the data.

Rate of Progress

Skip and Drill

Once the student progresses at the mastery level over an extended period of time (minimum of four weeks), the teacher may decide to implement the skip and drill technique developed by Lovitt and Hansen (1976b). Pupils proceed from one section of a book to another on the basis of comprehension and oral reading rates. They may skip stories if, on the same day, all three scores (accuracy, rate, and comprehension) are better than 25 percent of their baseline averages. A drill procedure is incorporated if their scores remain at or below baseline. Teachers often alter the contingencies for skipping or drilling stories, based on individual student needs.

Reading Comprehension

Oral Comprehension

The two major comprehension areas for which direct instruction and practice are offered are oral and written comprehension. For improving oral comprehension, the two most commonly used strategies are a backward chaining procedure and emphasis on question-type.

Backward Chaining Procedure. If the student is unable to respond to relevant questions at the end of each story, the appropriate questions are asked at the end of each page or paragraph if necessary. As success is experienced, the number of paragraphs or pages is increased until mastery is reached on comprehension questions asked at the end of the story. An example of a standard technique of this type is illustrated in Figure 7–4. In this example, the student was gradually prompted in this backward chaining fashion until the correct answer was given.

Question-Type Emphasis. The student may have difficulty with a particular type of comprehension question (that is, factual, sequential, inferential). If so, emphasis is placed on developing accuracy in answering that specific type of question.

Written Comprehension

Students are almost always transferred from answering oral comprehension to writing written comprehension questions during the direct instruction process. An exception might be made for a young student. Written comprehension is gradually introduced. For example, a student might answer ten comprehension questions orally. Then two of the same ten questions would be assigned for a written response for independent seatwork. The number of written questions would then be gradually increased while the number of oral questions would be decreased, until only written questions would be given.

Of course, the teacher must consider what kinds of measures of correct performance will be used. Some examples are accuracy of response, correct grammar, proper syntax, correct punctuation, correct spelling, and legibility of handwriting. If a number of measures are used, they should be introduced gradually for most students.

DISSEMINATION THROUGH CONSULTATION

This section contains four projects that illustrate how a direct instruction reading approach can be applied to group instruction and communicated to other regular and special educators. The first project illustrates how this instruction can be done with a small group in a resource setting. The second project is a report of how one R/CT shared the instructional model with another special educator who taught in a self-contained classroom for educable mentally handicapped students. The third project is an illustration of how an R/CT demonstrated a group instruction approach in a fourth-grade classroom. It also includes a report of the degree to which the classroom teacher used the model after the demonstration had ended. In the fourth project, the author worked as a teacher consultant to a regular classroom teacher. As the classroom teacher used a data-based model for reading instruction, the effects of various contingencies upon the reading performances of 18 students were tested. This group included two students who had been labeled as learning disabled.

Project 18: Data-Based Reading Instruction in a Small Group

R/CT: Anita Andrews

B. and G. were students receiving direct instruction in reading in the resource room. After consultation with their respective classroom teachers, it was decided that, although both students were making sufficient progress with individual reading instruction, both were lacking in group attending skills. The teachers decided to put B. and G. together for reading instruction. The instruction was given by the R/CT in the resource room.

How Students Were Grouped

B. was a third-grade student reading in *Enchanted Gates* (2^1) of the MacMillan Reading Series, and G. was a second-grade student reading in *Shining Bridges* (2^2) of the same series. A decision was made to place B. in *Shining Bridges* where G. was reading.

Measures of Performance

Each day both students read orally and were timed on a 50-word passage. From this passage, accuracy (the percent of errors made) and rate were computed. Both students then orally answered five comprehension questions each. Each student would answer three factual, one sequential, and one inferential question. Individual daily student records were kept.

Procedure. The students were seen for 30 minutes of daily reading instruction. Both B. and G. were required to master each story before proceeding to the next story.

> Accuracy: 94 percent correct
> Comprehension: 80 percent correct
> Rate: G. $\geq$ 40 CWPM
>   B. $\geq$ 30 CWPM

If one student was absent, then the other student practiced reading that day but would not be timed on the 50-word passage. The following day the entire story was read orally by both students. Both students were timed on the 50-word sample.

Results. This small group read 28 stories in *Shining Bridges,* the 2^2 reader, in two months. The average rate of progress is approximately 1.3 months' progress per month of instruction. One student, whose rate of progress over the entire year was 1.9 months' progress per month of instruction, was returned to his second-grade classroom, and special reading services were discontinued. The student had failed second grade the previous year. The second student averaged 2.3 months' progress per month of instruction for the entire year. She was a third-grade student now reading at the end of second-grade level. She continued to receive direct instruction at the end of the two-month period of group instruction.

Discussion

Project 18 serves as a model to illustrate how direct reading instruction can be expanded from individual to small group instruction. It would have been a good consultative strategy to offer this instruction in a regular classroom so the classroom teacher could be exposed to the instructional model. The R/CT offered the group instruction in the resource room because the students were from two different grade levels. The third-grade student may have suffered from peer harassment for receiving instruction with a second grader.

Project 19: Consulting with Other Special Educators

R/CT: Julie Keller

A special education teacher, who taught in a self-contained classroom for educable mentally handicapped (EMH) students, wanted to learn a more systematic approach for teaching reading. The R/CT offered to demonstrate some techniques for direct, data-based instruction. Consultation began with the R/CT watching the EMH teacher teach reading to a small group comprising four nonreaders in the six- to seven-year age range. Afterward the teachers met to determine which direct instruction techniques they might use with the group. The teachers continued to meet each day for a two-week period. In these meetings the following techniques were discussed and demonstrated: sound-sheet instruction; flash card drill; and oral reading with direct measurement. Problem areas were also identified, and the teachers worked out solutions together. The R/CT demonstrated all techniques without the students present. The EMH teacher then gave the actual instruction to the students.

Placement in the Curriculum

All members of the group were placed in *Blue Bananas,* which is the first preprimer of the Laidlaw basal reading series. About 20 new words are introduced in this book.

Soundsheet Instruction

Because the reading ability of the students was low, the teachers decided that emphasis should be placed on teaching phoneme/grapheme relationships. The R/CT demonstrated how to construct and use soundsheets for direct instruction. A set of rules for constructing soundsheets is shown in Appendix 7-A. Figure 7–5 contains an example of a soundsheet constructed for the first story in the *Blue Bananas* preprimer. As the students had already been taught five sounds, four of which were in *Blue Bananas,* the teachers decided to include these five sounds in the first soundsheet. The students could then begin sound drill with some sounds they already knew. The soundsheets were copied onto large charts so the teacher could point to the chart and the children could respond either as a group or individually. Ten different sounds were displayed on each chart.

For instruction, the teacher presented the sound chart and asked the children to produce the sound represented by each letter orally. The sound presentation technique was taken from the DISTAR reading program (that is, Englemann & Bruner, 1974) and is displayed in Figure 7–6. A criterion of 100 percent correct for each set of ten sounds for four consecutive days was set. The students were drilled and tested on ten sounds each day. The R/CT also demonstrated how to chart acquisition of sounds for each child.

Flash Card Drill

As the Laidlaw series places emphasis on sight word recognition, a flash card drill was added to instruction. The R/CT suggested that the words from the most recently read story, the story being worked on, and the subsequent story be practiced in isolation. This was done each day before reading the story. (Approximately 20 words are contained in an entire preprimer.) Drill consisted of having all students say the words simultaneously as the teacher pointed to them. Each student was then tested individually. After a day of instruction, the teachers decided to set a criterion of 50 percent correct. All students had to read the words at least this well before a story could be read.

Reading the Story

Because the stories in *Blue Bananas* are extremely short (approximately 50 words), it was decided that the children would read the first part of the story simultaneously. Again a DISTAR reading technique was used, that of the teacher clapping to cue the children to say each word. After each sentence the teacher would then randomly choose a child to read the sentence independently. The last 25 words of the story were saved for the time sample. Since the story had so few words, each child read the same sample. The R/CT suggested testing two children for rate and accuracy each day if time was limited. The teacher found that she was able to test each child every day.

The teachers decided that no comprehension questions would be asked in *Blue Bananas* because of the length and simplicity of the stories. They preferred to focus on accuracy and rate, and planned to include comprehension questions when the students began the second preprimer. The

R/CT explained what would be counted as reading errors and how to chart performance for accuracy and rate. (See Appendix 7-A.) The teachers discussed whether to set accuracy criterion at 92 percent or 96 percent of words correct. Although in most situations R/CTs have used 95 percent correct for accuracy, a student need only miss one word in a 25-word timed passage to score 96 percent. The EMH teacher decided to use the more stringent criterion of 96 percent. Three of the four students had to meet this criterion before the group could pass on to the next story.

Instruction

The EMH teacher began instruction on April 15 using only sounds, sound blending, and flash card drill. The children passed criterion for flash card drill, so she decided to add story reading on April 21. The R/CT suggested that all the sounds from the first story be mastered before the actual reading began. It was decided, however, that since many words used in the Laidlaw series are difficult to decode and since the children expressed eagerness to begin, this would not be done.

Reliability. The R/CT watched the teacher instruct on the first day and on four randomly selected, subsequent days over a period of seven days. She also obtained reliability measures on soundsheet and flash card testing, and rate and accuracy on three separate occasions. Absolute agreement between teachers occurred 95 percent or more of the time.

Results. The group continued to prepare for and read stories in *Blue Bananas* for the duration of the school year, which was approximately six weeks. The following fall term one student was returned to a second-grade class. The remaining three students reviewed *Blue Bananas* (first preprimer), and read *Runaway Monkey* (second preprimer). By January, two students were working in a group together and had completed ¾ of *Bluetailed Horse* (first-grade reader). The remaining student was beginning work in *Bluetailed Horse* in a small group with another student.

Discussion

This teacher consultant successfully taught a direct instruction reading approach to another special education teacher without taking over any responsibility for instruction. The teachers worked together to make accommodations for this slow group by altering sound drill to include some known sounds and eliminating initial emphasis on comprehension. It is important to reiterate that this was a group of students with virtually no reading skills. The teachers were concerned that the students not be overwhelmed with new instruction, so oral comprehension was postponed for the first few weeks of instruction. However, as a rule, comprehension practice should always accompany oral or silent reading.

The consultant demonstrated flexibility by proposing that all students need not be tested every day, but rather tested every other day. This flexibility may have been a key issue in the classroom teacher's decision to test the students every day. Daily measurement of student progress is a point that is crucial for effective data-based instruction. Yet it is a concept that is often difficult for teachers to accept. They are concerned that too much time will be spent in testing and not enough time will be allowed for instruction. Because they are not accustomed to reading daily student performance data as an indicator of progress, they often question the purpose of daily measurement.

Another important point for consideration is differential student performance. Initially, one student in this group made slower progress than other group members. Over time, she made adequate progress to remain with the group. If she had not, the group would have had to be reformed, putting the slowest student in individualized instruction or with another group of slower students. Teacher consultants must remain sensitive to the fact that forming a group does not create a constant, unchanging structure. Groups are dynamic, and individuals make progress at different rates.

Project 20: A Small Group in a Regular Classroom

R/CT: Polly Petry-Hill

This project was implemented as a demonstration in a fourth-grade classroom. The R/CT had the following three goals: (1) to demonstrate that data-based instruction could be used with a group of students; (2) to demonstrate that a systematic plan for behavior management could be woven into the instructional model; and (3) to offer the classroom teacher an instructional model that could eventually be used without assistance from the teacher consultant.

The R/CT gave the reading instruction to four boys in a small group. The boys were placed in the Laidlaw reading series in *Toothless Dragon,* which was the 1^2 reader. One student read aloud while the others followed along in their books. The length of the reading passages for each student varied randomly from one sentence to a full page. For measurement of performance, each student read a 100-word timed sample toward the end of the story. Performance was measured on the passage by recording the percentage of correctly read words and the rate (CWPM) at which each student read. After each story was read, oral comprehension questions were asked over the entire story. After three weeks, students wrote written answers as well.

All students had to meet the following criterion in order to pass a story: 95 percent correct words at 30 CWPM or better with at least 80 percent correct for comprehension.

Behavior Management

The students were seated around a table so the R/CT could easily see and reach each student. A diagram of the seating arrangement is depicted in Figure 7–7. Books were kept flat on the table to aid in determining the students' on-task behavior. This arrangement also facilitated a quick, quiet, and motivating method of signaling students to begin reading. The R/CT would signal each student's turn by placing her hand at the top of the student's book. Students were randomly selected to read. If they had the correct place in the book when they were signaled to read, the R/CT recorded a plus sign on a data sheet. A minus sign was recorded when the student was not ready to read. All recording was done in full view of the students. Positive comments were given when students received a plus sign. No comment was made when a minus sign was given, and the R/CT quickly called on another student to read.

Each Friday the group read for 15 minutes, instead of the usual 30 minutes. The remaining 15 minutes was allowed for free time. Any student who had three or more minus signs for the week lost five minutes of free time.

Results. Over a seven-week period of instruction, the group completed *Toothless Dragon,* which had 14 stories, and 26 out of 46 stories in *Tricky Troll,* the 2^1 reader. This is an average completion rate of approximately 8½ stories per instructional week. This is an average gain of approximately 3.14 months' gain per month of instruction. The students had to reread stories a second time on ten occasions. The students stayed on-task well; on only one occasion did a student lose free time.

Discussion

This teacher consultant met the first two goals she defined for this project. First, she demonstrated that a small group of students who were reading below grade level could make rapid progress in reading with the use of data-based, curricular instruction. For the second goal, she demonstrated that, with contingency management, these students could be taught to be ready to read with the correct place in the story when the teacher called upon them. She selected a reinforcement system that was easy to use in the classroom. A signaling system to call on students to

Figure 7–7 Seating Arrangement for Small Group Reading Instruction

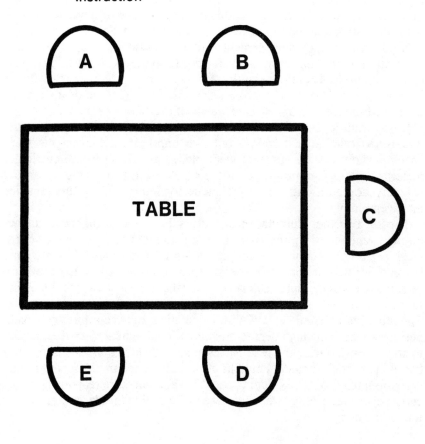

A, B, C, E, = Students
D = Teacher Consultant

read that was quiet and efficient was also developed. She praised appropriate responses and ignored inappropriate behavior. An important key was that, when a student was not ready to read, she quickly continued with instruction. This quick movement prevented students from complaining or arguing about not being ready to read.

The third goal, offering an instructional model for regular classroom use, was partially attained. The R/CT demonstrated that data-based instruction at the appropriate curricular level can result in rapid student progress. Over a seven-week period, she illustrated how to use the model in a regular class. At the end of this period, the classroom teacher took over the instruction, continuing to use a partial model of instruction. She used the contingency management plan and continued to give curricular instruction at the appropriate level. She discontinued the use of direct, daily measures. Therefore, students passed on to a new story without having met any expected performance criteria. This type of instruction continued for the remaining three weeks of the school year.

It was a disappointment that the classroom teacher did not adopt the data-based reading instruction, but two important achievements were accomplished: (1) the students were placed at a level in the curricular materials that was appropriate for their skill level; and (2) the classroom teacher adopted a data-based technique for implementing the behavior management plan.

The R/CT further identified some factors that she thought had an impact on the tremendous improvement that the students made over the seven-week period (3.14 months' gain per month of instruction). The students became actively involved in the group learning process. Each other's performance was measured by manipulating the stopwatch used for recording timed reading passages. Counts were kept of each other's reading errors. The students assisted the R/CT in calculating and recording their daily performances. This high degree of student involvement, plus their ability to stay on-task during the reading sessions, indicates that the entire data-based instructional model could have probably been implemented by the classroom teacher. The students could have taken more responsibility for counting and recording errors if this was a factor that the classroom teacher found unmanageable.

Project 21: Individual Oral Reading Performance within Data-Based Group Instruction in a Regular Classroom

Classroom Teacher: Kathleen Jensen-Browne

This project is reported from a working paper by Idol-Maestas and Jensen-Browne (1980) and reflects a consultation conducted in a regular classroom. The students chosen were 18 children—12 boys and 6 girls—from two fourth-grade classes in a small rural community in Illinois. The two classes were regrouped to represent a high and a low group for reading instruction. Students scoring below the fiftieth percentile on the Scott, Foresman placement test were assigned to the low group. The students in this project made up this low reading group.

Contained within this group were two girls who had been labeled LD by the school district. Both subjects were of average intelligence as measured by the Weschler Intelligence Scale for Children—Revised. Both scored more than one year below grade level for reading recognition and reading comprehension on the Peabody Individual Achievement Test and on the Woodcock Reading Mastery Tests. They received special services as well as attending regular class.

General Procedure

The class received reading instruction for 60 minutes every weekday morning. At the beginning of the study, the class was reading at the beginning of *Flying Hoofs,* the fourth-grade reader from the Scott, Foresman Series (1978). Each story was subdivided into 50-word passages. Every day, individual children read orally before the group of 18 children. A story was read daily, and the teacher recorded the oral reading errors for each student. In order to complete sentences or thought units, a child might have actually read more than 50 words, but the teacher recorded errors only on the 50-word passage. The following were recorded as errors: "substitutions; omissions; hesitations of more than 5 seconds; and insertions." (See Appendix 7-A for detailed definitions.) In addition, errors in reading proper nouns were counted only once if the same error was repeated throughout the passage. When a child misread a word, the teacher said, "What word?" If the child did not self-correct after five seconds, the teacher told the child to sound it out. If the child still did not call out the word, it was supplied by the teacher. The child repeated the word and then reread the sentence in which the error occurred.

Design

The effects of one reinforcer, three types of consequences, and various combinations of these, were examined in an attempt to reduce oral reading errors. The order and content of the resultant multiple phases were:

Baseline (A_1). General reading instruction procedures as described earlier in this chapter were used. These procedures remained constant throughout the project. (The length of the phase was five days.)

Phase B. When the students made an error, they lightly marked the word in the text with a pencil (nine days).

Phase C. In addition to marking errors in the book, the students charted the frequency of their errors (ten days).

Subphase C_1. One-half of the group charted errors. These children were in the homeroom of the reading teacher and received charting instruction first (five days).

Subphase C_2. The *entire* group marked their errors and charted the results (five days).

Return to Baseline (A_2). The children neither marked nor recorded errors. As in baseline conditions, the teacher recorded the errors (three days).

Phase D. In addition to maintaining error charts and marking errors, the students wrote each missed word on a drill card. On the day after the error was made, the students reviewed their drill cards with the class. The teacher held up the drill card, and the child whose card it was responded. Then the entire group read the word together (seventeen days, excluding seven days for vacation).

Phase E. The self-charting and word marking were dropped. The students continued to construct drill cards and practice error words (nine days).

Phase F. Prior to onset of this study, the students had special interest activities related to the stories in the reader. They had not read stories daily. As a reward for improved reading performance for the group as a whole, oral reading of stories was reduced from five to four days each week. The fifth day (Friday) was reserved for special interest activities (six days, including two Fridays).

Phase G. In addition to reduction of oral reading days, each student was assigned to whichever previous phase had produced the optimal performance for that individual. This addition included baseline condition if applicable (24 days).

Group Effects

A subject x phases ANOVA with repeated measures across phases was used to determine group differences across the phases. A Tukey HSD means comparison test was used to compare individual phases.

Individual Effects

Individual performance graphs reflecting accuracy across phases were monitored for the 18 subjects. For illustrative purposes, four individual performance graphs have been reported. (See Figure 7–8.) The four subjects were the two LD children, a poor reader, and an average reader from the group of 18 students. The poor and average readers were selected by

Figure 7–8 Frequency of Oral Reading Errors for Two LD Children and Two Regular Class Children

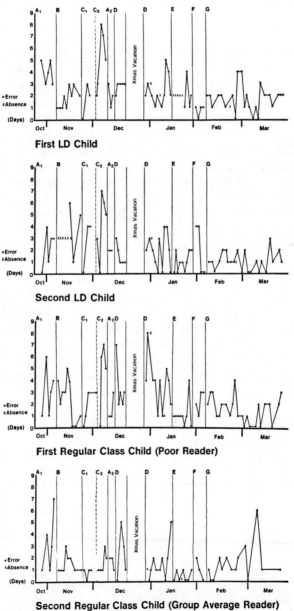

Source: Idol-Maestas and Jensen-Browne, 1980

the teacher, who used the basal series placement test as the determinant. The poor reader had one of the lowest scores in the group, and the average reader had a high score for this group of poorer readers.

Group Results

An overall significant difference was observed for phases (F = 4.21 (7,114), p < .004). (See Table 7–1.) The results of the mean comparisons for each phase are presented in Table 7-2. Phase E (error word practice), phase F (reduced number of instructional days), and phase G (placing each subject under optimal conditions) all produced significantly fewer errors (Tukey HSD, p < .01) than baseline condition. The differences between phases B, C, and D were not significantly different from baseline.

Significantly fewer errors (Tukey HSD, p < .05) were also made during phase E, when error words were practiced, than during phase B, when errors were marked. Significant differences also occurred between phase E and phase C (Tukey HSD, p < .01). Practicing error words produced fewer errors for the group than marking and charting errors. A significant difference also occurred between phase G and phase C (Tukey HSD, p < .05). Placing students under individualized optimal conditions resulted in fewer errors than having them mark and chart the errors.

The within-phase differences between phase C_1, when ½ of the group charted, and phase C_2, when the entire group charted, were not significant. There was also little difference between phase D prior to and after Christmas vacation. T-tests were used for comparisons.

For phase G, the students were placed under whatever previous phase had produced the fewest number of errors for each individual. The authors

Table 7–1 A Subject *x* Phases ANOVA with Repeated Measures Across Phases

Source	df		SS		MS	F	p
Model*	24		97.04		4.04	6.43	.0001
Subjects		17		78.53		7.35	.0001
Phases		7		18.50		4.21	.0004
Error	114		71.66		.60		
Total	138[P]						

*Model = Combination of subjects and phases.
[P]Total degrees of freedom reflect five missing observations.
   Source: Idol-Maestas & Jensen-Browne, 1981.

Table 7–2 Differences among Means across Phases

	A_1	B	C	A_2	D	E	F	G
A_1	—	.37	.20	.78	.44	1.19**	.95**	1.06**
B		—	.17	.41	.07	.82*	.58	.69
C			—	.58	.24	.99**	.75	.86*
A_2				—	.34	.34	.17	.28
D					—	.75	.51	.62
E						—	.24	.13
F							—	.11
G								—

** = $p < .01$
* = $p < .05$
Source: Idol-Maestas & Jensen-Browne, 1981

independently evaluated each student's performance chart and then compared the results. They consistently agreed upon the placement. Eight children were placed under phase E, which was to practice the missed words with drill cards. One child was returned to phase B, which was to mark the errors in the reader. Two children were placed under phase C, which was to mark errors and record them. Seven children were returned to baseline condition, where no interventions were in effect. For three of these children, a contingency was placed upon remaining under this condition. If errors were made three days in a row, they were placed under condition E, practicing with drill cards. One child returned to condition E after three days and another child during the second week. The third child remained under baseline condition. A summary of the frequency of assignment to each treatment condition is reported in Table 7–3. Sex differences were considered. The only outstanding difference was that five boys performed best under baseline conditions, while no girls were reassigned to this condition.

Individual Results

The daily number of errors across all phases for the two LD children, the poor reader, and the group average reader are depicted in Figure 7–8. The mean number of errors for the same subjects, plus those for the entire group, are reported in Table 7–4.

The first LD child made the fewest number of errors ($x = .8$) when the number of instructional days was reduced. As this was a constant for the remainder of the term, she was placed under phase B for her most optimal

Table 7–3 Assignment to Individualized Treatment Condition with Effects of Sex Differences Considered

Condition	Girls	Boys
A = Baseline	0	5
B = Mark errors	1*	0
C = Chart errors plus condition B	1	1
D = Practice error words plus condition C	0	0
E = Practice error words	4*	6

*= indicates one LD child is included in this grouping
Source: Idol-Maestas and Jensen-Browne, 1981

performance ($x = 1.6$). Thus, for the final phase of the study, she received instruction four days a week and marked the error words in the book. This student made the most errors during baseline conditions ($x = 4.0$) and during phase C_2 when the entire group charted errors ($x = 5.0$). She made noticeably fewer errors ($x = 2.0$) when only the children in her homeroom charted the errrors.

The second LD child made the fewest errors ($x = 1.0$) when she practiced the error words (phase E). Thus, for phase G, she received instruction four days a week and practiced errors. She made the most errors when she marked the errors ($x = 4.0$) and when the entire group charted ($x = 4.2$). Like the first LD child, she made fewer errors ($x = 2.6$) when only the children in her homeroom charted errors.

The poor reader also read most accurately when he practiced the error words ($x = 1.1$) and was reassigned to this condition for phase G. He made the most errors when the entire group charted their performance ($x = 4.5$). The same phenomenon occurred for the charting phase. This child made fewer errors ($x = 1.8$) when the children in his homeroom charted than when the entire group charted.

The group average reader also performed best when she practiced error words ($x = 1.5$). She made the most errors under baseline condition ($x = 3.2$). Again, there were differences between the subphases for charting. She did not chart when the children in the homeroom charted, and she made fewer errors ($x = .8$) than when she did chart ($x = 1.6$).

Discussion

Ten out of 18 fourth graders in this low reading group read most efficiently when they practiced words they missed during oral reading for four

Table 7–4 The Mean Number of Errors for Two LD Children, a Poor Reader, a Group Average Reader, and the Entire Class Across Phases

	Baseline (A₁)	Phase B	Phase C	Subphase C₁	Subphase C₂	Baseline (A₂)	Phase D	Phase E	Phase F	Phase G
First LD child	4.0	1.6	3.9	2.0*	5.0	2.0	2.5	2.0	.8	1.5[B]
Second LD child	2.2	4.0	3.6	2.6*	4.2	2.0	1.8	1.0	2.0	.9[E]
Poor reader	3.0	2.4	3.1	1.8*	4.5	1.7	3.6	1.1	2.3	1.6[E]
Group average reader	3.2	1.5	1.2	.8	1.6	1.6	1.8	1.5	2.3	1.3[E]
Entire class	1.8	1.4	1.5	.9	1.7	1.0	1.3	.5	.8	.7

* = charted errors during the first half of Condition C
B = placed under Phase B (mark errors)
E = placed under Phase E (practice error words)
Source: Idol-Maestas and Jensen-Browne, 1981

days a week. The effect of error word practice lends support to results reported by Eaton and Haisch (1974) and Jenkins and Larson (1979).

This is further substantiated by the significant decline in group errors under condition E, when all of the children practiced words compared to the following four prior conditions: (1) original baseline where children merely read orally and used a specific error correction procedure; (2) marking errors in the reader; (3) marking errors and graphing them; and (4) marking, graphing, and practicing error words. These results imply that, for most of the children, charting of errors was unnecessary. The lack of impact for self-recording is supported by Ballard and Glynn (1975) and Knapczyk and Livingston (1973). Ballard and Glynn found that self-assessment and self-recording used alone had no effect on story writing behavior. Knapczyk and Livingston reported similar results while examining use of token economies. Their subjects recorded their own data and used a token system to increase accuracy of reading assignments. When the self-recording feature was removed, the token system alone produced acceptable performance. It is important to reiterate that for two children who were not labeled LD, graphing and practice produced the best performance.

In further support of individual differences, one LD child read most accurately when she marked her errors in the reader. This is supported by a study (Houghton, Morrison, Jarvis, & McDonald, 1974) where immediate feedback and public posting of best performances (together with explicit timing) were an effective means of doubling the number of words contained in written compositions of second and fifth graders.

For five children, baseline conditions produced the most efficient oral reading for errors with no special contingencies. The overall group results indicated that when placed under individualized optimal conditions, the group made significantly fewer errors.

The overall group performance was also significantly better when the number of instructional days was reduced from five to four. There were no significant differences in group errors when assignment of children to optimal conditions was added to the reduction of instructional days.

In summary, the impact of time alone (eight weeks) over three conditions (B, C, D) produced no significant change in group performance. The final three conditions (E = error practice; F = 4 out of 5 instructional days; and G = 4 instructional days plus placement under individual optimal conditions) produced significantly fewer errors than previous conditions. There were no significant differences among the final three phases.

An analysis of individual performance reveals that remediation conditions should probably be individualized. Such determination of individualized best practice can be accomplished by taking direct and daily measures (Lovitt, Schaff, & Sayre, 1970) of all children's oral reading performance in a group setting. The results of this project indicate that classroom teachers can use a data base to make performance decisions for each individual child. They can also offer individualization within the confines of group instruction.

Finally, there was an unexpected result of using daily oral reading as a mode of instruction. For the first time at this school, a class finished the fourth-grade basal reader and completed ½ of a second fourth-grade reader.

MODIFICATION OF DIRECT INSTRUCTION APPROACHES FOR CLASSROOM USE

As Projects 18, 19, 20, and 21 illustrate, the precise strategies used for individual, direct reading instruction can be modified for use with groups. These projects also illustrate that classroom setting is an important factor that affects how the instruction will occur. The following is a summarization of different modifications that R/CTs used in these projects to accommodate the needs of student groups:

- Place students in close performance clusters rather than using strict criterial definitions for placing students in the appropriate curriculum.
- Reduce the length of the reading passage used to obtain a timed oral reading sample.
- Test students individually on the same timed reading sample.
- Use a group contingency for passing stories.
- Alter the criterion levels for passing stories to accommodate slower or faster students.
- Have remaining students practice when a group member is absent.
- Reduce the number of comprehension questions that are asked of each student.
- Reduce the number of performance measures.
- Use a preplanned seating arrangement with the teacher in close proximity to the students.
- Have students read simultaneously, except during the timed samples.
- Divide the story into equal-sized passages.
- Teach the students to measure and record their own progress.
- Practice flash card drill with the entire group.
- Use large charts or an overhead transparency for drill of error words or sounds/letters.

- Increase or decrease the number of sounds on each soundsheet.
- Reform groups if students' skill levels deviate too much from one another.

These strategies were implemented among four different projects. A teacher consultant must select strategies that are best suited for a particular group. The following are some additional strategies that a teacher consultant might use to facilitate group reading instruction:

- Have the students write the answers to the comprehension questions. This offers good practice in independent work completion, as well as provides extra time to obtain individual measures of student performance.
- Write extra comprehension questions so that individual students have a sufficient number of questions.
- Examine the kinds of comprehension skills that are required in the regular class. Incorporate these within the reading lesson.
- Use positive reinforcement to improve student performance.
- Allow students to preread comprehension questions prior to story reading to improve memory.
- Transfer higher level students from oral to silent reading tasks.
- Obtain an occasional time sample of oral reading for students who normally read silently. This can be done by having students record the time sample on a recording machine.

These strategies are merely illustrations designed to stimulate teacher consultants to devise ways in which effective, data-based reading instruction can be modified for use with groups of students.

COMMUNICATION EXCHANGE

Special educators who have been hired as teachers in resource rooms and special self-contained classes may begin to transform their job roles to include time for teacher consultation. Obviously, the best way to approach the issue of job transformation is to have administrative support from the superintendent of a school district, with a planned conscious effort to reeducate building principals, classroom teachers, and special educators. At a more minor level, some individual special teachers may begin to negotiate for changes in their job role descriptions, moving toward a teacher consultant model. For example, the majority of graduates from the R/CT Program at the University of Illinois negotiate for job role changes as they are seeking new positions. Some teachers strive to win support for consultation from building teachers and principals as they are working in resource positions.

Whether one negotiates for a new job or transfers from an old one, carefully planned communication of what the job entails is important. R/CT program graduates write job descriptions that reflect the skills they have for direct resource instruction and for teacher and parent consultation. Exhibit 7–1 on page 194 is an example of a typical job description.

Once time has been secured for teacher consultation, the teacher consultant must plan to alert building teachers systematically about available consultative services. Page 195 shows a memo that one R/CT sent to the teachers in her building to (1) inform them of the consultative services available; (2) find out how receptive they were to the idea of consultative services; and (3) clarify that the building principal supported the teacher consultant model.

Exhibit 7–1 Job Description Written by a Graduate of the Resource/
Consulting Teacher Program

The Role of a Resource/Consulting Teacher

Julie Keller

As a resource/consulting teacher, I would provide services to children having mild academic and behavioral problems in two ways:

1. working directly with the child in the resource room
2. helping the child indirectly by working with his/her teacher, parents, and peers

The direct services that I would provide would include:

1. testing the child in the curricular material used in the classroom to find appropriate placement;
2. giving the child daily, direct instruction in that material so that the child will be able to make an easier transition back to the classroom;
3. taking and charting daily measures of the child's performance to see if skills are being mastered;
4. basing instructional decisions on the data charted from these daily measures.

The indirect services that I would provide would include:

1. consulting with the regular classroom teacher to
   - help assess and place children using the curricular materials used in the classroom;
   - provide tests based on the classroom curriculum and give instruction on how to develop and use them;
   - assist in modifying the classroom curriculum, when necessary, to meet the needs of the child;
   - show how to take daily measures of a child's academic and social behavior;
   - help implement reinforcement contingencies for behavior management in the classroom;
2. establishing parent groups for discussion of and help with issues of concern to parents of mildly handicapped children;
3. training older peers, parent volunteers, and teacher aides to work with younger children as tutors so that they receive the individualized instruction they need;
4. offering inservice workshops for teachers that focus on special interest areas such as
   - constructing curriculum-based assessments;
   - using direct instruction techniques;
   - implementing programs for child management;
   - measuring daily performance data in a regular classroom

(Teacher's first name)

Dear (Teacher's First Name)

Even the coach of the champion Super Bowl team, the Oakland Raiders, has problems. One of his players, John Matuszak, jumped curfew before the big game and was found carousing on Bourbon Street at 3 a.m. Another player, Cliff Branch, skipped practice before the Super Bowl game. Even the best of mentors can use a little help now and then with behavior problems.

I'm interested in tackling any of your classroom problems (academic or behavior), even if you have a classroom of mostly "winners." Mr. Hoffmann suggested that I could see students four times a week (instead of five), leaving one period a day to help with classroom problems.

The following timetable could be a possibility if you're interested.

Period	Mon.	Tues.	Wed.	Thurs.	Fri.	Teachers' Names
1st	I	I	I	I	H	
2nd	I	I	I	H	I	
3rd	I	I	H	I	I	
4th	I	H	I	I	I	
5th	I	I	I	I	I	
6th	H	I	I	I	I	

I = Resource Room Instruction
H = Help a Classroom Teacher

Please mark your preference, and return to me by Friday. I will furnish complete details to those who are interested. Thanks.

Janet Ellis

_____ I do not want assistance. Continue to see my students five times a week.

_____ I would like assistance. See my students four times a week.

Please list those students needing help.

_____
_____
___ _____
_____

Appendix 7-A

Curriculum-Based Assessments in Reading*

These materials have been designed to describe the procedures
for constructing a reading assessment.

CURRICULUM-BASED ASSESSMENTS IN READING

Appendix 7-A is a description of how to construct *Curriculum-Based Assessments* (CBAs) for reading skill assessment. A philosophy of the Resource/Consulting Teacher Training Program is that assessment using curricular materials can provide the educator with more specific information than can be obtained from standardized tests. Students perform or fail to perform in specific curricula used by individual schools. Therefore, using those same curricular materials to construct tests for assessment is a more accurate way of describing how a student performs in comparison to other students in a particular classroom or school. In addition, students can be placed for instruction in a graded reader that is commensurate with their reading skills.

The 1979–80 trainees in the Resource/Consulting Teacher Program wrote the material. The actual procedures have been established by many persons affiliated with this program, primarily under the direction of Professor Joseph Jenkins during the mid-1970s.

Nancy Buechin	Margie Heintz
Polly Petry-Hill	Janet Ellis
Mary Pilosof	Kim Roberts
Barbara Bobek	Lynne Nicol
Kathleen Jensen-Browne	

---

*These rules and procedures have been adapted over time by many people working in the Resource/Consulting Teacher Training Program, Department of Special Education, University of Illinois from the mid-1970s to the present.

It has been revised by the following trainees in the 1980–81 program.

Charles Davis   Anna Diaz
Peggy Bullard   Chris Johnson
Julie Keller

SELECTING 100-WORD PASSAGES

The reading test is constructed by selecting 100-word passages from the first quarter of each of the basal readers for grades 1–6. The passages are randomly selected. The readers are ordered by difficulty and are referred to as book levels.

If you are using a traditionally constructed basal reading curriculum, you will find there are five first-grade books (3 preprimers, a primer, and a first level book = Levels 1 to 5), two second-grade books (Levels 6 & 7), two third-grade books (Levels 8 & 9), one fourth-grade book (Level 10), one fifth-grade book (Level 11), and one sixth-grade book (Level 12).

Each student is tested on three separate days. *Three separate 100-word passages* should be selected from the first quarter of *each* of the basal readers.

After identifying the selections to test, mark the beginning of the section with an arrow → and count off 100 words. A bracket] should be placed at the end of the 100-word passage. The slash / should only be marked on the teacher's copy.

If the last sentence in the passage is longer than 100 words, make a slash on the sheet to indicate the end of the 100-word sample and a bracket] at the end of the sentence. Sometimes you may *have* to have students read to the end of the paragraph so that they have read enough material for you to ask five comprehension questions.

Twenty-five or 50-word passages must be taken from the preprimer and primer levels. If a 25- or 50-word passage is used, it is multiplied by 4 or 2, respectively, to get a 100-word passage score.

Xeroxing the pages for each 100-word passage will make administering the CBA easier. Comprehension questions should be included on this page.

After xeroxing the passages, label them with the book level number (1–12), the day (1–3), and T (teacher) or C (child).

Example: B_6D_1C Book 6 (Level 2.1)   or B_1D_3T Book 1 (Preprimer)
Day 1 (of testing)   Day 3 (of testing)
C (Child's copy)   T (Teacher's copy)

TAKING RATE OR CORRECT WORDS PER MINUTE (CWPM)

To get a rate measurement you will need a stopwatch or the classroom clock to time the student on each 100-word passage. Start the stopwatch when the student begins to read and stop it when the student finishes reading the *100th* word (at /).

When the student finishes reading the 100-word passage, record the time it took to read it in seconds. For example, 1 minute and 35 seconds would be recorded as 95 seconds.

You will later convert this to CWPM by multiplying accuracy by 60 and dividing it by the total seconds.

$$\text{Rate (CWPM)} \quad = \quad \frac{\text{Accuracy} \times 60}{\text{Total Seconds}}$$

PROCEDURES FOR RECORDING ERRORS

These procedures have been adapted from Haring, Lovitt, Eaton and Hansen (1978, p. 53).

Errors

Omissions

   a. If the student leaves out the entire word = *one* error.

       Example: The cat drinks milk.

       Student reads: The drinks milk. = one error

   b. If the student omits the entire line; if possible, redirect the student to the line; this is counted as one error.
       • if you are unable to redirect the student, count is as *one* error, not the number of words in that line. Subtract the number of words in the line from the *total number of words* read in the passage.

       Example: The cat drinks milk—the student omits the sentence; count as *one* error. The total number of words in the timed sample would be 96 not 100 words.

Substitutions

If the student says the wrong word = *one* error
   a. Proper Nouns—if mispronounced, count as an error the first time; accept as correct all subsequent presentations of the same noun.

Example: John ran home. The student says Jan instead of John four times; this is only counted as *one* error.

b. Deletions—of 'ed' or 's', if the student deletes these suffixes in his/her speech patterns, do *not* count as an error. (The reader may choose to make a note of this for subsequent oral language instruction.)

Additions

If the student adds a word or words not in the sample = *one* error.

Repetition

Do *not* score as an error.

Self-Corrections

Do *not* score as an error.

Pauses

After five seconds, supply the word and count it as an error.

Any Helps *count as an error.*

Example: redirecting students when they omit a line; counts as *one* error.

Be certain that the student says the whole word, not just a series of separate sounds in the word, before counting it as correct.

Note: Do not prompt, praise, instruct, or encourage during the time sample. You may encourage the child after samples are taken, but be nonspecific. Do not praise for specific behaviors like reading fast or accurately.

Give these directions to the student: "I'd like to see what a good reader you are. Some of these words might be hard, but don't worry; read as well as you can. Begin reading here → and read all the way to here]. Begin now."

To Determine Accuracy:

1. Subtract the number of errors from the total number of words read. (The total number of words will be 100 unless the student has omitted a group of words.)
2. Take the number of words read correctly and divide this number by the total number of words read in the sample to get a percentage.

Example:
a. 100 words read − 4 errors = 96 correct words

$$\frac{96}{100} = 96\%$$

b. 97 words read − 4 errors = 93 correct words

$$\frac{93}{97} = 95.9 \text{ or } 96\%$$

c. 50 words read − 4 errors = 46 correct words. Converted to a 100-word passage score: 46 × 2 = 92 correct words

$$\frac{92}{100} = 92\%$$

COMPREHENSION QUESTIONS

After each passage is read by the student, the teacher orally asks the student five comprehension questions to which the student must orally respond. The answers to these questions must be derived from the 100-word time sample. If the one hundred words end in the middle of a sentence, questions may cover information extending to the end of that sentence or even to the end of the paragraph. The end of the passage is marked by a bracket.

The questions must be of three types: three factual, one sequential, and one inferential. *A factual question* is one that asks for information specifically stated in the time sample (i.e., What did Jane get for her birthday?). *A sequential question* is one that asks about the order of events in the time sample (i.e., What happened after the dog escaped? or What did mother do before she went to the store?). *An inferential question* is one in which the answer is not directly stated in the time sample. The student must use clues gained from the mood, tone, or wording of the time sample (i.e., Why do you think Andy couldn't catch any balls?).

Before administering the CBA, the teacher must write up the questions and answers. It is important to write specific answers to reduce judgmental decisions regarding the student's comprehension skills. For inferential questions, feasible answers should be written and the teacher should indicate which answers are acceptable. For example, acceptable answers for the inferential question written above would be (if not specifically stated in the story): because his hair was too long and he couldn't see; his hair kept getting in his way and he couldn't concentrate on catching balls. Unacceptable answers would be: because he wasn't a good ball player; because he didn't care.

In asking the questions the teacher may repeat a question if the student requests it or if the teacher thinks the student has not understood the question. However, the questions cannot be reworded or interpreted by the teacher. If a question is repeatedly missed by several students, the teacher may wish to consider rewriting the question for future CBAs.

Wordage of the questions should adhere as strictly as possible to the words used in the time sample. In instances where this is not possible, words of appropriate vocabulary level should be used (i.e., preprimer and primer books).

After the comprehension questions have been written, they should be attached to each 100-word passage.

The acceptable criterion for comprehension is 80 percent or four correct out of five. Refer to the placement section for further information.

CBA PERFORMANCE RECORDING FORM

The first step is to determine the starting level of testing. Using information from informal observation, past performance record and teacher recommendation, determine the book (level) immediately before the point at which the student is reading. This is the base point to begin testing. Testing will continue through the level where the student would be at the actual year-end grade level. For example, a third grader should read sample passages through the 3^2 book.

Once the information on the top of the form is completed and the appropriate 100-word passages from the curriculum are prepared, you are ready to begin.

Begin with passages selected for Day 1. Enter the date. The child and the teacher read from separate copies. Have the students read only the passages within their appropriate testing range (as determined above). Skip the other sample passages not in the testing range. Enter the number for each book level after *book number.*

Using a stopwatch or minute hand on a clock, direct the child to read. Use tally marks on the record sheet to record errors as they occur. Students read from → to]. Stop the stopwatch when the reader reaches the slash mark (/), but allow the child to continue reading to the]. Read the stopwatch and record the number of seconds in the space after *seconds.* Subtract the number of error tallies from 100 and record this number after *correct/100.*

Some of the passages are only long enough for 50-word samples. When this occurs you need to double the number of errors and seconds that take place (or quadruple *with* the 25-word passage). Using the rate formula find correct words per minute and record in the appropriate space.

CBA PERFORMANCE RECORDING FORM

STUDENT'S NAME _____ AGE _____ GRADE _____ TEACHER _____

EXAMINER _____ CBA CURRICULUM _____ CLASSROOM CURRICULUM _____

	BOOK NUMBER															
DAY 1	WORDS															
	ERROR TALLY															
	CORRECT/100															
DATE	SECONDS															
	CORRECT WORDS/MIN															
	% COMPREHENSION															
DAY 2	WORDS															
	ERROR TALLY															
	CORRECT/100															
DATE	SECONDS															
	CORRECT WORDS/MIN															
	% COMPREHENSION															
DAY 3	WORDS															
	ERROR TALLY															
	CORRECT/100															
DATE	SECONDS															
	CORRECT WORDS/MIN															
	% COMPREHENSION															

At the end of each sample, ask the child the five comprehension questions you have prepared. Convert the number correct to percentage and record on the sheet.

Proceed through all levels on Day 1. Repeat the same procedure on Day 2 and Day 3. Using the form, circle the median (middle) scores for accuracy (correct/100), rate (correct words/min), and comprehension for each book level. For three days of testing, you will have selected a middle score for each skill area (accuracy, rate, comprehension), in order to reflect the most stable estimate of the student's performance.

PLACEMENT IN THE CURRICULUM

This form is used to make a placement decision. It is designed to be used in conjunction with the *CBA Performance Recording Form.* After circling the median scores on the *Recording Form,* the median scores are plotted on the graphs on the *Placement in the Curriculum Form.*

The information to be recorded on the *Placement in the Curriculum Form* is:

1. Enter the name and grade of the student, the school, the name of the examiner and the curriculum used.
2. Enter the dates of the three days of testing.
3. Plot the median scores for each tested level for *correct words per minute, reading accuracy,* and *comprehension. (Note:* The book levels are located at the top on the horizontal axis of the graph. The numbers reflecting measured performance appear on the vertical axis of the three graphs.)
4. Connect the data points (dots) representing each median score.
5. Place the student in a reader (book level). This is done by selecting the highest book level in which the student meets these criteria:
   a. Reading accuracy is 95 percent or better
   b. Comprehension is 80 percent or better.
   c. Correct words per minute is 30 CWPM or better if the child is in grades 1–3. It is 50 CWPM or better if in grades 4–6. If the child is reading on the preprimer level, it is 25 CWPM or better.
6. On the line following *Placement,* write the name of the reader (book level) and the grade level of the book in which the student has been placed.
7. After *Comments,* enter any additional behaviors that you observed that might be helpful for instruction.

PLACEMENT IN THE CURRICULUM FORM

Name: _____   Grade: _____   School: _____   Examiner: _____

Assessment Dates: (1) _____   (2) _____   (3) _____

Placement: _____

Comments: _____

Book Levels: 1 2 3 4 5 6 7 8 9 10 11 12 13 14

Correct Words Per Minute: 150 140 130 120 110 100 90 80 70 60

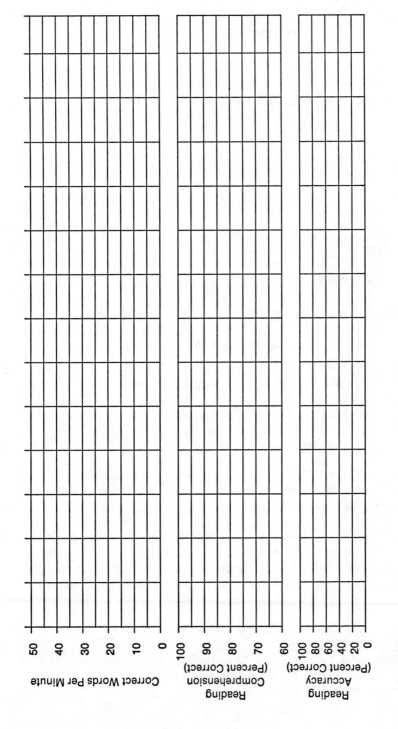

Correct Words Per Minute

50 40 30 20 10 0

Reading Comprehension (Percent Correct)

100 90 80 70 60

Reading Accuracy (Percent Correct)

100 80 60 40 20 0

Curriculum: _____

Appendix 7-B

Sound Sheet Construction*

SOUND SHEETS

I. General Statements

A. Initially use sound(s) found in phonetically regular words or found in commonly used irregular words that follow a pattern. Examples of commonly used irregular words that follow a pattern are:

old	ank
hold	prank
mold	spank
bold	Hank
cold	shank
told	bank

B. Derive the sounds from the words found in the student's books rather than the teacher's manuals. This will ensure the correct order of sound introduction.

C. Decide prior to the sound sheet construction which specific information about sounds will best meet the student's need. This will determine how you will "set up" the sound sheets. For example: Does the student need additional help with sound combinations as

---

*These rules and procedures have been adapted over time by many people working in the Resource/Consulting Teacher Program, Department of Special Education, University of Illinois from the mid-1970s to the present.

well as single sounds? If so, you will incorporate combinations from the text such as:

augh	kn	n't
oat	ere	ing
ake	ike	

D. We suggest that you refer to the inside, front cover of Carnine and Silbert's *Direct Instruction Reading* for sounds that are commonly used. Various researchers, authors, and other specialists do not necessarily agree; there is no one correct list to refer to for all sound(s) combinations.

E. You *must* use the order of sound(s) presented in the specific reading series being used with the student. Begin with the first preprimer, then the second preprimer and so on through the sequence of levels. *Usually* all new sound(s) combinations have been introduced by the end of the second-grade reader.

II. Construction of Sound Sheets

A. List sounds to be introduced at each level or in each book in the curriculum in the order presented. The only exception to this procedure will be when more than one sound is introduced for one letter combination. In this case you will include all introduced sounds in succession on the sound sheet for that particular letter combination. For example, in *Curbstone Dragons,* the student will learn that there are three different sounds for *"ea."* Although the student has already learned two of these *"ea"* sounds at an earlier level, the cumulative number of different sounds for *"ea"* will be included on the sound sheet. The sound sheet will include *ea, ea, ea* as in pl*ea*se, gr*ea*t, br*ea*d.

B. Each sound sheet should consist of 20–30 (maximum) different sounds. All of these sounds will be introduced in the first 2–3 rows of sounds. Then they should appear again but in a different order in the next 2–3 rows. Then again, and so on down the page until there are 100 entries. Thus, each sound sheet will consist of 10 rows and 10 columns of sounds.

C. When more than 30 sounds are introduced in a level (book), divide the list into halves or thirds (or more, if necessary) and construct a separate sound sheet for each segment. One sound sheet should contain those sounds introduced in the first half (or third), the next should contain those sounds introduced in the second half of the book. Label each sound sheet so that you know which sound sheet goes with which book or segment, e.g., Pug—1st half, pages 1–30; Green Feet—2nd third, pages 24–42.

III. Implementation

A. General Comments

1. Sound sheet practice should range from 3–5 minutes per reading session.
2. Sound sheet practice is considered an instructional intervention (independent variable) and would appear on the student's instructional format sheet prior to implementation.
3. Previously charted oral reading data should indicate a need to introduce such a technique, i.e, word accuracy has been below the criterion line for at least a five day period or longer.

B. Direct Instruction Using Sound Sheets

1. Instruction/Practice Period
   1.1 Select a segment of the sound sheet page that contains all the different sounds introduced (First 2–3 rows, Second 2–3 rows, Third 2–3 rows, etc.).
   1.2 Point to each letter(s) combination and say, "what sound?". Wait five (5) seconds for a student response before saying the sounds. Move at a consistent pace across columns and rows until all 20–30 different sounds have been reviewed. Return to the ones that were problems and have the student review.
2. Test/Time Sample Period
   2.1 Select another segment of the sound sheet that contains all the sounds. This segment is to be the test sample. You will record the number of errors. You will say, "what sound?". give no corrections and continue until each different sound has been sampled. Wait five (5) seconds for hesitations then proceed without comment.
   (Optional: You may wish to use a stopwatch to record the number of seconds as well as errors and then compute rate data.)

3. Record/Chart Data
   3.1 Chart data before proceeding to the next activity.
      3.1.1 *Errors* charted as

$$\frac{\text{Number of Sounds} - \text{Number of Errors}}{\text{Number of Sounds}}$$

      3.1.2 *Rate* charted as

$$\frac{\text{Number of Sounds} - \text{Number of Errors} \times 60}{\text{Number of Seconds/Minutes}} = \frac{\text{Sounds}}{\text{Per}}{\text{Minute}}$$

4. Criteria
   4.1 A decision rule (criterion for mastery) must be set prior to implementation as to when a student may proceed to the next sound sheet in the sequence. We suggest three consecutive days of 100 percent mastery. You may wish to use another decision rule. Discuss this aspect with others with whom you'll be working.
   4.2 A student receives instruction and time-sample testing on all sound sheets in the reading series being used with that student. This must occur in the sequenced order of the reading series.

Chapter 8

Consultation: Improving Social Behavior at School

Inappropriate social behaviors disrupt classroom learning and are a common reason for teachers to refer students for special services. Students who have been labeled as behavior disordered are expected to exhibit classroom behavior problems. In addition, many other mildly handicapped students (LD and EMH) also have social behavior problems that affect classroom performance.

Disruptive classroom behaviors are not merely characteristic of special education students. Other students have social behavior problems. Sometimes entire groups of students are unmanageable or disrupt learning. Effective instruction cannot occur unless there is effective classroom management. Consulting teachers can provide an invaluable service by establishing individual and group behavior management programs. This consultative assistance can be provided to teachers in their classrooms as well as in other school settings, such as lunchrooms, playgrounds, parking lots, gymnasiums, hallways, study halls, and on school buses.

A key factor in helping teacher consultants manage school behavior is a thorough knowledge of the principles of behavior modification and applied behavior analysis. Consultants must be able to define social behaviors as entities that can be observed and measured. They should know how to quantify those behaviors so that they can be recorded on a charting system (1) that can be used in a regular class or school setting; (2) that can be used by classroom teachers to analyze the effects of selected child-change strategies; and (3) that can be easily communicated to students and others who are concerned with student progress Teacher consultants must be familiar with the behavior change literature to a point that they can readily select any number of possible strategies to alter student behavior. They must be capable of applying those remedial strategies to school and classroom settings. They must fully understand the powerful effects that reinforcement and punishment have on student behavior. Finally, they must

211

be able to train other teachers to apply the principles of behavior management in their classrooms. Some important references that illustrate how classroom teachers have used these principles can be found in Greenwood, Hops, Delaquadri, and Guild (1974), Hops and Cobb (1973), and Madsen, Becker, and Thomas (1968).

This chapter contains a series of projects that were completed by R/CTs. All projects center around altering and managing social behaviors in school settings. These consultation projects were implemented in various classroom, playground, and lunchroom settings.

EFFECTS OF TEACHER ATTENTION ON CLASSROOM MANAGEMENT

When consulting and classroom teachers work together to solve classroom management problems, they may find that they eventually alter teacher behavior as well. Some teachers may attend more to unwanted student behaviors than they do to more desirable ones. Thus, students who are not accustomed to being praised for good work may not think themselves capable of good work. Instead, they resort to obtaining teacher and peer attention by exhibiting undesirable and disruptive behaviors. Thus, when collaborating teachers begin to arrange for changing problematic behavior, they also change some interactive skills of the teacher.

There is a supportive body of research in the applied behavior analysis literature that points to the powerful effect teacher attention can have on student behavior. In fact, the first article in the first volume of the *Journal of Applied Behavior Analysis* is an analysis of the effects of teacher attention on study behavior (Hall, Lund, & Jackson, 1968). Percent of time spent studying was tested under conditions where teachers were instructed to attend to appropriate study behavior by verbalization and physical contact, and to ignore nonstudy behaviors. This strategy was proven effective with one first-grade and five third-grade students. For two students, follow-up observations were also collected. These postchecks indicated that higher study rates were maintained after the formal management programs had been terminated.

In the same issue that the Hall et al. (1968) study appeared, another classic study (Thomas, Becker, & Armstrong, 1968) demonstrated that approving teacher responses served to reinforce appropriate classroom behaviors. Every time approving teacher behavior was withdrawn, disruptive behaviors increased. The subjects were 28 well-behaved children in a primary public school class. These results were also supported by earlier work of Becker's (Becker, Madsen, Arnold, & Thomas, 1967) in which problem children in public schools were systematically managed by teaching teachers to use praise and smiles to reinforce good behavior.

In a later issue of the same journal, another article reported success in instructing beginning teachers to use reinforcement to control their classrooms (Hall, Panyan, Rabon, & Broden, 1968). Reinforcement included teacher attention, length of between-period break, and a classroom game. Again, study behaviors were increased, and disruptive behaviors were decreased. For one first-year teacher who was taught to deliver contingent praise, study rate increased by a mean rate of 72 percent.

Two interesting directions emerged in the literature following reports on the effectiveness of contingent teacher attention. One was a report (Broden, Bruce, Mitchell, Carter, & Hall, 1970) that positive teacher attention had been found to generalize from student to student. When a teacher delivered contingent praise to one student, the work production of a second, nonreinforced student was found to increase. A second direction was that some researchers began to teach children to modify teacher attention by the behavior they exhibited in regular classes (Graubard, Rosenberg, & Miller, 1971).

The consultation projects (Projects 22, 23, and 24) reported in this section are examples of how different teacher consultants have used contingent teacher attention to alter disruptive behavior and poor work habits of problem students in regular classrooms.

Project 22: Working through a Multidisciplinary Team Approach

R/CT: Janet Ellis

In this project, Janet Ellis guided a teacher to use contingent praise to improve on classroom behavior of a student who had a history of receiving special services. She approached the consultation through a multidisciplinary approach working with several individuals including the child's parent. Parental involvement enhanced the program by adding home reinforcement in the form of daily report cards (Lahey, Gendrich, Gendrich, Schnelle, Gant, & McNees, 1977) to the contingent teacher attention program.

In this project, the teacher consultant worked with several individuals who were concerned about a boy who had been receiving special education services in a learning disabilities resource room and remedial reading through a Title I program. He had been integrated into a second-grade classroom and had demonstrated multiple problems in academics and social behavior. In the first multidisciplinary team staffing, these individuals met to discuss G.'s problems and to determine a set of remediation strategies. G.'s performance was summarized by each individual as follows:

- *Classroom teacher*: G. performed consistently at mid-first-grade level in reading and spelling. He did well in math and manuscript handwriting. He was easily frustrated; he frequently cried, left the classroom, copied other students' work, and engaged in various other forms of off-task behavior.

- *Title I reading teacher*: G. scored K.5 on the Slosson Oral Reading Test and 1.3 on the Wide Range Achievement Test. Both tests were given in October 1979. No curricular assessment data were available because G. was unable to read passages from the first preprimer of the MacMillan basal reading series. He had difficulty identifying letter/sounds. Vowel sounds were especially difficult for G.

- *Mother*: G. was easily frustrated with nonacademic tasks within the home as well. He had had behavior problems for a long period of time.

- *Teacher consultant*: G. was off-task (not looking at the teacher when she was talking; not looking at assigned books and papers) anywhere from three minutes, 40 seconds to eight minutes, 3 seconds over a five-day period. These observations were made during the same fifteen-minute period each day. He copied from his neighbors' papers between 9 and 25 times, averaging 15 times per each fifteen-minute observation on five separate days.

Each of these individuals agreed to be responsible for some aspect of an educational plan for G. The classroom teacher would praise appropriate behavior, ignore inappropriate behaviors, try to give G. tasks of short duration, and give him as much individual attention as possible. The Title I reading teacher would continue to review the contents of first preprimer work on a group of word lists, offer practice on letter/sounds, continue working on handwriting activities, and coordinate G.'s remedial reading program with his classroom reading assignments. The mother would continue to help G. with his math at home. The teacher consultant would continue to observe G. in his classroom daily from 11:00 to 11:15 A.M. She would also serve as consultant to the classroom teacher and notify members of the staffing team of any changes in G.'s behavior management program. The LD teacher would no longer see G. for special services.

The remainder of this report will focus on the collaborative efforts of the classroom teacher, the teacher consultant, and the parent to increase G.'s appropriate classroom behavior. The teacher consultant chose the following four techniques to accomplish this:

1. Give the classroom teacher specific guides for reinforcing G.'s appropriate classroom behavior.
2. Delineate the precise behaviors that the classroom teacher considered to be appropriate.
3. Send daily reports to G.'s mother informing her of his progress.
4. Have G.'s parents deliver reinforcement at home for good daily reports.

An explanation of these techniques follows:

Guides for Reinforcing Good Behavior

The classroom teacher and the teacher consultant met to plan the best ways to handle G.'s inappropriate classroom behavior. The teacher consultant wrote a summarization of those plans, which are displayed in Figure 8–1. These were given to the classroom teacher to serve as a reminder of what to do when G. responded appropriately or inappropriately. Copies of these guides were sent to all members of the multidisciplinary staffing team.

Appropriate Classroom Behavior

The classroom teacher and teacher consultant met to determine appropriate classroom behavior as perceived by the classroom teacher. They wrote four general goals followed by a series of specific behaviors to describe each of the four goals. These were as follows:

Goal 1. G. will demonstrate acceptance of class/school rules.

- G. will raise his hand when he has a question or needs teacher help.
- G. will wait his turn for teacher help.
- G. will remain in line once the class has lined up.
- G. will stay at his table at lunchtime until his table is called.
- G. will go the bathroom before the first bell in the morning.
- G. will go to Title I for reading at the correct time (11:15).

Goal 2. G. will decrease the number of hostile statements and actions toward teacher and classmates.

- G. will respond to teacher in a pleasant way when the teacher is helping him do something.
- G. will pass out books or papers to his classmates, handling and placing them gently on classmates' desks.

Figure 8–1 Sample Guides for Reinforcing Good Behavior that Were Provided for Classroom Teacher by a Teacher Consultant

---

Consultation on G.
Provided for (Classroom Teacher)
By Janet Ellis, R/CT 10-22-79

PRAISE
1. Praise G. immediately (or as soon as possible) after a desired behavior.
2. Be specific with your praise.
3. Say G.'s name when you're giving praise to get his attention.

Examples of Praise:
1. "G., I like the way you're listening to directions."
2. "I can see you're really trying, G. That's great!"
3. "You're doing a nice job on your spelling today, G."
4. "G., thank you for waiting so patiently for me. I'll be right there!"
5. "You've got a good start, G."
6. "I like the way you answered me so nicely, G."
7. "Good! You tried! Now let me show you the way it should be done."
8. "Good! You're back in your seat. Let's get to work now." (Give help if necessary.)

REPEAT
1. If G. does not appear to hear instructions, repeat them.
2. If G. does not understand instructions, try saying them in a different way.

IGNORE
1. Ignore any crying or tantrums.
2. If G. knocks over his chair, leave it. He'll have to pick it up.

TALK OVER
1. Ask G. to try to wait patiently for your help. You'll be there as soon as possible. (Whenever you see his hand up, recognize him, and tell him you'll be right with him.)
2. "Growing Up Corner"—Tell G. you don't want him leaving the room anymore. Pick a place in the room he can go to "cool off." Let him know it's okay to get upset sometimes. Tell him, "Go there when you need to. Come back to your desk as soon as you can."

BE GENTLE. BE POSITIVE. GOOD LUCK!

Copies to building principal, Title I reading teacher, and social worker.

Goal 3. G. will be able to follow teacher directions the first time they are given.

- G. will get materials ready for spelling the first time teacher gives directions to do so.
- G. will get materials ready for math the first time teacher gives directions to do so.
- G. will get materials for reading the first time teacher gives directions to do so.
- G. will get materials ready for every subject the first time teacher gives directions to do so.

Goal 4. G. will be less dependent on others for support and approval.

- G. will say, "I need some help, I don't understand how to do this," or "I forget how to do this," rather than "I can't do this."
- G. will try (attempt to do) an activity before asking for help.

The classroom teacher selected four of these behaviors for G. to work on at a time. The teachers kept an ongoing record reflecting which behaviors were being currently remediated, which behaviors were being maintained without direct reinforcement, and which ones were to be worked on in the future. Once a given behavior was established as one that G. consistently performed, direct reinforcement was discontinued, the behavior was monitored for maintenance, and new behavior was added to the list of behaviors to be reinforced. This list always contained four behaviors. The direct reinforcement consisted of daily report cards and home reinforcement.

Daily Report Cards and Home Reinforcement

Reports were sent home daily to G.'s parents summarizing his performance on the four target behaviors. An example is presented in Figure 8–2. If all four behaviors were positive, the teacher reminded the parents to reinforce G. by circling the asterisk notation at the bottom of the card. The parents then let G. do something special that he would like to do that evening. Some examples were reading a story, getting five cents extra spending money, and watching extra television.

These techniques were introduced over approximately nine weeks. For the first three weeks, the teacher consultant taught the classroom teacher to praise the student specifically and to ignore his poor behavior. During the last six weeks, the teachers faded the precise praise to a more natural

Figure 8–2 Daily Report Card Sent to Parents To Inform Them of Student Progress

Behavior Report Card

	Yes	No
1. Student was polite and respectful to the other children.	_____	_____
2. Student showed interest in his assignments today.	_____	_____
3. Student participated in the activities today.	_____	_____
4. Student was attentive to teacher's requests and orders today.	_____	_____
*Student should be rewarded.	_____	_____

Date_____ Teacher's Signature_____

teacher behavior and added the use of daily report cards to inform G.'s parents of his daily progress. The precise conditions and results follow.

Baseline Condition (A)

The teacher gave general classroom praise, which seemed to be sufficient for most students. During a 15-minute period of observation over a five-day period, the teacher specifically praised G. one time.

Results. G. was off-task anywhere from 180 seconds to 483 seconds. (See Figure 8–3.) He copied from his neighbors' papers from 9 to 25 times during these same observation times. (See Figure 8–4.)

Condition B

The classroom teacher was asked to praise G. immediately for desired behaviors. She used the guidelines for praise shown in Figure 8–1, which include saying G.'s name and referring to specific behaviors when praising. She was also asked to repeat any instructions that G. did not hear or understand and to ignore inappropriate behaviors, such as crying, tantrums, and knocking over chairs. This condition lasted three weeks.

Results. During the observation periods, G. was off-task anywhere from 0 to 180 seconds per period. (See Figure 8–3.) The mode (most frequent) and median (absolute middle score) time spans were 0 seconds. He copied his work from others from 0 to 13 times per observation period. (See Figure 8–4.) The most usual response was not to copy.

Figure 8–3 Effects of Teacher Attention and Parental Reinforcement on Number of Seconds Spent Off-Task

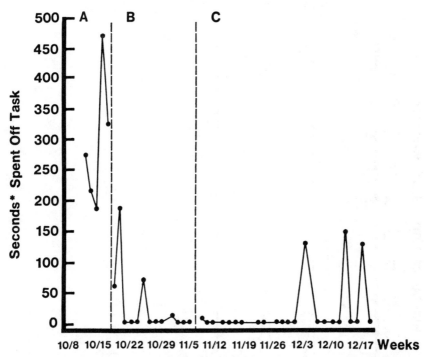

Condition C

During this six-week period, the teacher was asked to praise G. with more natural praise, similar to that she used with the other students in the classroom. The behavior report cards described earlier were sent home daily and focused on four target behaviors at a time. The parents delivered contingent home reinforcement.

Results. For the first 13 days of observation, G. was never off-task during the observation time. During the subsequent 10 days, he was off-task on 3 days, averaging 130 seconds. (See Figure 8–3.) Over the total 23 days of observation, G. copied from others' work four times on the first day. After that, he did not copy anyone's work. (See Figure 8–4.)

Discussion

A consultative group (comprising a classroom teacher, a parent, and a teacher consultant) reduced G.'s off-task and work copying behavior to a

Figure 8–4 Effects of Teacher Attention and Parental Reinforcement on Work Copying Behavior of a Second-Grade Boy

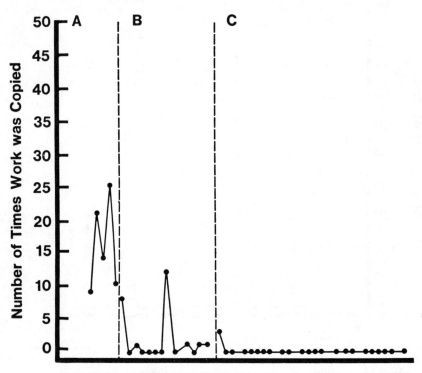

A = Baseline Condition
B = Teacher Praise/Ignore
C = Natural Teacher Praise and Daily Report Cards

level of infrequent occurrence. The most important strategy that the consultant used was to involve several members of the multidisciplinary team in this student's behavior management program. She altered the amount, timing, and the quality of attention the classroom teacher gave the student by providing specific guidelines to assist the teacher in using contingent ignoring and praising. A considerable amount of research has been reported in the applied behavior analysis literature demonstrating that contingent teacher attention does alter child behavior (that is, Broden, Bruce, Mitchell, Carter, & Hall, 1970; Hall et al., 1968; Madsen, Becker, & Thomas,

1968; Thomas, Becker, & Armstrong, 1968). The consultant then faded highly structured teacher praise and actively involved the student's parents by using daily report cards and contingent home reinforcement. Chapter 9 contains more information on and discussion of this type of home reinforcement program.

Another important strategy that this consultant used was to focus on changing a small number of behaviors at a time. The student exhibited many behaviors that were annoying. When the classroom teacher was asked to identify and specify them, a total of 14 behaviors were produced. These behaviors were subdivided into four goal areas, and only four behaviors were concentrated on at a given time. When teachers identify many problem behaviors for a student, teacher consultants can assist in specifying and organizing these behaviors. A suggestion is usually made that the teacher select a small number of behaviors that are most annoying or cause the most problems for overall classroom management. These behaviors are fitted into a behavior management plan first. Additional behaviors are added as the student's behavior improves on the initial set.

A final strategy that this teacher consultant used, that is generally useful, is to obtain daily measurement of student behavior during small periods of time. The consultant observed in the classroom from 11:00 to 11:15 every morning. The time period was small enough to fit easily into the consultant's schedule, but large enough to measure behavior change and thus provide a data base for making decisions about effectiveness of programmed interventions.

Project 23: Teaching a Classroom Teacher To Contingently Attend and Record Pupil Behavior

R/CT: Anita Andrews

The teacher consultant also used teacher praise to increase desired classroom behavior, but she experimented with the effect teacher movement in the classroom might have on appropriate behavior. In contrast to Project 22 where the consultant recorded behavior, in this project the classroom teacher was taught to collect the behavioral observations.

D. was a first-grade girl who was referred to the teacher consultant by her teacher for off-task behaviors. This R/CT met with the teacher to discuss D.'s behaviors. The two agreed to keep data on the following behaviors: (1) getting out of seat; (2) talking with neighbors; (3) bothering neighbors physically; and (4) playing at desk and not doing work.

The teacher wanted a program that would be the least disruptive in the classroom and one with which performance data could be recorded. The teacher wanted the program to be in effect only when D. was doing independent seatwork, while the teacher was working with other students in reading groups.

Baseline (A)

The R/CT explained the procedure for keeping baseline to the teacher. The teacher marked the bottom of every other page in her reading manual. While she was working with other students in small reading groups, she would look up at D. when she came to those "marks" and record whether D. was on-task or off-task. The teacher used a recording form provided by the R/CT. She defined on- and off-task behaviors as the following:

- *On-task*: D. was in seat, was not talking, was not physically touching another student, and was working on assigned lessons.
- *Off-task*: D. was out of seat, was talking, was touching another student, was playing at desk, and/or was not doing assigned lesson.

The teacher would record a " + " for D. being on-task and a " − " for D. being off-task. This record was kept for a one-hour period each morning.

Results. For a five-day period, D. was off-task an average number of eight times per hour. The average number of on-task behaviors was one per hour. (See Figure 8–5.)

Condition B

During this phase, the teacher looked up at the bottom of every other page (which she had marked) and praised students who were on-task. The R/CT had talked with the teacher about being specific with praise, (that is, "I like the way Terry is sitting in her seat." "Billy is doing his work so quietly and neatly."), rather than making general praise statements. The teacher continued to record D.'s on- and off-task behaviors.

Results. D.'s off-task behavior decreased from an average of eight to six times per hour. Average on-task behavior increased from one to two times in the same hour over a five-day period. (See Figure 8–5.)

Condition C

When the teacher came to the mark at the bottom of every other page, she got up and circulated around the room. While walking up and down the rows, she praised the children who were on-task. When she again sat down at the reading table, she would look at D. and record whether D. was on- or off-task.

Figure 8–5 Off- and On-Task Behavior of a First-Grade Girl
Illustrating the Effect of Teacher Movement

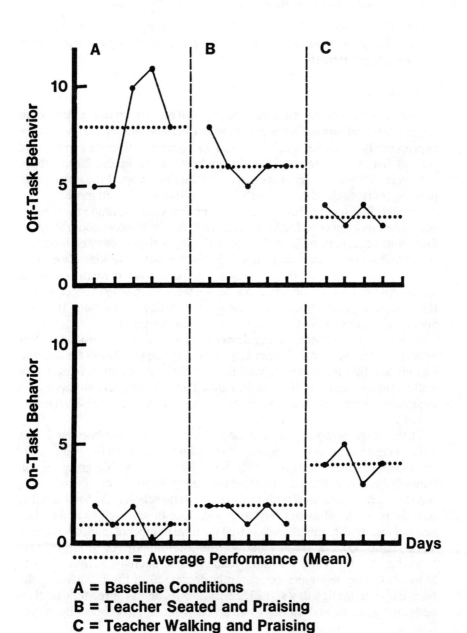

.... = Average Performance (Mean)

A = Baseline Conditions
B = Teacher Seated and Praising
C = Teacher Walking and Praising

Results. Off-task behavior again decreased to either three or four times per hour for four days. On-task behavior also increased again to an average of four per hour. (See Figure 8–5.)

Reliability. Three reliability checks were conducted by the teacher consultant. They were taken in each phase, for both behaviors. Agreement was always 100 percent.

Discussion

These teachers discovered that the physical movement of the classroom teacher affected this girl's classroom behavior. The student behaved more appropriately when the teacher looked up from a small reading group and praised her while she was working independently in the large group. However, when the teacher moved down the desk rows of the large group praising individuals, this student's behavior improved even more.

A delightful aspect of this project was the innovative solution the teacher consultant thought of to facilitate data collection by the classroom teacher. Sometimes teachers balk at the idea of using a timing device to remind them to observe because of the noise that is produced. Marking the bottom of every other page of the teacher's manual produced relatively equal increments of time for observation, which were evenly distributed across the one-hour period used for small group reading instruction. It was a simple, quiet device that required little preparation time.

As an additional note, timing devices are available that produce a low noise for sounding time. Pocket calculators can be purchased for approximately $30 that include a stopwatch and an alarm as well as features for arithmetic calculation. But, as illustrated in this project, sophisticated equipment is not necessary to obtain reasonably accurate measurements of behavior.

The management program was appealing to the teacher because it was easy to implement, and it was effective. As a follow up to the project, the classroom teacher began to use the same procedure with a group of students in her class. She recorded whether they were on- or off-task using the same procedure used with D. A large chart recorded the total number of daily off-task behaviors for the group. Free time activities and a class activity for reinforcement on days that the total number of marks decreased were set up. Over a six-day period, the total number of group off-task behaviors for the same one-hour reading class decreased from 27 to 14 behaviors. The behaviors consistently decreased in the following order from day one through day six: 27, 22, 21, 20, 16, and 14. Free time or class activities were earned on days two through six as the off-task behaviors decreased every day.

Project 24: Management of Disruptive Behavior in a Regular Classroom

R/CT: Mary Petry-Cooper

In this project, this teacher consultant also used teacher attention and daily report cards to decrease disruptive work habits of a third-grade boy. She monitored attending behaviors of both the teacher and the student.

K. was a third-grade boy whose teacher expressed concern about his disruptive work habits. K. frequently roamed around the classroom; sometimes left the classroom without permission; talked and played with peers, which sometimes developed into arguments; and sought inappropriate teacher attention. For example, the student might ask the teacher questions that he already knew the answers to. As a result, this student frequently did not complete his assignments, even though he was only expected to do one-half of the work normally assigned to classroom peers.

The teacher consultant defined K.'s disruptive classroom behavior as the following:

- *Attending* is sitting in seat, looking at work or writing, talking to teacher or peer about work, or standing or sitting near teacher while work is checked.
- *Not attending* is not staying in seat, not looking at work or writing, or talking to teacher or peer about something other than work.

Interactions between K. and his teacher were also observed. They were defined as the following:

- *Positive teacher attention*—Teacher shows approval of K.'s behavior with words or actions; teacher explains or answers K.'s questions and teacher gives directions that further clarify work assignment.
- *Negative teacher attention*—Teacher shows disapproval of K.'s behavior by word or action, including reminders about working behavior.

Baseline (A_1)

For eight days, the R/CT observed K. in his classroom. Attending and nonattending behaviors were recorded using a momentary time sampling with one-minute intervals. Teacher attention (positive and negative) was recorded using partial interval time sampling.

Results. The average daily occurrence of attending behavior was 27.27 percent of the intervals observed. Eighteen instances of negative teacher attention occurred over the eight-day period ($x = 14$ percent of the intervals recorded). One occurrence of teacher praise (x = .63 percent of observed intervals) occurred in eight days. (See Figure 8–6.)

Note. As indicated in Figure 8–6, a substitute teacher taught the class on the third and fourth days. This had no differential effect on either attending or teacher attention. On the sixth day, observations were recorded while the student was attending a small, teacher-directed reading group. As expected, this radically improved attending behavior and is the only high data point of the baseline phase of Figure 8–6. Small group instruction did not differentially affect teacher attention. On the seventh day, the classroom seating arrangement was altered. The R/CT was unaware of the change until she arrived to obtain the observational data. This change had no effect on K.'s attending behavior and increased teacher attention for a single day.

Condition B

The R/CT and the classroom teacher defined and explained in detail to K. a set of acceptable and unacceptable working behaviors. These rules were written on a card and taped to K.'s desk. Teacher praise and tokens

---

Figure 8–6 Effects of Teacher Praise, Token Economy, and Daily Report Cards on Attending Behavior and Teacher Attention

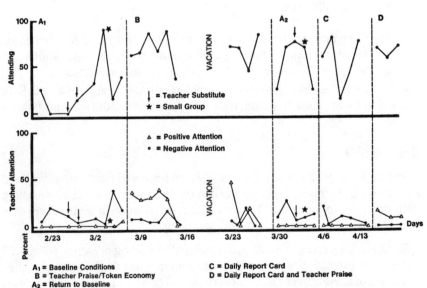

A₁ = Baseline Conditions
B = Teacher Praise/Token Economy
A₂ = Return to Baseline

C = Daily Report Card
D = Daily Report Card and Teacher Praise

(paper clips) were awarded to K. when he displayed good working behavior and were withdrawn when poor behaviors were displayed. For the first two days, the R/CT modeled the use of the token economy program. She then provided feedback to the classroom teacher as she took over giving and removing tokens. The reinforcement schedule for token exchange was: 15 tokens = five minutes spent in a free-choice activity; and 20 tokens = K. could invite a friend to join him in the free-choice activity when all assignments were completed.

Results. K.'s attending behavior increased to 67.2 percent of observed intervals, an average increase of 39.95 percent over baseline conditions. Teacher praise increased to an average of 20 percent of observed intervals, and negative teacher attention was reduced to almost one-half of that of baseline conditions (from 14 percent down to 7.4 percent).

Condition A₂

Conditions were returned to those in baseline. The observations again included one day with a teacher substitute and one day when K. was in a small reading group.

Results. Attending behavior dropped to an average of 50.2 percent of observed intervals. This was still almost twice the amount of attending recorded during original baseline conditions, but it represented a 17 percent drop from the praise/token reinforcement condition. Positive teacher attention again dropped to 0 percent and negative attention rose to 11.8 percent of observed intervals.

Note. No differential results occurred with the teacher substitute or in the small reading group.

Condition C

As a result of school parent/teacher conferences, K.'s parents expressed a desire to become involved in K.'s behavior management program. It was agreed that the classroom teacher would give K. short, daily reports of his behavior and work habits. These were taken home to his father. K.'s father agreed to praise good work habits as specified by the daily report and to discuss poor work habits and behavior with K. to encourage improvement.

Results. K. attended to his work 55.8 percent of observed intervals, and teacher praise remained at 0 percent. Negative teacher attention dropped slightly to 7.2 percent.

Condition D

In addition to the daily report card being sent home, the classroom teacher agreed to praise K. when she saw that he was attending to work. The paper clip system had been cumbersome for the teacher, and K. had expressed dislike for it since other students in the class did not earn tokens. The R/CT shared the data collected thus far for teacher attention hoping that this would influence the teacher to remember to praise K. The classroom teacher had not previously seen any charted data.

Results. Positive teacher attention rose to an average of 9.67 percent of observed intervals, with no occurrence of negative teacher attention. K.'s attending behavior rose to an average of 64.3 percent.

Reliability. Reliability checks were obtained during both baseline conditions. For attending behavior, interobserver reliability was 92 percent agreement. For positive teacher attention it was 100 percent, and for negative teacher attention it was 91 percent.

Discussion

Teacher praise and token reinforcement were found to be effective in increasing this student's attending behavior. The R/CT found that this classroom teacher was more likely to attend to problem behaviors than to praise appropriate behavior. Praise was increased when reminders (that is, paper clips) were used in condition B and when the effectiveness of praise was demonstrated in condition D. The teacher's attention to inappropriate behavior decreased when she gave more attention to appropriate behavior.

Although a token economy using paper clips as the immediate reinforcer helped to improve this student's attending behavior, it was not a strategy that the classroom teacher used comfortably. It did serve as a useful device for teaching the classroom teacher to praise good behavior contingently. When the teacher was shown charted data reflecting positive and negative attention given to K., she stopped giving negative attention. Her positive attention remained higher than both baseline conditions, but it was not as high as it was in the more rigid structure of the token economy program (phase B).

Another important consultative strategy used in this project was the modeling technique the R/CT used to teach the teacher how to praise and deliver the tokens. When suggesting a new and unfamiliar technique, simple modeling can be a more efficient approach than merely describing what the teacher should do. Special attention should be given to how the teacher reacts to the suggestion of modeling. It may be better to model the technique in private rather than in the actual classroom in front of the students.

During the final phase of this project, K.'s attending behavior increased 37.5 percent above the initial baseline condition. The R/CT recorded attending behavior of three other randomly selected students in the same class for four days; she found that their attending averages were 54.5 percent, 58.5 percent, and 23 percent of observed intervals. So, although in some classrooms K.'s attending behavior might still be considered low, it was above average for his specific classroom environment when a token economy and teacher praise were used.

STUDENT SELECTION OF REINFORCERS

It is not unusual for teachers who are unaccustomed to using contingent reinforcement as a management technique to make a common error. They might select reinforcers based on what they think students should like. Then the reinforcers prove to be something teachers like, but not necessarily what students like. This could lead to the conclusion that contingent reinforcement does not work. It is important to obtain student input when selecting reinforcers. Some teachers offer students a list of possible suggestions, allowing students to make the final selection. Others tell the students to consider what they might like as rewards, but that the teachers will be involved in the final selection.

In the following consultation projects (25 and 26), students were actively involved in selecting reinforcers. Project 25 illustrates a behavior change for a single second-grade student who made a list of preferred activities. In Project 26, a group of ninth-grade students was allowed to select preferred activities from a suggested list.

Project 25: Reducing Inappropriate Classroom Talking

R/CT: Audrey Sommerfeld

A teacher consultant worked with a second-grade teacher to eliminate inappropriate talking behavior in L., a seven-year-old boy. Observational data were collected in the second-grade class during three morning periods for independent seatwork, group reading, or work at the class center. The observation periods were from 15 to 20 minutes per day and were randomly varied across the three class periods.

Target Behavior

The target behavior of "talk-outs" was any verbal response initiated by the student and directed to the teacher or classmate(s) without raising the hand or without teacher permission. Any work-related question that was directed toward the teacher or classmates was not considered as inappropriate, even though it may have occurred without permission.

Target Behavior Aim

The collaborating teacher agreed to aim for 15 or fewer talk-outs for each school day, including mornings and afternoons.

Measurement Techniques

A tally count was used to count the number of talk-outs during each 15- to 20-minute period. Each time the student talked inappropriately, the R/CT recorded a tally mark. The time of each observation period was also noted.

Baseline (A)

Frequency of talk-out behavior was recorded for ten days.

Results. L.'s average number of talk-outs were 23 per 15- to 20-minute period. (See Figure 8–7.) The baseline was extended from five to ten days because the number of talk-outs was so variable (range: 1 to 41).

Intervention B

The classroom teacher asked the student to make a list of five things he enjoyed doing in class. After he had written the list, the student and the classroom teacher chose one activity together. The teacher and student agreed that the teacher would record the number of talk-outs every day. At the end of each day, they examined the tally, and, if L. had talked inappropriately 15 or fewer times, he engaged in the chosen activity for five minutes. L.'s mother was informed of this management program, and she supported this idea. Weekly progress reports were sent home.

Results. L.'s average number of talk-outs were six per 15- to 20-minute period. (See Figure 8–7.) Although he was reaching the criterion of 15 for this observational period, he was not meeting this criterion for the entire day. The average number of daily talk-outs was 19. Therefore, no free time activity was earned.

Intervention C

The classroom teacher felt that L. could not wait for the entire day to receive reinforcement, so she decided to split the day in half. The criterion was changed to 16 talk-outs for the day, with 8 in the morning and 8 in the

Figure 8–7 Number of Talk-Outs During a 15- to 20-Minute Period in a Second-Grade Class

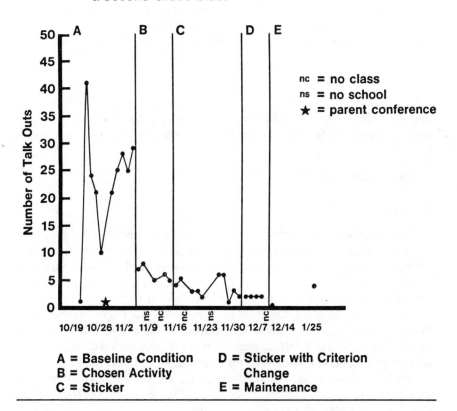

A = Baseline Condition   D = Sticker with Criterion
B = Chosen Activity   Change
C = Sticker   E = Maintenance

afternoon. L. was given a scratch-n-sniff sticker at the end of the morning if he talked out 8 or fewer times. He received another sticker at the end of the day if criterion was reached for the afternoon.

Results. L.'s talk-outs averaged three for the 15- to 20-minute observational periods. (See Figure 8–7.) Average number of total talk-outs was six in the morning and four in the afternoon.

Intervention D

Because L. was doing so well, the collaborating teachers decided to reduce the numbers of stickers awarded each day. L. was told that if he talked out in class ten times or fewer for the entire day, he would receive one sticker at the end of the day.

Results. L.'s average number of talk-outs were two per 15- to 20-minute period. The average number of daily talk-outs was 3.75. (See Figure 8–7.) Stickers were awarded for each of the four days of this condition, but an interesting phenomenon occurred. On one of these days, L. forgot to pick up his sticker, but he continued to perform at teacher expectation.

Maintenance

Contingent reinforcement was discontinued. L. was told that he was doing a good job and should keep it up, but that he would no longer be given stickers. Data were collected every other day for one week by the R/CT.

Results. See Figure 8–7.

Discussion

These teachers demonstrated that they could abruptly reduce L.'s inappropriate talking in class by using contingent reinforcement. Although offering L. a contingent activity of his choice reduced talk-outs during the observation period, his total number of daily talk-outs did not decrease satisfactorily. Reinforcement was delivered at a more frequent pace of twice a day. Even though simpler reinforcement (stickers) was used, L.'s talk-out behavior was reduced during observation and for the entire day. Gradual reduction in reinforcement delivery of stickers led to maintenance of appropriate class talking with no contingent reinforcement.

The R/CT was careful not to intervene with any reinforcement program until she was certain that the baseline data were stable. On the first day that baseline data were collected (Figure 8–7), only one disruptive talk-out occurred. This illustrates the importance of obtaining multiple daily measurements of a behavior. Had the teacher consultant based her conclusions on a single visit to this classroom, she could have erroneously decided that talking was not the "true" problem. Again, on the fourth day of baseline, the downward data trend indicates that the problem was being eliminated without a planned intervention. However, a total of ten days of baseline data clearly indicated that this student did talk out frequently as an overall average. Sometimes it is difficult to obtain a baseline measurement of adequate length because teachers are eager to try a particular intervention or to solve the problem. Teacher consultants must insist that adequate measurement is obtained. Of course, for serious disruptive behaviors that are occurring at a frequent rate, a three-day baseline measurement is probably sufficient, especially when the classroom teacher is eager for something to be done.

An essential strategy that this R/CT used was to encourage the classroom teacher to allow the student to decide which free-time activity he preferred. It is wise to inform students that the teacher will be involved in final selection of activities, as this can reduce unrealistic selection or disappointment in teacher credibility should the teacher veto some activities after student selection. The rule is to obtain student preference for reinforcers but to make the final selection together.

Another consultative strategy used in this project was informing the parent of the behavior management program. Because the parent in this project was supportive, there may have been some encouragement given at home for L. to decrease talking behavior. This was probably not a confounding variable in the reduction of talk-out behaviors, as the parent was told about the program after five days of baseline measurement. Talking behavior occurred more frequently immediately after the parent conference.

Finally, the most appealing attribute of this project is the inclusion of the maintenance phase and the changing phases building toward it. An activity that took classroom time was used initially. Then two changes were made. The teachers discovered that this student needed more frequent reinforcement. They also selected a reinforcer that was easy to deliver. Then, they again returned the student to a more infrequent reinforcement schedule. Finally, the desired behavior was maintained without reinforcement.

Teacher consultants must be cautious to select and suggest reinforcers that can be easily delivered in classroom settings. The reinforcers should be as close to social reinforcement as possible and should be paired with social praise. An exception to pairing would be with a student who clearly dislikes teacher praise.

Project 26: Reducing Disruptive Classroom Behavior in a Ninth-Grade Math Class

R/CT: Julie Haizman
Teacher: Tsivia Cohen

The teacher of a remedial math class for ninth-grade special education students and the teacher consultant agreed to design and implement a program to reduce disruptive group behavior. There were ten students in the class, and the teacher reported that several students did no work for most of the hour. She said that she could never give directions or explanations to the group because it was never quiet in the room. After one observation visit by the teacher consultant, the teachers defined on-task and off-task behavior as follows:

- *On-task behavior*—All class members sitting in their seats, attending quietly to teacher directions, raising hands to answer questions, asking relevant math questions, independently working on math problems, or talking to a neighbor about math problems.
- *Off-task behavior*—Any class member exhibiting any of the following behaviors: (1) talking while the teacher is talking to the class; (2) being out of seat for any reason including sharpening pencils; (3) eating or passing out candy; (4) talking to another student about anything other than math; (5) kicking, hitting, or throwing things; (6) making noise (that is, whistling, popping chewing gum, tapping, dropping books, moving desk); (7) smashing (insulting others); (8) cussing; (9) cheating; (10) coming to class late; (11) talking back; and (12) yelling.

Baseline Condition (A_1)

General classroom procedures remained constant throughout the project. Students were given daily grades for behavior and were issued "violations" for inappropriate behavior. These violations were recorded on index cards and were counted against student grades. The amount of total time the class was on-task for the 50-minute class period was recorded. Frequency counts were also collected for the number of occurrences for each of the 12 defined off-task behaviors for each of the students. Baseline measurements were taken for three days.

Results. Over three days, the group average for on-task behavior was 5.67 minutes over a 30-minute period. (See Figure 8–8.) The average occurrence of each of the 12 off-task behaviors is reported in Table 8–1.

Condition B_1

The students were told that the amount of time they were working was being recorded. A class hand-out explained that each time the entire class was found to be working for a total of 30 minutes in the 50-minute period, they would be given the remainder of the hour to indulge in a preferred activity. These activities and the 12 off-task behaviors were listed on the hand-out. (See Figure 8–9.) The teacher also discussed the use of activity time delineating behaviors that were acceptable and unacceptable. The students were told that the consultant would record time with a stopwatch. Each time anyone engaged in an off-task behavior, the stopwatch would stop. The class was not permitted to ask the observing consultant how much time was remaining.

Results. For a period of nine days, the group average for on-task behavior was 26.5 minutes per day. They earned activity time on five of nine

Figure 8–8 Number of Minutes Spent On-Task and Amount of Activity Time Earned by a Class of Ninth Graders

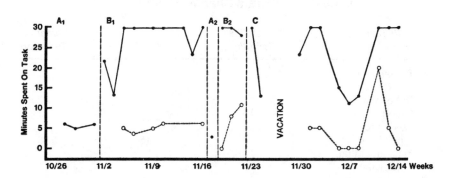

A_1 = Baseline
B = Earned Activity Time
A_2 = Baseline with Substitute Teacher
C = Phase Out of Teacher Consultant
○ = Amount of Activity Time Earned

days for a total of 27 minutes. The average amount of earned activity time was 3.1 minutes with a median of .75 minutes. All 12 off-task behaviors were decreased. (See Table 8–1.) The percentage of decrease for each behavior ranged from 50 percent to 91 percent.

Reliability. On two days the classroom teacher and the consultant both measured duration of time spent on-task. Interobserver reliability was 93 percent.

Return to Baseline (A₂)

A partial return to baseline measurement was obtained. A substitute teacher taught the class for one day. All other baseline conditions remained the same.

Results. The group was on-task for three minutes.

Condition B₂

Condition B_1 with earned activity time was continued for three more days.

Results. The group average for on-task behavior was 29 minutes. Free time was delivered on two days for a total of 18 minutes.

Table 8–1 Average Daily Frequency of 12 Off-Task Behaviors in Baseline and Phase I Conditions with Percent of Decrease to Illustrate Change Effect

Off-Task Behaviors	Baseline Conditions	Phase I	Percent of Decrease
1. Talking when teacher is	32	4	88
2. Out of seat	15	3	80
3. Eating	11	1	91
4. Talking to neighbor	47	15	68
5. Kicking, hitting, throwing	8	3	63
6. Making noise	19	9	53
7. Smashing	25	8	68
8. Cussing	12	2	83
9. Cheating	3	5	83
10. Being late	4	2	50
11. Talking back	14	4	71
12. Yelling	29	12	59

Condition C

In order to return total responsibility for the management program to the teacher, the teacher consultant no longer collected observational data. The frequency count of individual off-task behavior was terminated. The classroom teacher continued to monitor the number of minutes spent working. All other conditions remained the same.

Results. Over 11 instructional days, the average amount of time spent on-task was 23 minutes; the mode was 30 minutes. Total amount of free time earned was 35 minutes over four days.

Discussion

On-task behavior for this group was considerably increased from an average of 5.6 minutes to 26.5 minutes per 50-minute period. This is a 480 percent increase in time spent on-task. All of the 12 off-task behaviors were substantially reduced as well. A combination of factors probably influenced this change in class behavior, the effect of (1) being measured with a stopwatch by the teacher consultant; (2) being rewarded with earned activity time; and (3) having the class rules clearly specified. It is interesting to compare the overall conditions of the classroom before and after inter-

Figure 8–9 Sample List of Classroom Rules That Was Given to Each Member of a Ninth-Grade Math Class

The *Whole Class*—30 Minutes of Working

1. In seat
2. Listening to directions for day
3. Working alone or quietly with partner
4. Daily quiz

Behavior that will stop the clock:

1. Talking while I'm talking
2. Being out of your seat
3. Eating, passing out candy
4. Talking about things other than math
5. Kicking, hitting, throwing things
6. Making noise (whistling, popping gum, tapping)
7. Smashing
8. Cussing
9. Cheating
10. Coming in late
11. Talking back
12. Yelling

To get an A: No violations; no stopping the clock. Every time you stop the clock, it comes off your grade.

The time that is left at the end of the hour is your time.

Some things you may do with it: talk quietly; play math games; use calculator; do extra credit (for extra As); use felt tip pens; read.

vention. Before and during baseline conditions, the philosophy of student management centered around use of punishment, in the form of recording violations and lowering grades for bad behavior. In comparison, the use of contingent activity time centered more on positively rewarding good student behavior. Also, even though the students only earned the activity time about one-half of the time, their on-task behavior improved substantially.

The partial return to baseline condition used in this project is not a "true" return to baseline compared to intervention conditions because the teacher factor was altered. It did demonstrate that with a new teacher and no class rules the class again became disruptive. The result prompted the classroom teacher to think about providing precise student management plans for substitute teachers as well as providing lesson plans.

These teachers used an interesting communication strategy. They facilitated communication with the students by using the students' language for describing behavior. For example, "smashing" was used as a target behavior because it was the students' term for insulting other people.

They also set a realistic goal for this disruptive group of students. They required that a minimum of 30 minutes of the 50-minute hour be spent on-task in order to earn activity time. This was a more attainable goal than requiring good behavior for the entire period. It also allowed sufficient time for delivery of reinforcement. They planned to set a future goal for which they would lengthen the required amount of time spent on-task.

The teacher consultant was present in this classroom for four weeks for the 50-minute class. During this time, she observed and recorded student behavior. Simultaneously, the classroom teacher collected occasional reliability data demonstrating that she could obtain behavior measurement while she was instructant. The consultant systematically planned for transfer of teacher recording responsibilities from the consultant to the classroom teacher. The data in the final phase of this project indicate that the classroom teacher did a good job of collecting this information, as well as implementing the management procedures.

CLASSROOM GAMES TO MANAGE GROUP BEHAVIOR

Classroom games that are based on contingency management can be a useful technique for consulting teachers in managing disruptive classroom behavior. One such game, "the good behavior game" (Barrish, Saunders, & Wolf, 1969), is an alternative approach to changing teacher attending behaviors directly. Instead, the good behavior game involves subgroup competition for natural classroom privileges other than teacher attention. Jenkins and Pany (Note 1) have delineated the general procedure of the good behavior game as designed by Barrish et al. (1969). The procedure is the following:

- Select target behavior; define in observable, measurable terms (like out of seat or talk-outs without permission).
- Collect baseline data.
- Determine criterion performance level (a minimal acceptable number of demerits for winning).
- Select potential reinforcers, preferably privileges or events natural to the classroom or school setting (extra recess or free time, early dismissal, victory badges to wear).
- Divide class into teams.
- Implement in the following way: (a) Define target behaviors in specific terms to the class; (b) Record a demerit for a team every time *any*

member of the team talks out or is out of seat; and (c) Tally the demerits for each team at the end of the defined period. The team with the fewer number of marks is the winning team. If neither team exceeds the set limit, then both teams are winners.

• Modify as needed; as behavior or levels stabilize, *gradually* lower criterion number of points or extend period during which behavior is measured.

One variation might be to use the entire class as a single team. Another might be to assign team points at the start of the period. These could be recorded by tally marks on the classroom blackboard. Points would then be erased each time a disruptive behavior occurred.

Jenkins and Pany (Note 1) also remind educators that certain students may try to "beat the system" by purposely causing team demerits. Some solutions that they suggest include the following: (1) placing those students on their own separate team; (2) having individual or group consequence of detention or extra homework assignments for teams that lose; (3) removing the student from the setting or excluding from game participation; and (4) making the student subject to expulsion from the team by vote of team members, if the student causes the team to lose for two consecutive days. Educators should be careful about making work completion a punishing event, however, especially with students who are already failing to complete work.

Consulting teachers and classroom teachers may find the good behavior game a viable solution for management of groups and of some individuals within groups. Barrish et al. (1969), Harris and Sherman (1973), and Medland and Stachnick (1969) have validated the effectiveness of this game approach to group management. The following consultation project is an example of how a teacher consultant used this approach in a combination third-/fourth-grade classroom.

Project 27: The Good Behavior Game for Class Management

R/CT: Tina Holler

A teacher for a third-/fourth-grade combination class expressed concern to this R/CT about the general behavior of the students in her class. The teachers met to determine the precise behaviors that were troublesome. They decided that out-of-seat behavior would be the easiest and most important behavior to control, partially because it is so disturbing and partially because it is obvious and easy to measure. They defined out-of-seat behavior as moving around the room for purposes *other than* seeking assistance with work from teacher or others, sharpening pencils, obtaining or returning materials, or special cases with teacher permission.

Baseline (A)

The classroom teacher recorded the number of out-of-seat behaviors that occurred each morning, without the students' knowledge. Baseline conditions lasted for three days.

Results. Frequency ranged from 35 to 43 with an average of 40 occurrences. (See Figure 8–10.)

Intervention B

The class was divided into teams by separating the assigned seats into two groups. An imaginary line was drawn down the middle row of the seats. Seat assignments for problem students were randomly distributed throughout the classroom. Data were kept with a blackboard tally so that the class could monitor its own performance. Criterion rules were established. If a team with the least number of out-of-seat and disturbing behavior had fewer than ten tallies, this group received library passes for 15 minutes during the afternoon. If the entire class had only one mark, the class received ten minutes free time. If the entire class had no marks, the class received 15 minutes free time. This phase continued for 15 days.

Note. On the first day, the classroom teacher expanded the disruptive behaviors to include tattling and shouting. When the recording was done on the blackboard in front of the students, they began to exhibit these two new behaviors. At the end of the first day, the classroom teacher immediately included them in the unwanted behaviors without conferring with the consultant.

Results. The frequency of out-of-seat and disruptive behavior ranged from 9 to 30 disturbances with an average of 18 occurrences. Even with the addition of two more behaviors, the mean of inappropriate behaviors dropped over 50 percent. (See Figure 8–10.)

Intervention C

Conditions remained the same as in the previous phase, except criterion changes were implemented. If *each* group had five or fewer marks, the entire class received 15 minutes of free time. If the winning group had five or fewer marks and the other group had more than five, the winners received 20 minutes of free time. Criterion for library passes remained the same.

Results. Frequency ranged from 7 to 25; average number of disturbances was 17.

Figure 8–10 Decreasing Out-of-Seat Behavior by Using the Good Behavior Game

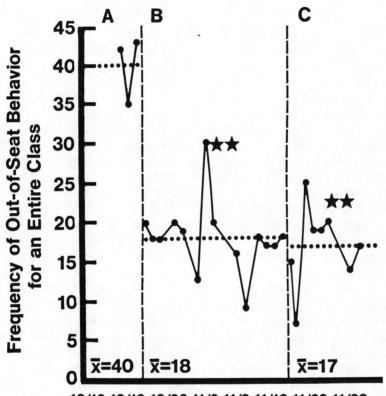

A = Baseline
B = Good Behavior Game
C = More Lenient Criteria Were Added
★ = No Class

Discussion

In this project, the teacher consultant showed a classroom teacher how to use the good behavior game (Barrish, Saunders, & Wolf, 1969) to manage classroom behavior. Criterion levels for each team and the entire class were set using library and free time as reinforcement. The effect of the game itself was demonstrated by a dramatic reduction in disruptive behavior.

The classroom teacher set the criterion at levels that she wanted for acceptable classroom behavior. The teacher consultant was certain that these were too stringent and suggested setting them at more lenient levels. The classroom teacher wanted to measure the effect of peer reinforcement in the behavior game so the consultant did not insist on criterion levels that were realistically within the group's reach. The consultant felt that this was a small point on which to differ, and she wanted to protect the quality of the collaboration between the two teachers. Had a "true" changing criterion design been used, the criterion levels would have been set closer to the baseline level of the classroom. Then they would have gradually been *changed* to more stringent levels.

In the second intervention, the criterion levels were raised to a less stringent level, but they were still not as high as the teacher consultant wanted. Again, the teachers negotiated the point, as one favored an increase in stringency, and the other favored a decrease. The ability to negotiate and give in on minor issues is an important clue to being a good teacher consultant. A consultant who is unwilling to be flexible may not be contacted for consultation in the future. In this particular case, the consultant's willingness to negotiate paid off. Since this project, the classroom teacher has sought the consultant's assistance with other classroom problems.

Teacher consultants and managers of behavior should be aware of a phenomenon that occurred in this project. Once the classroom teacher implemented the good behavior game, she discovered that unexpected behaviors occurred as result of playing the game. The students appeared to be disruptive because they wanted to make certain that the teacher recorded the data properly. The classroom teacher altered the definition of targeted behaviors to accommodate this phenomenon. The consultant might have balked at this alteration because of the deleterious effect it would have on comparing behaviors between baseline and intervention. In doing so, she might have also alienated the classroom teacher. The classroom teacher might have concluded that the consultant was more concerned with conducting classroom research than in solving classroom problems. This consultant wisely responded positively to the change, because it seemed important for maintaining classroom control and teacher collaboration.

Even though the good behavior games can be said to be an alternative approach to altering patterns of teacher attending, the following teacher consultant found that negative teacher comments were, in fact, reduced when the game was introduced.

Project 28: Reducing Negative Teacher Comments with the Good Behavior Game

R/CT: Janet Ellis

In this project, the building principal asked the teacher consultant to assist a classroom teacher with her language arts class. Initially, the consultant worked with a small group for reading instruction in the regular classroom. After two weeks, the consultant suggested that the classroom again be structured as one large group for reading because (1) it was apparent that this teacher would not assume responsibility for smaller group instruction; and (2) the consultant had collected baseline information indicating that the teacher/student interaction for the remainder of the large group was negative.

Baseline (A)

Frequency of negative teacher comments was measured while the R/CT was giving small group instruction and the classroom teacher was working with the rest of the group. Any teacher comment that included a negative form such as "no, don't, won't, or stop it," was counted as a negative comment. Measurement was taken during a five-minute period for ten instructional days.

Results. As reflected in Figure 8–11, frequency of negative teacher comments ranged from 4 to 12 comments over the same five-minute time period. The average number of negative comments was 7.5.

Condition B

The teachers decided that the entire class would complete vocabulary worksheets prior to reading each story as a group. The "good behavior game" was implemented to manage group behaviors. The class was divided into two teams. The following classroom rules were established: (1) bring necessary materials to class; (2) raise hand for permission to talk; and (3) remain in seat until permission to rise is given. If either team had fewer than six violations from 12:35 P.M. to 2:00 P.M., that team could have 15 minutes of activity time. Any team that had more than six violations continued to work for the 15-minute period. The rules were posted in the classroom, and the game rules were explained to the students. The teacher consultant gave the teacher the following list of suggestions to facilitate group management:

- *Circulate* around the room to help students during independent seatwork.

Figure 8–11 Effect of the Good Behavior Game on the Number of Negative Teacher Comments During a Five-Minute Period

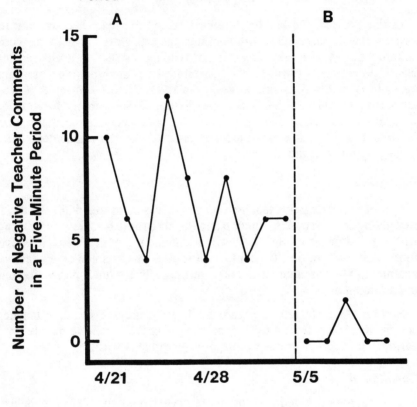

A = Baseline
B = Good Behavior Game

- *Praise* the class and individual students when they perform well.
- *Be consistent* in tallying violations and with praise.

Results. For a period of five days, the consultant continued to monitor negative teacher comments during the same five-minute period. On four days, the teacher made no negative comments during the five minutes, and she made only one on the remaining day. (See Figure 8–11.)

Discussion

Even though the consultant monitored the number of talk-outs made by the two teams, the most discriminating data collected were negative comments made by the classroom teacher before and after implementation of the good behavior game (Barrish, Saunders, & Wolf, 1969). At least during the five-minute observation period negative teacher comments were virtually eliminated.

A noteworthy strategy used by this teacher consultant was to select a method that would enable the classroom teacher to manage her entire class during reading instruction. Once the teachers agreed to use this management system, the consultant wisely asked the teacher to determine which class rules were most important. The following initial list of rules was lengthy and primarily stated in negative form:

• Homework must be done.
• Bring materials to class.
• No talking without permission.
• No yelling.
• No fighting.
• No throwing of objects.
• Stay in seats.

The consultant suggested that they begin with fewer rules and that other behaviors could possibly be added later. The teacher was asked to select the most important rules. These are the three rules listed under Condition B. The rules that were used were stated positively. Both teachers agreed that these three rules probably covered most of the problem behaviors initially selected by the teacher.

In summary, teacher consultants may find that using group management games to alter classroom structure positively affects teacher behavior as well. However, teacher consultants must be diplomatic and considerate when measuring teacher behavior. If the data can be shared with the teacher in a positive and constructive manner, then it should be shared. However, teacher consultants are not teacher evaluators. Their purpose is to assist and support classroom teachers. If focus on alteration of teacher behavior will hurt the consultation, then focus should be placed on altering student behavior.

MANAGING BEHAVIOR OUTSIDE THE CLASSROOM

Consultative efforts need not be limited to within-classroom interactions between teacher consultants and classroom teachers. Consultation can also be offered as support for management of small and large groups of students in all school settings. School lunchrooms, playgrounds, and school buses are examples of settings in which behaviors of students in a school can be systematically managed. Projects 29, 30, and 31 are examples of how the consultative services of an R/CT have been expanded to include the overall school setting.

Managing Individuals

In Project 29, a student with antisocial behavior was observed during playground interactions with other students. The teacher consultant taught the student to self-evaluate his own playground behavior. Some research studies have reported self-monitoring of behavior to be an effective change agent in altering behaviors for study (Broden, Hall, & Mitts, 1971), oral group reading (Hallahan, Marshall, & Lloyd, 1981), and oral and written reading tasks (Glynn & Thomas, 1974).

Project 29: Self-Recording to Improve Social Behavior on the Playground

R/CT: Becky Musch

N. was referred by his classroom teacher because of acting out behavior. He had verbal arguments with the classroom teacher and the physical education teacher, and he had arguments with other students that sometimes led to fights. The teacher also reported that N. would be disruptive to get the attention of the other students. After observing N. at recess for five days, the R/CT determined the target problem area to be "antisocial" behavior. Antisocial behavior was defined as any behavior initiated by N. that (1) caused other students to express displeasure verbally; (2) caused students to complain to the teacher; and (3) caused agressive physical contact, such as hitting, pushing, or throwing objects at people.

Baseline

The R/CT observed N. at morning recess (9:55 to 10:15) for seven days and recorded whether N. had exhibited any antisocial behavior. The R/CT had no direct contact with N., so he was not aware that he was being observed. The classroom teacher was given a form to note any occurrences of antisocial behavior she noticed or heard about during afternoon recess.

Intervention

The R/CT discussed her observations with N., getting his reactions to some of the incidents that had occurred, and talked about alternative and preferred behaviors he could have exhibited in the same situations. She told him that she would continue to observe his behavior at recess, but that she also wanted him to think about his own behavior and how well he got along with other students. At the end of each recess period, he was to rate himself on a 3–2–1 rating scale. (See Figure 8–12.) In addition, they talked about his behavior after recess. During this time, the R/CT would point out good behaviors that he exhibited during recess (that is, "It was nice of you to let the other boy have a turn on the swing.").

Results. During the seven days of baseline, N. exhibited antisocial behavior three out of seven recess periods in the morning or 43 percent of the recesses. Incidents included trampling other childrens' sand tunnels and trying to take a board that was being used by two other students. The classroom teacher reported two similar incidents during the afternoon (29 percent of the recesses). In total, N. had at least one incident every day for six out of seven days. During the intervention phase, neither the classroom teacher nor the R/CT observed any antisocial behavior during morning or afternoon recess. N.'s self-ratings were always 2 or 3. He never rated himself as having made other students angry. The frequencies were four ratings of 3, meaning he perceived himself as playing and sharing with other students during morning recess, and two of these highest ratings were for afternoon recess. He gave himself two ratings of 2 for morning recess, meaning that on these occasions he saw himself as playing acceptably, but still in need of improvement.

Discussion

For morning recess, this student's antisocial behavior was decreased from a 43 percent rate of occurrence to nonoccurrence. This R/CT combined several factors to achieve this result. She talked to the student about his behavior; he realized that he was being observed at recess; and he was asked to evaluate his own behavior.

When the R/CT talked with N. about his behavior, he commented that the other students sometimes did things that made him angry. The R/CT reported that all of the playground incidents she had observed were caused by something that N. had done that made another student angry. Because of this conflict in perception, the R/CT asked N. if he ever thought that the things he did might sometimes make people angry. He admitted that he had not thought of this before.

It is also interesting to note N.'s self-ratings. On two occasions, he gave himself ratings of 2. When he was asked what he had done that needed improvement, he said he had kept to himself and did not play with anyone else. Although he and the R/CT had not discussed playing alone as a

Figure 8–12 Self-Rating Scale Used by a Student to Increase Acceptable Social Behavior

Week of _____

_____ Morning Recess   _____Afternoon Recess

HOW WELL I GOT ALONG WITH
OTHER STUDENTS AT RECESS

3 = I played with other kids and shared.
2 = I did o.k., but I could have done better.
1 = I did things that made other kids angry.

MONDAY	TUESDAY	WEDNESDAY	THURSDAY	FRIDAY

problem, it is interesting that he considered playing with other students a desirable trait.

A useful technique was the problem-solving strategy this R/CT selected to determine where the problems were occurring. The classroom teacher had initially complained that N. had arguments with teachers and students. To specify the problem better, the R/CT observed N. in a variety of settings that included the classroom, the playground, and a physical education class. She encountered some obstacles that influenced her choosing the playground for observation. The R/CT had difficulty setting up a time in her schedule that coincided with times in which N. had behavior problems in the classroom, and the physical education class met infrequently. For the four occasions that she did observe during class and physical education, no specific problems were observed, except that N. was off-task slightly more than other students.

During recess, which lasted for 20 minutes, there were no structured activities, and the students (approximately 140) were supervised by a single classroom teacher. For five days, the R/CT kept an anecdotal record of N.'s morning recess activity. During this time, she observed N. engaged in play activites that sometimes led to pushing and fighting with other students. Most of these incidents appeared to be initiated in some way by N. This initial, anecdotal observation was the key determinant that led the R/CT to choose antisocial behavior as the targeted problem area. After writing three behavioral definitions of antisociability, she obtained a seven-day baseline measurement of occurrence of these behaviors on the playground.

The teacher consultant also used a unique way of obtaining a reliability measure of her observations. She asked the classroom teacher to observe the student during afternoon recess. This second observation confirmed that N. did exhibit antisocial behavior during morning and afternoon recesses, although the frequency was higher in the morning. She also used the same technique for the self-recorded data during the intervention. The ratings were consistent across recess times, even though the classroom teacher only had the student fill out the self-recording on two out of six possible occasions.

Follow-Up Data

For three more weeks, follow-up data on self-reports were collected by the classroom teacher without assistance from the teacher consultant. During morning recess, N. had five ratings of 3 (got along well and shared), five ratings of 2 (did okay, could have done better), and no problematic incidents. He was absent three mornings. During afternoon recess, he had seven high ratings, one okay rating, one fight resulting in a rating 1, and four absences. For both morning and afternoon recess, only top ratings were self-assigned during the final weeks of follow up.

Managing Groups

The good behavior game discussed earlier is one approach to managing group behavior. Many other strategies exist as well. Considerable evidence has been collected that points to the effectiveness of using positive reinforcement to manage group behavior. In a review of 57 group contingency studies, Wilcox and Pany (Note 2) reported that positive reinforcement techniques were used nearly 75 percent of the time. Group contingency programs with positive reinforcement are pleasant for teachers and students, and therefore could be effective strategies for consulting teachers to consider. As an additional asset, they could be used to influence positively school attitudes toward the consulting teachers.

Another important consultative strategy is to select positive reinforcers that are socially useful in class or school settings. This would exclude use of edible and tangible reinforcers that are expensive, undesirable to the teacher or parents, or difficult for school personnel to deliver efficiently and easily. Some social reinforcers for managing disruptive classroom behaviors that have been used in previous group studies are points (Ascare & Axelrod, 1973); points and classroom privileges (Barrish, Saunders, &

Wolf, 1969); early dismissal (Harris & Sherman, 1973); free time (Grandy, Madsen, & deMersseman, 1973); extra recess (Hall, Fox, Willard, Goldsmith, Emerson, Owen, Davis, & Porcia, 1971); movie and recess (LaForge, Pree, & Hasazi, 1975); and field trips and ice cream (Walker & Hops, 1972).

Consultation Project 30 is an example of how contingent recess time was used to improve lunchroom behaviors. The students were a small group from a special education class. It is interesting to note that teacher behavior was altered in this project.

Project 30: Altering Lunchroom Behavior of Special Education Students

R/CT: Chris Bedford

The R/CT sent a memo to all teachers in her building offering assistance with any student behavior problems. A special education teacher asked the R/CT to assist her with her class. The class was a self-contained class for EMH students. The teacher reported that four of her students were causing problems in the lunchroom almost on a daily basis. One student was near the point of being excluded from lunchroom privileges for the remainder of the year. The lunchroom management policy was that students serving as monitors reported to the teachers when students were disruptive. It then became each teacher's responsibility to take appropriate action. This teacher had been sending the disruptive students to a time-out room for ten minutes after lunch on days that they were disruptive in the lunchroom.

The students in this project were four first graders who had been placed in the EMH room for the majority of each school day. Inappropriate lunchroom behavior included running around the lunchroom, hitting or pinching other students, throwing food or objects, and shouting and screaming. If a student exhibited any of these behaviors on a given day, a poor report was given to the teacher. Otherwise, a good report was given. Frequency of good and poor reports was monitored by the R/CT for the five days.

Results. The total percentage of good reports from student monitors ranged from 25 percent to 75 percent with a mean of 50 percent (See Figure 8–13.) Student A always had a poor report; Student B had one poor report; and Students C and D each had two.

Intervention B

The usual schedule in the EMH room allowed for 20 minutes of story reading after lunch for all students not in the time-out room. In an effort

Figure 8–13 Individual Responses and Percentage of Good
Behavior Reports for Four Students in the School
Lunchroom

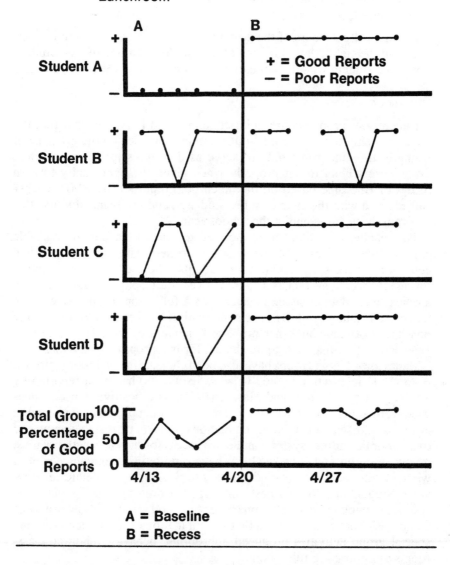

A = Baseline
B = Recess

to discourage so much playtime, the teacher discontinued the afterlunch recess that most classes had. The R/CT suggested that each student who got a good report from the lunchroom monitors be allowed 5 minutes of recess before coming in to work. The EMH teacher said that 15 minutes might be even better, so it was established that each student who got a good report from the lunchroom monitors was allowed to go outside for 15 minutes of recess or 15 minutes of selected free time in the classroom if the weather was poor.

Results. All members of the group earned recess on seven out of eight days. On the eighth day, three out of four students earned recess. Student B was the student who did not earn recess on one day. (See Figure 8–13.)

Discussion

Lunchroom problems are quite common, and it was evident that the threat of being sent to the time-out room or being denied the privilege of eating in the lunchroom did not serve as deterrents for these students. They were willing to act properly when given the opportunity to earn recess or free time based on the lunchroom reports. The EMH teacher was pleased with the change in her students, and she planned to use this program through the end of the school year.

The teacher consultant used a memo to remind teachers of available consultative services, and she was able to help with a school problem centering around special education students. She used the existing monitoring lunchroom system as a source of generating pupil data, resulting in a quick, easy data collection system. As a follow up to this project, the teacher consultant and the special education teacher met to discuss the possibility of changing other problem behaviors by focusing on earning privileges rather than using punishment for inappropriate behavior.

Behaviors of large groups have also been changed in lunchroom settings. A cafeteria intervention study (n = 455 students) has been reported by Muller, Hasazi, Pierce, and Hasazi (1975). The positive consequences used were a daily point system, which the building principal explained to each class; display of point accumulations on a chart; results announced over a public address system; and extra recess for the class with the most points. Axelrod and Paluska (1975) have reported that announcement of winners was not always enough, at least for increasing academic performance. Students performed best when special privileges and prizes were added to announcement of winners. Greenwood, Hops, Delaquardi, and Guild (1974) have also verified that a combination of rules, feedback, and special group activities produced appropriate behavior for three classrooms as opposed to rules alone.

The following consultation project (Ellis & Idol-Maestas, 1981) is similar to the Muller et al. (1975) study in that points and winner announcements were used. It is different in that individualized special activities were also used. The special activities were chosen by individual teachers and their students. The building principal also offered a class-selected field trip as an end-of-the-year grand prize. Special activities were chosen as a consultative effort to bring together all of the building teachers to support this lunchroom intervention study.

Project 31: Lunchroom Behavior Change in Rewarded Children

R/CT: Janet Ellis

There were 441 children in this project, aged 5 to 12 years, who used the lunchroom in an elementary school. They were subdivided into 19 classes, including one kindergarten group and two special education classes. The ethnic group proportions were 65 percent Anglo-American, 33 percent Afro-American, and 2 percent Asian-American. All children ate lunch with their respective classes, and each class was assigned a table in the lunchroom.

At the beginning of the study, the lunch hour was divided into two shifts. Two weeks later, it was split into three shifts of 20 minutes each. The students were evenly distributed by sex and ethnicity across the shifts. Four lunchroom supervisors—housewives in the neighborhood—were hired by the school principal to supervise the lunch period.

Definitions of Behaviors

Four desirable target behaviors were chosen. The target behaviors were the following: (1) walking into the lunchroom; (2) waiting quietly for lunches; (3) walking up to get lunches; and (4) talking quietly while eating lunch.

Walking into the lunchroom was defined as orderly movement of a class to its assigned table in the lunchroom without running or pushing. Waiting quietly for lunches meant that the entire class sat at its assigned table without any yelling until the table was called to get lunches. Walking up to get lunches was defined as an entire class getting up from its assigned table and lining up, without running or pushing, to get lunches from serving tables at the front of the lunchroom. Talking quietly while eating was defined as no yelling while sitting at assigned tables for eating.

Scoring Procedures

Observations and scoring of behavior were done by the lunchroom supervisors who moved about the lunchroom during the hour. One supervisor collected data each shift. The four supervisors alternated this responsibility. A diagram of the lunchroom was made so that lunchroom supervisors could easily record their observations by class-assigned table for each of the four behaviors. A plus (+) was assigned for achieving each of the target behaviors, and a minus ($-$) was assigned for any infractions.

Each day's observations were recorded on a raw data sheet that reflected the four target behaviors for each of the 19 classes. The raw data were converted to percentages, using the total score possible as the denominator and the total plusses earned as the numerator ($\times$ 100) for each behavior. A combined percentage score representing all desirable behaviors for the entire 441 students was also calculated.

Baseline

The lunchroom supervisors recorded individual class performance for the four defined target behaviors. Baseline was limited to three days, because the percentage of total desirable behaviors for the school was low (30 to 49 percent).

Intervention

A lunchroom behavior incentive program was presented to the school faculty. Each teacher was given a list of the defined target behaviors, and the recording system was explained. They were also told that the class(es) with a perfect score (plusses for every day for all four behaviors) at the end of each week would earn the title of "Best Class During The Lunch Hour." The honor would include the following: (1) a poster with the winner's name hung in the lunchroom; (2) the principal announcing the winner(s) over the public address system; and (3) a certificate to the winning class(es), which could be posted in their room.

The building principal chose to offer an additional reward of a special activity for any class that had four wins. (These special rewards were individualized according to the interests of each particular class.) As an end-of-the-year bonus, the class with the most wins would be awarded a special field trip. Teachers announced this plan to their classes, and intervention scoring began the next day.

After two weeks, the lunchroom schedule was changed from two 30-minute shifts to three 20-minute shifts, in order to reduce the number of students in the lunchroom at one time. The demographic representations (ethnicity and sex) remained proportionate.

Return to Baseline

After 11 instructional weeks, the incentives were withdrawn, while observations were continued for another two weeks. Teachers were told that due to the improvement and continued good behavior of the classes during the lunch hour it was no longer necessary to give classes rewards. They were told that the certificates, special activities, and announcements of winners would be discontinued. The principal made the same announcement over the public address system so that all students would be aware that they would no longer be rewarded for good behavior. They were told that the lunchroom supervisors would continue to record each class' behavior at lunch, but the children would not receive any of the previous rewards. Lunchroom supervisors were given the same information as the teachers and students. Only the authors and the principal were aware that this action was part of the study design and not an arbitrary end to rewards.

Return to Intervention

For the final three weeks the intervention condition was reinstated.

Reliability. A total of seven reliability checks on supervisors' scoring were done throughout the study. The R/CT did the first reliability check during baseline. The remaining checks, three during the intervention phase and three during the return to baseline, were conducted by two trained undergraduate observers. They were asked not to reveal their observations to the lunchroom supervisors and to avoid any discussion with them. Reliability was computed by dividing the number of agreements by the total number of agreements plus disagreements, and multiplying the quotient by 100. The results are reported in Table 8–2.

Results for Total Appropriate Behaviors. During baseline, 37 percent of the total measured behaviors for all groups of students were appropriate (range: 30 to 49 percent). In contrast, behaviors were appropriate 83 percent of the time over an 11-week period when the intervention was in effect (range: 76 to 100 percent). When the intervention was removed, there was a declining trend across the phase from 100 percent to 78 percent in total appropriate behaviors, even though the decline is not represented by average phase performance (x = 92 percent; range = 88 to 97 percent). The lunch hour schedule change had little effect upon total appropriate behaviors. There was a positive data trend prior to the schedule change, and it continued after the change. The daily performance of the combined groups is reported in Figure 8–14.

Results for Walking into Lunchroom. A 55 percent positive change occurred between the last baseline data point and the first data point of the intervention. The average percent of occurrence of walking into the lunchroom appropriately was 62 percent (range: 45 to 48 percent) for baseline compared to 99 percent (range: 95 to 100 percent) for the intervention phase. Appropriate walking-in behavior maintained at 100 percent during return-to-baseline except for the last day (75 percent). The students continued to walk in appropriately (100 percent) when the intervention

Table 8–2 Reliability Checks between Lunchroom Supervisors and Independent Observers

Dates:	1/15/80	1/22/80	3/19/80	3/26/80	4/17/80	4/24/80	5/1/80
Behaviors	Baseline		Intervention		Return to Baseline		
Walking in	95%	100%	86%	95%	100%	100%	100%
Waiting quietly	90%	90%	90%	90%	90%	100%	100%
Walking up	95%	100%	95%	85%	90%	90%	95%
Talking quietly	86%	90%	86%	81%	81%	81%	90%
TOTAL	92%	95%	89%	88%	90%	93%	96%

Source: Ellis and Idol-Maestas, 1981

phase was repeated. The schedule change had no effect upon the data trend. (See Figure 8–15.)

Waiting Quietly

The intervention also had a noticeable effect upon waiting quietly for lunches to be served. There was an approximate 72 percent positive change in the data from the last baseline data point to the first intervention data point. The phase averages were 20 percent for baseline and 92 percent for the intervention. The schedule change had little or no effect, as depicted in Figure 8-15.

Waiting quietly maintained during return to baseline (x = 95 percent) with the exception of decreased behavior (75 percent) on the final day of the phase. Waiting quietly maintained a stable, positive pattern that ranged from 88 percent to 100 percent for the final return of the intervention.

Walking Up. Appropriate behavior for walking up to the serving area to get the lunches was also positively influenced by the intervention. A 62 percent change in the data was observed between the final baseline data point (x = 49 percent) and first intervention data point (x = 99 percent). As with the previous dependent measures, the schedule change had little effect upon the walking up behavior. Likewise, this behavior maintained across the return-to-baseline and return-to-intervention phases.

Talking Quietly. The same positive shift was observed between baseline (x = 31 percent) and intervention (x = 83 percent) data, with a 69 percent change between final baseline and first intervention data points. The effect of the schedule change was minimal. Return to baseline caused a down-

Figure 8–14 Effects of Lunchroom Management Strategies on Total Percentage of Appropriate Behaviors for All Students

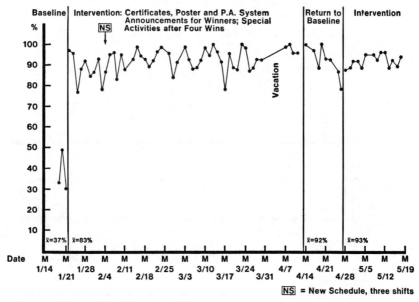

Source: Ellis and Idol-Maestas, 1981

ward data trend from 100 percent to 65 percent (x = 81 percent). However, occasional data fluctuations during the intervention reflect a similar range. The data trend did improve again when the intervention was reinstated (a 27 percent increase for the first six days), but the total average performance remained constant (81 percent).

Group Wins. All but one class were "winners" and received certificates at least once. One second-grade class won rewards every week during the first intervention phase and two out of three weeks during the reinstated intervention phase. Another second-grade class won nine times during the 11-week intervention and every week during the reinstated intervention. In contrast, one fifth-grade class never won a reward. The frequency of wins by individual classes and by lunch hour sessions is reported in Table 8–3. The classes who ate lunch during the second hour won significantly more often ($F [2, 16]$ = 6.02, p <.01) than the classes who ate lunch during first and third hour. A Scheffe multiple comparison test was used to compare individual groups.

Figure 8–15 Comparison of Baseline to Intervention Effects for Management of a School Lunchroom as Measured by Four Dependent Measures (Walking Into the Lunchroom, Waiting Quietly for Lunches, Walking up to Get Lunches, and Talking Quietly While Eating)

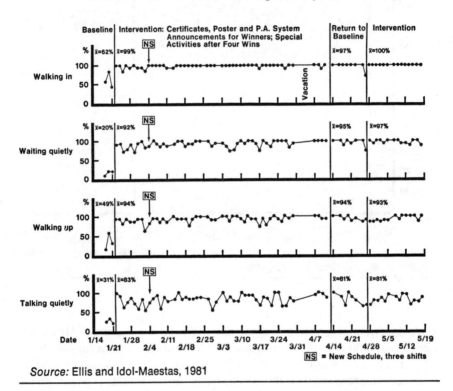

Source: Ellis and Idol-Maestas, 1981

Discussion

Rewarding good behavior within a group contingency plan resulted in improved lunchroom behavior for students in this elementary school. When the contingencies were removed, the students continued to maintain good behavior for almost two weeks. At the end of the two-week period, the frequency of good behavior decreased. A reinstated intervention increased the good behavior. The reinstatement of the intervention was strongly requested by the classroom teachers and the building principal. The request probably indicates their enthusiasm for the program, as the appropriate behaviors did not decline until the end of the return-to-baseline phase.

Table 8–3 Total Number of Wins for Each of 19 Classes by Lunch Hour Session

	Grade Level	Number of Wins*	Group mean
First lunch hour	EMH	7	3.7
	EMH	6	
	Kindergarten	2	
	First	1	
	First	5	
	First	3	
	First/second	2	
Second lunch hour	Second	9	7.5
	Second	5	
	Second	11	
	Third/fourth	5	
	Fourth	8	
	Fourth	7	
Third lunch hour	Third	6	3.3
	Third	3	
	Third	3	
	Fifth	6	
	Fifth	2	
	Fifth	0	

*Maximum number of wins possible is 11.

Source: Ellis and Idol-Maestas, 1981

A qualifying aspect of this project is how the students walking into the lunchroom were influenced by teacher interest in having a "winning" class. By the fourth week of the intervention phase, all teachers were walking with their students into the lunchroom. They had previously left their classes at the lunchroom door or at the top of the stairs leading to the lunchroom. This added teacher interest was considered to be a favorable result of the study, even though it was a confounding variable for the first dependent measure.

Another limitation is that the interobserver reliability of the fourth dependent measure (talking quietly) remained low (81 to 90 percent) throughout the study. This could have been due to a target behavior definition that was not clear enough to all observers, or it may have been due to differentiating vantage points of the observers. The lunchroom supervisors moved about the lunchroom more frequently than the undergraduate observers.

In summary, Projects 30 and 31 are examples of how consulting teachers can offer services to entire school populations. The effective use of contingent rewards positively changed lunchroom behavior, but a more important result was that classroom teachers worked cooperatively with each other and their student groups in order to effect group behavior changes. The consulting teachers demonstrated that contingent rewards can be selected that are easy to administer, and are rewarding to students and their teachers.

SUMMARIZATION OF CONSULTATION STRATEGIES

The consultation projects presented included strategies that were used to manage behavior of individual students, small groups of students, and large groups of students. The effects of teacher attention and contingent group management were stressed as useful devices for effective management. Emphasis was placed upon training teachers and students to measure and record behavior. Various combinations of consultation strategies were used to accomplish these changes in student and teacher behavior. The following is a summative list of the most important of these strategies:

Observing Student Behavior

- Use anecdotal records to help identify behavior problems.
- Observe students in a variety of settings if several people are complaining about problem behaviors.
- Collect observational data in small units of time.
- Devise simple methods for teachers to collect observational data, such as marking appropriate time intervals in the teacher's instructional manual.
- Teach students to record their own behavior.
- Use student language to define behaviors.
- Provide teachers with recording forms.
- Obtain reliability measures to ensure that the behavior observation is dependable.
- Ask teachers, principals, aides, parents, and other students to collect reliability information.

- Obtain reliability information by asking classroom teachers to observe during another part of the day as well as during the same observational time.
- Use existing recording systems as a source for collection of observational data. Some examples are attendance records, teacher grade books, and previous report cards.

Changing Student Behavior

- Identify specific goals and objectives for behavior changes.
- Focus on changing a small number of behaviors at a time.
- Establish classroom rules.
- State classroom rules positively and clearly.
- Offer strategies that can be used with other students in the classroom.
- Select reinforcers that are easy to deliver in classroom settings.
- Select reinforcers that can be paired with or are similar to social reinforcement.
- Use home reinforcement programs and daily report cards to involve parents in school consultation projects.
- Alter teacher behavior by training teachers to praise and ignore student behavior contingently.
- Model the management strategy before expecting a teacher to use the strategy.
- Use teacher movement in the classroom to control behavior.
- Use awards and recognition to enhance student performance.
- Use classroom games to manage student behavior.
- Teach students to evaluate their own behavior.

Working with Others

- Involve a multidisciplinary team to manage student behavior.
- Remind the members of the team of their responsibilities in the management program.
- Be willing to give in and negotiate when selecting remedial strategies.
- Transfer observational and instructional duties from teacher consultant to classroom teacher.

COMMUNICATION EXCHANGE

Lack of communication between the classroom teacher and teacher consultant may be the reason for an exceptional child failing in a regular classroom. Seaton, Lasky and Seaton (1974) have identified some problem areas that may result in a communication gap between teachers and specialists. The general areas were 1) giving evaluations of exceptional children that were little more than a label, 2) offering brief explanations of what to do with a problem student, 3) failing to come into the classroom, and 4) providing sufficient time for teacher conferences. They offered a set of guidelines to facilitate communication on these problem areas:

1. Provide and define specific areas for remediation rather than a general diagnostic label.
2. Take the time to provide a rationale to the teacher from any given procedure.
3. Prepare a written explanation so the teacher can review it if necessary. The specialist probably took notes when first exposed to the ideas involved, and teachers should be allowed this same opportunity.
4. Demonstrate how the procedure is to be done using the teacher or a child as an example.
5. Slow the rate of speaking and increase the redundancy. When new and complex information is received, the rate of processing is slowed and benefit may be derived from decreasing the rate of presentation and reviewing the information presented.
6. Supply a written step-by-step set of directions for any procedure or activity. Expecting someone to remember unfamiliar procedures may be unrealistic and inefficient.
7. In some cases it may be beneficial for the teacher to try out the recommended procedures while the specialist is readily available to help.
8. Try to schedule in advance a time to have a conference. Let the teacher be prepared and able to give full attention to the information exchange.
9. Follow-up with the teacher as well as with the child. Frequently, unanticipated questions or difficulties arise when attempts are made to incorporate special procedures into the classroom situation.

Source: Reprinted from *Teacher Specialist—A Communication Gap* by H. W. Seaton, E. Z. Lasky, and J. B. Seaton, with permission of *Education*, 1974, pp. 90–91.

Chapter 9

Teacher Consultation
with Parents

A key to effective educational programming for children is to actively involve their parents. This involvement should always occur during the initial stages of assessment and planning of an educational program for mildly handicapped children. The Education for All Handicapped Children Act (PL 94–142) specifies this minimal degree of parental involvement. The act says that parental consent must be obtained prior to testing students to determine whether they qualify for special education services. It further, specifies that parents should be encouraged to participate in developing their child's educational program if that child is eligible to receive special education services. This educational program, referred to as an IEP, is defined as:

> . . . a written statement for each handicapped child developed in any meeting by a representative of the local educational agency or an intermediate educational unit who shall be qualified to provide, or supervise the provision of, specifically designed instruction to meet the unique needs of handicapped children, the teacher, the parents or guardian of such child, and whenever appropriate, such child, which statement shall include (a) a statement of the present levels of educational performance of such child, (b) a statement of annual goals, including short-term instructional objectives, (c) a statement of the specific educational services to be provided to such child, and the extent to which such child will be able to participate in regular educational programs, (d) the projected date for initiation and anticipated duration of such services, and appropriate objective criteria and evaluation procedures and schedules for determining, on at least an annual basis, whether instructional objectives are being achieved . . . (*Federal Register*, August 23, 1977).

Once a legislative mandate such as this has been officially released, the actual policies regarding interpretation and implementation of the mandate are the responsibility of state and local educational agencies. Precise policies may vary from school district to school district based on individual interpretation. Parental involvement in the IEP process is one of many examples of components of PL 94–142 that are subject to this interpretive variation. Even though a school district may have a clearly defined policy for parental involvement in the IEP process, variation across individual parents can also be expected. Some parents may be involved in the planning of their child's educational program, and others may give the required signature with limited understanding of and input towards their child's program.

The same observation can be made of the degree to which classroom teachers are involved in the IEP process. This depends on school district policy, knowledge of teachers and their willingness to participate, and the willingness of special educators to involve teachers and parents actively in this process.

Currently, school districts are required to meet these minimal requirements for both parental and teacher involvement in student assessment and educational programming. Regardless of whether PL 94–142 remains in effect over the coming decade or whether it is rescinded, parental involvement in children's IEPs should remain a constant. A sound set of policies for any local or state educational agency should include this important element. School districts that employ a teacher consultant model would be wise to consider a model that encompasses consultation with parents of consultees as well as regular classroom teachers. Assigning this responsibility to teacher consultants could ensure that parents and classroom teachers are active participants in the educational programming process. It could also reduce the degree of involvement that is dependent on individual teachers and parents.

ROLE OF THE TEACHER CONSULTANT

The major responsibility of the teacher consultant working with parents is to serve as a liaison between parents and teachers of mildly handicapped students. Involvement with students' parents should be shared by both the classroom teacher and the teacher consultant, but some specific responsibilities can be assumed by the consultant. When a student is referred for special services, the consultant can interpret educational test data for the parent. Knowledge of standardized tests, CBAs, and behavioral observation will assist the consultant in offering a clear description of a student's academic and social skills.

If an IEP is to be developed for the student, the consultant can help the parent become involved in IEP planning. Explanations for proposed educational programming can be given to parents by the consultant. The consultant can also solicit information from the parents that could enhance the child's program. Some examples of this information include the following: (1) kinds of child management techniques used in the home; (2) potential problems with illnesses, school attendance, transportation, school-related fears, and so on; (3) sources of motivation and positive reinforcers for the student; (4) parental attitudes toward establishing home reinforcement and/or instructional programs; (5) previous school histories; and (6) preferrable ways of establishing an ongoing communication system between home and school.

During the IEP meeting, the teacher consultant can serve as a support person to parents, assisting them with stating their needs and clarifying unclear points. If the consultant has already talked with parents before the IEP meeting, the parents may feel more welcome and comfortable during the actual program planning.

Once a program has been implemented, the role of liaison to the home is important. The teacher consultant, working collaboratively with the classroom teacher, provides feedback to the parents that reflects the progress the student is making at school. Teacher consultants who use a data base for making instructional program decisions and for assessing student progress will find this an invaluable tool for facilitating communication.

The classroom teacher and teacher consultant may determine that a home program can be coordinated with the school program to improve pupil progress. The teacher consultant is then instrumental in establishing home-based programs with a sufficient monitoring system for assessing effects.

Essentially, the consultant does the following: (1) elicits information from parents; (2) serves as a liaison between parent and school; (3) interprets test data; (4) serves as a support person for the parent; (5) provides specific feedback on ongoing pupil progress; (6) establishes home programs; and (7) works closely with both classroom teachers and parents. The role of the home consultant can be adopted by others who might serve as consultants to classroom teachers. Some examples of others who could assume this role are building principals, social workers, school psychologists, classroom teachers, and social workers. If any of these other persons expresses an interest in any of the several aspects of being a home consultant, the teacher consultant should be willing to work cooperatively, assume less direct responsibility, give others the freedom to assume responsibility, and ensure that an accountability system is established so that each person is certain of his or her commitment to the home consultation.

THREE SUBCOMPONENTS OF HOME CONSULTATION

The remaining content of this chapter will elaborate on three general areas of home consultation: 1) giving parents systematic feedback, 2) developing home reinforcement systems, and 3) developing complementary home instruction.

Giving Parents Systematic Feedback

Parents of school children, especially those whose children have difficulty in school, have a right to know how their child is progressing in school. Sending grade reports at the end of grading periods is not sufficient feedback for any parents, but this is especially true for parents of children who are having difficulty in school. Such parents should be given continuous and frequent feedback on the academic and social progress of their children. When data-based instruction is used, the home consultant has a concrete set of feedback information to share with parents. The consultant can use charts and graphs to illustrate a student's progress or lack of progress.

A progress chart that delineates the child's progress over time in school can be helpful in giving clear, specific information to parents. An example of this type of chart is presented in Chapter 4 and depicts the reading progress of a second-grade student. (See Figure 4–3.) This student was initially more than one year below grade level and with direct instruction achieved grade level reading by the year's end.

This type of progress chart can be used for any skill area. Figure 9–1 is an illustration of the basic framework of a progress chart reflecting progress over time. The basic components of the chart include the skill or curricular levels (point A or the ordinate of Figure 9–1) over the period of time spent in instruction or school (point B or the abscissa of Figure 9–1). Any set of content materials or learning objectives that are hierarchically ordered could be fitted onto this type of progress chart. The same is true for time spent in school or instruction. This could reflect a period of several days, weeks, months, or the year. Point C in Figure 9–1 represents the rate of progress that would be expected of a student who completes each level of material at the expected point in time. Point D is the point where a student might be performing when instruction was begun that was preceded by an appropriate curricular placement. Point E is the rate at which the student

Figure 9–1　A Basic Framework for Constructing a Progress Chart that Reflects Student Rate of Progress in Relation to Normal Expectations

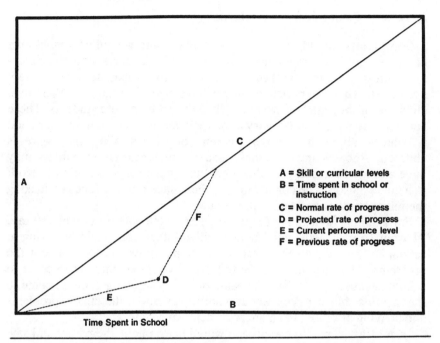

A = Skill or curricular levels
B = Time spent in school or instruction
C = Normal rate of progress
D = Projected rate of progress
E = Current performance level
F = Previous rate of progress

Time Spent in School

had been progressing before instruction. Point F reflects the rate at which a student should progress in order to achieve a normal rate of progress.

A progress chart could be used that merely contains points A and B without a reference to normal rate, but this certainly would not reflect the same degree of referential information that a complete six-point chart would contain. Three excellent sources that contain illustrative examples and discussions of this type of progress chart are Deno and Mirkin (1980); Jenkins, Deno, and Mirkin (1979); and Lew, Mesch, and Lates (1982).

Many other types of progress charts can be used to report student accomplishments to parents. The projects contained in this book will supply the reader with a variety of charting options for depicting pupil progress. One general guide for using charts and graphs to explain student progress to parents is to use a display system that is easy to read and explain.

A final strategy for using charts with parents is to provide them with a photocopy. If they take this copy home, it could be rewarding to them and to their child. It could also serve as a useful device for changing parental attitudes about parent/teacher conferences.

Increasing Parent/Teacher Contacts

Consultants should recognize that contact with school personnel may be undesirable for some parents of mildly handicapped students. Sometimes these parents have had previous negative encounters with school personnel. Those experiences might have been in regard to their own children, or they might have been when the parents were students. These parents may have grown weary of hearing about what a failure their child is, what a failure they are as a parent, or what a failure they were as children. Recognizing that these underlying, negative encounters may have already occurred puts the consultant in a stronger position to work as a home liaison. The consultant can then place primary focus on making the initial home contact a positive one.

For example, a negative focus would be to telephone a parent and say, "I want to meet with you about problems that your child is having at school." The most likely parental reaction will be to inquire about the problems. This reaction may be followed by (1) deciding not to come to school because it is always the same old story or (2) agreeing to come to the meeting, but worrying about what to say about the child's problems and arriving at school in an angry or defensive state.

In contrast, a positive approach would be to phone the parent and say, "I would like to talk with you about how your child is progressing at school." Interestingly, when some teacher consultants have called to report on pupil progress, parents have been surprised to hear of positive progress and not of problems or complaints. If the latter approach is taken first, the parent contact is initiated under positive circumstances. Then, if problems should arise later on, communication has been facilitated.

Another way to increase the frequency of parent/teacher contacts is to use various forms of communication. Telephone calls, letters, memos, daily or weekly report cards, and periodic progress reports are some examples of alternative forms. The use of these varied choices occurs frequently in the home consultation projects reported later in this chapter.

Structuring Meetings with Parents

Some preliminary thought should be given to the type of place where meetings are held. A room with a table surrounded by chairs is a good way to bring people together physically to work. The table offers a working surface where graphs and charts can be displayed and a space for taking notes. Meetings around tables also aid in eliminating hierarchical seating arrangements where persons with more authority or power sit in the best chairs. Another example of a problematic seating arrangement is to meet in a teachers' lounge, sitting in chairs of various heights and sizes distributed throughout a large room. In contrast, people sit closer together when they are clustered around a table, and this can create an atmosphere that says, "We are all here to work together."

A second strategy for structuring meetings and for increasing parent/teacher contacts is to plan for meeting duration. Parents should be told how much time will be required for the meeting, and a time should be selected that is agreeable to all parties. At the beginning of the meeting, the consultant should remind everyone of the allotted time and briefly indicate what is to be covered in the meeting.

The meeting should also reflect two-way communication between home and school. The consultant should take enough time to share pupil progress information, but also plan to allow time to listen actively to what the parents want to say. Announcing the objectives and the time frame at the beginning of the meeting may also be helpful to parents. There are parents who will want to talk about their problems for the entire meeting. One way to accommodate this is for the consultant to give the feedback information during the first part of the meeting and then allow sufficient time for the parent during the latter half of the meeting. Of course, the initial announcement for agenda content and time should include a reminder that time for parent feedback is a part of the meeting agenda.

When it is necessary to meet with parents to discuss problems that their child is having, positive aspects of the student's progress should be discussed along with the problems. It is preferable to report on the positive aspects first and then discuss the problem areas. Discussion of problem areas should be done in a problem-solving rather than a condemnatory manner. An example of the latter would be to say, "Do you know what your child has done?" which places indirect blame on the parents. The more positive, problem-solving approach would be to say, "We are having difficulty getting J. to complete his class assignments. I was hoping that we could all talk together (classroom teacher, parent, and consultant) and decide on the best course of action for us to take." Notice that any "blame" is directed toward teacher/consultee management of the problem, rather than on the parent or the student.

Further discussions of facilitating home/school communication and for improving parent conferences can be found in Kroth (1975) and Kroth and Simpson (1977).

Developing Home Reinforcement Programs

Home consultants work with students' parents to develop contingent home reinforcement for desired academic and social behaviors of problem students. A home program could motivate a student to perform well at school. It could also be solely for developing appropriate home behaviors.

Several projects throughout this book contain examples of using home reinforcement to encourage better schoolwork and behavior. In Chapter 6, there are two classroom consultation projects that contain home reinforcement. In Project 12, the consultant sent notes home to the parents to inform them when their child completed classroom assignments. The notes also contained a reminder to praise the child when the note contained positive results. In Project 16, the consultant and classroom teacher established a home reinforcement program where parents allowed their son to attend athletic practice on the weeks that spelling grades were acceptable. Also included in this project is a discussion of the problems that the consultant encountered. The problems centered around getting the parents only to deliver reinforcement contingently and maintaining a consistent communication network between the parents, the classroom teacher, and the consultant. The Communication Exchange section of Chapter 4 will give readers some suggestions for improving this type of communication problem.

In Chapter 8, there are three consultation projects for improving social behavior that utilize home reinforcement. Report cards sent home daily or weekly were used in Projects 22, 24, and 25. In Project 22, the reinforcement was formally delivered at home in the form of preferred home activities. In Project 24, a father was instructed to praise and to discuss poor work habits. The reports only provided parents with pupil progress information in Project 25.

Regardless of whether the home program is designed to change school behaviors or home behaviors, there are some common elements for both program types. These elements are the following:

- Encourage parents to participate in home programs by emphasizing the importance of establishing constancy in child management rules between school and home.
- As in teacher consultation, assist parents in defining specific behaviors to change.
- Suggest reinforcers that are easy for parents to deliver, that are inexpensive or preferably free, and that are attractive to the child.
- Establish a consistent communication system between home and school.

- Provide written guides for parents to follow that are concise and easy to read. (If the parents cannot read well, use a set of ideographic reminders.)
- Design a method for collecting behavioral information that is easy to record.
- Actively involve the child in recording the behavioral information.
- Use a consistent schedule for follow-up contacts. Parents should not be made to feel that you are spying on them, yet they should be able to anticipate when they will hear from you again.
- Develop a vehicle for parents to use to report progress or, even more important, lack of progress.
- Once a program has been successfully launched, encourage the parents to try to expand the program to eliminate other troublesome child behaviors.
- Introduce parents to other families who are working on similar home programs. This may help them feel more comfortable, and groups of parents may share and discover some effective reinforcement strategies.

Developing Complementary Home Instruction

Besides having parents deliver contingent reinforcement to students for desired behavior, parents can also be involved in complementary home instruction. This strategy is particularly useful for students who need repetitious practice on a skill before it is mastered. Home instruction should complement school instruction. The parent who acts as a teacher should not be asked to devise or test new instructional strategies. Rather, the home instruction should be a replication of a technique that has been successfully used with the student at school.

Home instructional programs should include the following four basic elements: (1) a formative plan that involves all participants; (2) a guidance and training procedure for parent tutors; (3) a recording procedure; and (4) a communication network.

The Formative Plan

The planning process for home instruction should involve the parent who is to give the instruction, the child, the classroom teacher, and the home consultant. All should clearly understand what is to be done, and all should agree that they are willing to support the program. Some consultants asked everyone to sign a contract agreeing to fulfill the part of the program for which they are responsible. Project 35 contains a good example of how such a contract was used for a home reading program.

Guidance and Training Procedure

Sufficient time should be spent in preparing and training the parent to give home instruction. Resource/consulting teachers who used cross-age tutor programs found that if they did not devote enough time to train tutors adequately, they spent extra time retraining once the program had been initiated. The same principle applies to preparing parents for home tutoring. The number of training sessions should be based on a concept of mastery. The consultant should always demonstrate first, and then have the parent try successive steps of the program. Sufficient training has occurred when the parent demonstrates mastery and 100 percent implementation of the task. Some consultants and parents prefer to train in simulation without the student; others prefer to train directly with the student. A recommended procedure is to have an initial session without the student where the instructional procedures can be discussed and the parent can ask questions. This should be followed by direct training sessions where the parent practices with the student while the consultant supervises. Projects 32, 33, 35, and 37 contain examples of how parents were trained to use precise instructional techniques before program implementation.

Training sessions should also be supplemented with guides for parents to follow. These guides should reiterate the precise steps involved in the instructional procedures. Projects 36 and 34 contain examples of how these training guides have been used for home programs.

Recording Procedures

The training sessions should include preparation for obtaining measures of student performance. Consultants have been successful in training parents to obtain fairly elaborate measures of academic performance, as illustrated in Projects 32 through 37. A good rule to follow is to ask parents to measure and record no more than the amount and type of measurement with which they feel comfortable. This should be determined during training, not prior to it, as parents may think that they can do less than they really can.

Classroom and special education teachers often react the same way when a training effort is initiated. It is not unusual for them to think that too much measurement will be difficult to manage. Precise training has been found to alter these initial attitudes. Teaching parents to measure and record instructional performance data is facilitated by the principle of extending existing programs from school to home, rather than initiating new ones. One important strength of this approach is that the student is already accustomed to the procedures. In some cases, the student may already be used to recording the data, which could facilitate the home practice.

Communication Network

As in home reinforcement programs, consultants must be especially attentive to establishing a sound and consistent communication network. To reiterate, the parent should know when and how the contact will be made prior to its initiation. A system should be developed that is efficient and easy to use. Some examples are telephoning at predetermined times, sending notes from home to school and vice versa, and school or home visits. Examples of how consultants have used these systems are illustrated in Projects 12, 16, 22, 24, 25, and 32 through 37.

HOME INSTRUCTION PROJECTS

The following projects are reports of how consultants established complementary home instructional programs. They vary across academic subject areas, procedures, and ages of students. The projects are divided into three subject areas: (1) reading; (2) spelling; and (3) mathematics. The ages of the students range from six to fifteen years.

HOME CONSULTATION AND READING INSTRUCTION

These home reading projects are all examples of how a precise instructional technology was transferred from school to home. A variety of reading materials was used including basal readers, a supplementary direct instruction program, and a supplementary high interest/low reading reading level series.

Project 32: Supplementary Home Reading Instruction

R/CT: Mary Pilosof

This R/CT saw S., a first grader, for direct instruction reading in the resource room. When instruction began in September, S. was placed at the beginning of the third preprimer in the Holt, Rinehart & Winston basal reading series. Placement criteria were 95 percent correct for word accuracy and 80 percent correct for comprehension. By March, S. was reading in the second reader of first grade (1^2). At this time the R/CT had a meeting with S.'s mother to report on his progress. S.'s mother was interested in working with her son at home. The R/CT decided to have her practice with S. on new vocabulary words and listen to S. read each story in his reader prior to reading it at school.

Procedures

The mother and the R/CT met a second time to practice an instructional procedure for vocabulary word drill. No special procedures were used for practice story reading. S.'s mother merely agreed to listen to him read. The guide shown in Exhibit 9–1 was given to the mother, and it reiterated the practice procedure.

Materials. S.'s mother was provided with the basal reader, and the R/CT agreed to send home the practice cards each Thursday. The cards were sent on Thursday to remind S.'s mother to return the previously used set and performance data on Friday. The practice cards sent each week represented the vocabulary words from three to four stories ahead of the story S. was currently working on in the resource room. This resulted in approximately 30 to 35 words per week. The R/CT also provided S.'s mother with a data sheet to use for recording correct and incorrect words.

Baseline Results. During the five instructional days prior to the home intervention, S. read two stories to the R/CT. For the first story, it took two days for him to meet criterion for both reading comprehension and

---

Exhibit 9–1 Guide for Practice Procedures

> *Step 1:* Present each card to S. to read.
> *Step 2:* Make two stacks of cards as he reads. Put correctly read words in one stack and incorrectly read words in the other.
> *Step 3:* Record on a data sheet the number of correct and incorrect words read each day.
> *Step 4:* Practice the incorrect words two more times.
>
> A word is counted as incorrect when:
> 1. S. says something else instead of the word printed on the card.
> 2. He omits "ed" or "s" sounds at the ends of words.
> 3. He does not call out the word within five seconds.
> 4. He tries to sound out the word.
>
> If any of these responses occur, say the correct word to S. and have him repeat it after you. Then put that card in the stack for incorrect words.

oral reading rate (CWPM). For the second story, it took two days to master rate, but comprehension had not been mastered by the third instructional day. (See Figure 9–2.) S. reread stories for a total of three times per week. The average for rate of first time readings was approximately 28 CWPM. The average for comprehension on first readings was 40 percent.

Home Program Results. After the home program was started, there was a significant improvement in both comprehension and rate. (See Figure 9–2.) There was a total of six story rereads over four instructional weeks, compared to three in one week during baseline. The average for first readings for reading comprehension was 86 percent correct, compared to 40 percent during baseline. For rate, it was 43 CWPM compared to a baseline average rate of 28 CWPM.

Figure 9–2 Improved Oral Reading Comprehension and Rate as a Result of Home Practice on Vocabulary Words

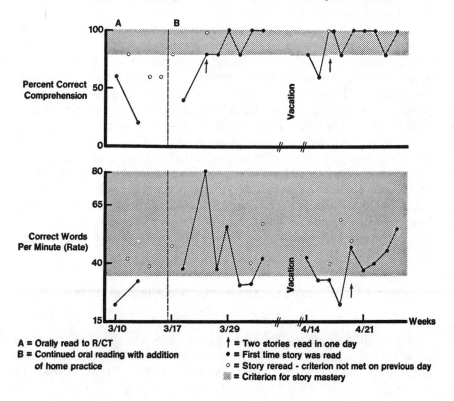

A = Orally read to R/CT
B = Continued oral reading with addition
    of home practice

† = Two stories read in one day
● = First time story was read
○ = Story reread - criterion not met on previous day
▓ = Criterion for story mastery

Discussion

This student's rate of passing stories in a basal reader was influenced positively by a home reading program. Likewise, his speed of reading and accuracy of comprehension improved considerably. The home intervention program was relatively simple, involving vocabulary word practice and noncontingent oral reading.

The home program was data-based as well. The mother kept a record of her child's accuracy in reading vocabulary words. In addition, every two weeks the R/CT shared S.'s school performance data with his mother. This no doubt served as reinforcement to both S. and his mother. The R/CT took responsibility for providing guides for instruction, data sheets, and for sending instructional materials home every week. S.'s mother was responsible for returning completed data sheets to school and for giving home practice.

As well as demonstrating that parents can measure progress of their children, the teacher consultant also illustrated that home reinforcement programs can become an integral part of remedial programs used at school. She devised a measurement strategy that ensured that she could assess the effect of the home program.

As a final note, this consultant established a pattern of frequent contact with this student's mother to ensure good communication. First, she met with the parent to plan and then again to practice the instructional technique. Second, she contacted the mother on a weekly basis by sending materials and data back and forth between school and home. Frequent contact is essential to ensure that a home program is actually working. If a parent or child becomes discouraged because the program is not working or if they are not implementing the program, frequent home contact will give the consultant information so program alterations can be made.

Project 32 represented how a home reading program can be established for a young child, even though the strategies could certainly be used with older students. Projects 33 and 34 report how home instructional programs have been established for older children. Project 33 centers on improving reading progress of a fifth-grade student from a self-contained classroom for EMH students.

Project 33: Increasing Curricular Progress with Home Instruction

R/CT: Peggy Bullard

M. was a fifth-grade student from an EMH class who attended a resource room for group instruction with three other students. All members of the group were older students who were poor readers. The R/CT was the instructor and was using a direct instruction reading program, *Corrective Reading (Decoding A)* (Englemann, Becker, Hanner, & Johnson, 1980), for the curriculum. Each lesson included a decoding lesson at the blackboard, practice reading isolated words, and an oral story reading with comprehension questions.

Baseline

When M. missed a group lesson because of school absence, he was encouraged to come back to the resource room sometime during the next afternoon he was back at school to read the story independently. He could not read the story orally with the teacher because of lack of R/CT time. Because of his class schedule, he was never able to read the missed lesson before it was time for the group to read a new lesson. As a result, he received no feedback, and the story was always read out of sequence. This situation lasted for five instructional weeks.

Results. During these five weeks, M. was absent four times and completed 13 of the 17 stories that the group read (76 percent completion).

Intervention

The R/CT met with M.'s mother and explained the baseline conditions. The R/CT and mother agreed that the mother could listen to M. read stories aloud at home. This was done each time M. was absent from school and missed the group lesson. Missed lessons were sent home with M., accompanied by a note reminding his mother of what to do. On three occasions, M.'s mother came to school to pick up the work. M. was to read the entire story once and then reread a 100-word sample from the story. The 100-word passages were marked in advance by the R/CT. M.'s mother recorded the number of errors made in the 100-word sample on the top of each lesson sheet, along with a list of error words. This was returned to school the following day.

Results. During six instructional weeks, M. was absent five times, but by reviewing those five lessons with his mother he completed all 22 stories that the group read. The average word accuracy for home reading was 98 percent correct, compared to 98.6 percent correct for school readings.

Discussion

Home consultation ensured that an older student completed all reading lessons in spite of school absences. Involving a parent in solving a common problem like school absences was a simple solution to a problem that could have been complex.

The R/CT reported that a major reason for the success of this project was the good relationship the EMH classroom teacher had established with M.'s mother. The degree of success of any home project depends on such good rapport between parents and teachers. The positive relationship probably had an effect on the student as well. He always promptly returned the lessons to school and verbally reported on the number of errors he had made. Teacher consultants must be especially sensitive to the possibility that teacher/parent relations can have an effect on student motivation and behavior.

Project 34: Increasing the Amount of Time a Student Spent Reading

R/CT: Chris Bedford

Project 34 is another example of how reading practice can occur at home. The R/CT was interested in increasing the time this student spent reading and structuring a supportive triad consisting of the student's classroom teacher, his mother, and the teacher consultant.

R. was a sixth-grade student who was repeating sixth grade and had been transferred to the R/CT's school because of parental request. He attended an LD resource room for reading and math instruction. At the time of this project, he was reading in the fourth-grade reader of the Laidlaw reading series. R.'s parents were pleased with his reading progress in the resource room and had been encouraging R. to read at home. In the semester prior to this project, the R/CT had provided the parents with a strategy for correcting R.'s reading errors. The home consultation project was initiated because the R/CT was concerned that R. was reading materials that were too difficult for him. She feared that he would become discouraged if the gap between difficulty levels of school and home materials was too wide.

Before implementing the program, approval was obtained from R.'s teacher. The R/CT wrote a note to the teacher and asked her to sign it to indicate approval. (See Figure 9–3.) The original parent contact was made via telephone, so a follow-up note was sent to the parent reconfirming the following instructional plan. (See Figure 9–4.)

The Instructional Plan

R. chose a book from a high interest/low vocabulary, paperback series, graded 3.5 to 4.5. Five daily assignments, each consisting of 5 to 7 pages, were listed on an index card. A column was included by each assignment for the number of errors made in the 100-word sample for that assignment. Two copies of the book were sent home with R., one for him to read and

Figure 9–3 Note Written by an R/CT to a Classroom Teacher to Share Plans for a Home Instructional Program

---

February 16, 19___

Mrs._____,

I feel that since R.'s parents are so concerned about his reading and are working with him at home, it would be good to offer some guidance for reading at home. I was thinking of having him select books from a graded interest series (PAL Paperbacks) ensuring that he practice with materials written at the grade level he is reading. I would, however, be very open to any suggestions that you might have (i.e, library books or a series you might have).

What this would involve would be for R. to read aloud three to five pages to his parents every night. His parents would count the number of mistakes he makes in a 100-word marked page. They would record the errors as a tally. R would then bring this information to me at the end of each week. I will chart the information.

I would like to begin this program next week. If you have any suggestions or questions, I'd be most appreciative. Thanks so much for your help.

Chris Bedford

---

a copy for his parents. The parent copy was marked near the end of the selection specifying a 100-word passage with an arrow at the beginning, and a /100 at the end of the 100 words. The procedure included the following steps:

- *Step 1.* R. orally read the assigned pages to his parents.
- *Step 2.* R.'s parents followed along in their copy of the book.
- *Step 3.* If R. made an error, but not within the 100-word passage, his parents corrected him using the error correction procedure illustrated in Figure 7–2.
- *Step 4.* When R. reached the 100-word passage marked in his parents' book, they recorded the number of errors R. made on the assignment card.
- *Step 5.* When the fifth assignment was completed, R. brought the assignment card to the R/CT, who charted the data.
- *Step 6.* If R. did not meet the word accuracy criterion of no more than six errors, he reread the story on subsequent days until criterion was reached.

Results. For the first three weeks of this program, R. met criterion on all occasions. His word accuracy scores ranged from 94 percent to 99 percent, which was consistent with his performance at school. R. always brought the completed assignment card back to school each week.

Figure 9–4 Sample Letter Written to a Student's Parents to Reiterate a Home Instructional Program That Was Agreed Upon by His Parents and the Resource/Consultant

---

Letter to Parents

February 20, 19___

Dear Mr. and Mrs._____,

I was glad that we had the chance to talk yesterday concerning R.'s progress. I feel that structured home reading will really be a benefit, and I'm glad you agree.

As we discussed, R. will use one copy of the book, and you will use another. Your copy is marked with an → at the beginning of the 100-word passage and with /100 where the passage ends. There is a marked time sample like this for every section in the book.

R. is to be corrected for reading errors before and after this 100-word passage. He is not to be corrected when reading the 100 words. During this time, you will count the number of errors he makes. Please use the error correction procedure I sent you last semester. If R. corrects himself within five seconds, a word is counted as correct. Things that are counted as wrong include:

1) calling out the wrong word (i.e., *bat* for *bath*)
2) skipping a word or line
3) losing the place (If this happens, show him the place.)
4) leaving off or putting on endings to words (i.e., *call* for *called*)

On the assignment card is a place to record pages read and errors. Either write the number of errors or record tally marks for errors in the space provided for errors.

Example:	*Pages*	*Errors*
	pg. 3–5	5

Please have R. bring the card to me each Monday. I will record his scores for the week.

If you have any questions or problems, please feel free to call me at 217-4963. Thank you so much for your help.

Sincerely,

Ms. Bedford
Resource/Consulting Teacher

P.S. If R. makes more than six errors, have him read the same story the next day.

Discussion

The home reading program was successful because R. demonstrated that the reading progress he had made at school could be generalized to a home reading session with his parents. Again, the R/CT attributed the success of this program to the parents' cooperative attitude and their willingness to provide the program as structured by the consulting teacher.

This consultant made certain that the plans for the home program met with the approval of the classroom teacher. She also made certain that what was agreed upon with one parent over the telephone was confirmed with both parents by sending a letter home reiterating the contents of the home program. The consultant also took responsibility for ensuring that the reading level of materials was suitable for this student. She provided instructions, materials, and assignment cards.

Even though the consultant asked the parents to collect performance data, she took the ultimate responsibility of charting the data. This strategy served several purposes. It ensured that the data were collected, because it had to be returned to school; if it were not collected, the consultant would know within the week. It gave the student the responsibility of bringing the data back to school. Finally, it served as a means of communicating a strong interest in the student's home progress.

Teaching others to collect student performance data is not always easy. Some people may fail to recognize the importance of obtaining continuous feedback on student performance. Others may simply find that the measurement procedures are too difficult to implement. This consultant carefully selected one reading behavior—oral reading accuracy—for these parents to measure. At school, this student's progress was monitored by measuring several daily behaviors including word accuracy, oral and written comprehension, speed of reading, and number of stories completed over time. Yet the consultant chose one of these behaviors for home measurement that would occur naturally when children read with their parents: the child makes an accuracy error and the parent corrects the error. Data-based instruction can occur in environments other than resource rooms, but, as illustrated, consultants must be careful to structure situations that can be monitored by others.

Project 35: Home Instruction for a High School Student

R/CT: Charlie Davis

Project 35 is also a home instructional program for reading, but in this case, the student involved was a 15-year-old high school student. The reader should note the similarities between this project and the previous projects for younger students.

This home project was initiated when A., a 15-year-old male in tenth grade, expressed interest in doing readings at home for extra credit. This student suggested that his mother could serve as a reading tutor. The R/CT phoned A.'s mother to discuss the possibility of organizing a home reading program for A. The R/CT suggested that all parties sign a contract stating the conditions of the home study program and that A. assume all managerial responsibilities. A.'s mother agreed but stipulated that the following must occur: (1) A. must be responsible for arranging all tutoring sessions; and (2) the project contract must include an option to terminate tutoring if A.'s mother had to assume managerial duties (that is, nagging A. to do his reading).

Tutor Training

A.'s mother came to school to receive initial training for being a reading tutor for direct, data-based instruction in the Harcourt Brace, Bookmark reading series. During the first part of the meeting, the contents of a program contract were discussed, and a first draft was written. The second half of the meeting was used to present an overview of direct instruction techniques for reading. A.'s school progress charts were used as a model for instruction.

On the following day, a second training session was held at school. The formal contract was signed by the student, the parent, and the consultant. (See Figure 9–5.) A.'s mother practiced using direct instruction reading techniques, while A. read to the R/CT and his mother. (A discussion of this model of instruction can be found in Chapter 7.) Both the R/CT and A.'s mother recorded performance data for speed and accuracy. A. wrote the answers to ten comprehension questions from one story read earlier to the R/CT. The responses were independently scored by A.'s mother and the R/CT.

Reliability. During the practice session in which A. read two oral, timed samples, there was 100 percent agreement in scoring between teacher and mother for word accuracy and CWPM. They also agreed on the scoring of the comprehension questions.

Home Instruction

Home instruction began the following week. A. orally read stories to his mother and answered written comprehension questions. His mother measured A.'s performance on accuracy and rate with 100-word timed samples and scored responses for written comprehension. A. charted the information on a graph.

Results. Over a three-week period, A. and his mother had six practice sessions. The average score for accuracy was 97 percent correct (range: 96 to 98 percent). For rate, the average was 136 CWPM (range: 109 to 148.5). For written comprehension, responses were always 100 percent

Figure 9–5 Independent Reading Contract Used to Obtain
Commitment from the Student, Parent Tutor, and
Program Consultant to an Independent Reading
Program

Direct Instruction Reading Program
Urbana High School
Spring Semester

Independent Reading Contract

Date:

   I, _____, do hereby choose to begin an
independent reading program. In order to make sure that the program is
fair and successful for all people involved, I agree to the following
conditions and responsibilities.

_____ CONDITIONS _____

1. All reading that will be done for credit will be done with
   my independent tutor.

2. To get credit for the reading that I do, I will keep my
   charts up to date and will present them and written
   answers to all comprehension questions each week to my
   program consultant.

3. For the first _____ weeks of the program, I will read at
   least _____ segments of reading with my independent tutor.

4. After this _____ week period, I will increase my reading
   to at least _____ segments of reading per week with my
   independent tutor.

_____ RESPONSIBILITIES _____

1. I will set up all reading sessions with my independent tutor
   in advance. All sessions will be held at a time acceptable
   for both of us.

2. I will be present and prepared for all reading sessions. In
   the case that I must miss a reading session - for any reason -
   I will make arrangements with my independent tutor before the
   session to reschedule it when it is convenient for my independent tutor.

   Having read these conditions and responsibilities, I agree that
they are fair and that I will follow them as shown above. Failure to
follow these standards will be cause for ending the program.

(left margin, top to bottom) Initialed: (tutee) ,   (tutor)   (program consultant)

correct. This performance pattern was similar to how this student was reading at school.

Reliability. The R/CT visited the home on two occasions to view the reading sessions and to collect reliability information. The first time, there was a one-second discrepancy for rate and a slight difference in calculation for CWPM. The consultant and A. practiced on more timed reading samples until 100 percent agreement was reached. On the second home visit, agreement for oral reading rate was 100 percent. There was 100 percent agreement for scoring of accuracy and comprehension on both occasions.

Follow up. This project continued through the remaining two months of the school year. In total, A. completed 27 extra reading assignments by reading at home with his mother. His overall rate of improvement for the year was 2.85 months' gain per month of instruction.

Discussion

This R/CT responded to a student's request to accomplish more independent work by devising a home consultation program. He trained a parent to be a direct instruction reading teacher and made certain that the performance data she collected were accurate.

The home consultant also used a formal contract to specify clearly the conditions and requirements of the home program. The contract delineated the amount of credit to be given by the teacher for work completed and the managerial responsibilities that this student had to assume. (See Figure 9–5.)

The consultant trained the parent first without the student present and then with the student. This was a sound strategy because the first sessions allowed the parent to ask questions and discuss points without the student being present. The second sesson provided a "real situation" by having the student present.

This project was similar to the three previous projects (32, 33, and 34) because a complementary home program was used. The high school student exhibited the same basic behavior of reading aloud to parents. This project was slightly more complicated, because the parent presented the entire reading program package including measurement of word accuracy, speed, and written comprehension. Thus, the home program was identical to the school program for the student.

All four projects demonstrate how a teacher consultant can involve parents in a home reading program. In all of these projects, parents offered some form of instruction that complemented their child's school reading program. In all four cases, consultants taught and encouraged parents to use data-based, reading instruction.

HOME CONSULTATION AND SPELLING INSTRUCTION

A natural academic subject in which to encourage parents to offer home instruction is spelling. Many students study their weekly spelling lists at home, often with parental assistance. In fact, in some classrooms students are expected to study spelling words at home, and practice time during school hours is not offered. Also, many students who experience academic difficulties are poor spellers. All of these reasons point to the idea of implementing home instructional programs for spelling. Project 36 is an example of how a teacher consultant taught a parent to improve her son's poor spelling grades.

Project 36: From Failure to Excellence with a Precise Study Technique

R/CT: Janet Ellis

At the beginning of the school year, J. displayed severe problems with spelling. He was referred by his classroom teacher for resource instruction in spelling and reading.

Baseline

J. took weekly spelling tests on Friday of each week in his classroom. A new list was used each week.

Results. Baseline data were collected for three weeks. For the first week, J. spelled no words correctly on an 18-word spelling word list. For the second week, he spelled one word out of 18 words correctly. For the third week, he again spelled no words correctly on a third 18-word list.

Word Analysis and Rewrite

J. and the R/CT devised a "word analysis technique" for spelling. Each week the R/CT gave J. a trial test each Wednesday in the same way the classroom teacher gave the Friday final test. She pronounced each spelling word, used the word in a sentence, and then repeated the word. Then together the R/CT and J. analyzed and rewrote any misspelled words. The word analysis and rewrite procedures are delineated in Figure 9–6 in steps one through six. This condition lasted for nine instructional weeks.

Results. J. took final tests on six Fridays; no tests were given on the remaining three Fridays. He earned two grades of A+, two A's, one A–, and one B+. He correctly spelled from 85 percent to 100 percent of the words correctly on the final test. (See Figure 9–7.)

Figure 9–6 Sample Procedures for Testing, Analyzing, and Rewriting Spelling Words Used in Resource Instruction and Given to Student's Parent for Home Instruction

---

Procedure for Studying Spelling Words

On Wednesday night
   I. Give J. a spelling test. Pronounce each word, and use it in a sentence. Pronounce it again.
   II. Examine the completed test. If a word is spelled correctly, say, "You spelled ___ correctly. Good!" Then, go on to the next word.
   III. If a word is misspelled:
      1. Underline the parts of the word J. spelled correctly, complimenting him for the part he spelled right.
      2. Circle the parts of the word that are incorrect.
   IV. If he can, have him sound out his misspelled word. Say, "What did you spell?" His response—*dintance.* You say, "The word is *dentist.*"

REMIND J. TO TRY TO SOUND OUT THE WORD HE'S SPELLED WHEN HE'S TAKING THE TEST TO BE SURE IT'S THE SAME WORD THE TEACHER IS SAYING.

      3. Write the correct spelling next to his misspelled word, underlining small, embedded words. *Emphasize* small words within the spelling word or tell him other words he knows that will help him remember how to spell the word.
      4. Have J. write the word correctly next to your spelling of the word.
      5. Continue down the list following the above steps.
      6. When you finish, you can count up the number of words that J. spelled correctly and say, "Good! You spelled 11 out of 17 words correctly!"

On Thursday night
   Give J. the words again in test form. Briefly go over any errors, reminding J. of "clues" to remember the words AND to read what he has written when he finishes writing a word. Compliment J. for correctly spelled words and for any improvement.

On the Wednesday trial tests, he failed seven out of nine tests, but there was an impressive acceleration in the data trend indicating that J. steadily spelled more and more words correctly over time. (See Figure 9–7.) The percent of correctly spelled words on the test ranged from 0 to 60.

Home Practice

During the previous phase, the R/CT and J.'s mother had frequent telephone conversations to discuss J.'s impressive improvement in spelling. Since J. was doing well over an extended length of time, the R/CT decided to ask J.'s mother to help him practice the words at home, using the word analysis and rewrite technique. (See Figure 9–5.) On January 18, 1980, the R/CT sent a note to J.'s mother asking if she would cooperate.

Figure 9–7 Number of Words Spelled Correctly on Final and Trial Spelling Tests Illustrating the Effect of a Study Technique Used First in the Resource Room and Then at Home

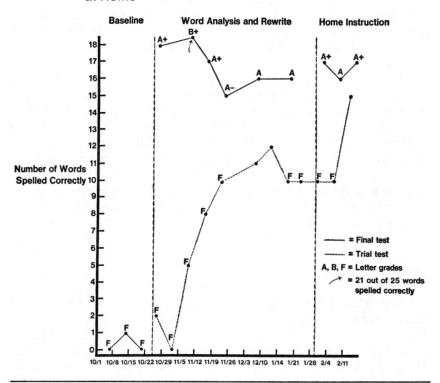

Five days later, J.'s mother came to school, and the R/CT demonstrated the word analysis technique. The mother practiced each step with J., using words from later spelling units while the R/CT observed. The R/CT gave her the contents of Figure 9–5 to use as a guide at home. All agreed that J. would bring the words that he and his mother practiced to school each Thursday morning. The R/CT agreed to send home notes or telephone to report on J.'s weekly progress. Home practice continued for three weeks, as depicted in Figure 9–6.

Results. J. earned two A+ grades and one A grade on final tests. On the trial tests, he spelled 56 percent of the words correctly on two tests (still failing grades) and 83 percent correctly on the third test.

Discussion

This R/CT significantly changed a student's consistent pattern of poor spelling to one of consistent excellence. She initially taught the student to use a word analysis technique to determine the kinds of spelling errors he was making and to correct misspelled words. When the student was performing well over a long period of time by using the technique, the consultant transferred the occurrence of the study sessions from a school to a home setting. The transfer to home instruction led to two important results: (1) R/CT instructional time previously used for practice of spelling words with the student was now available for classroom consultation or direct instruction in another subject; and (2) the parent was given a proven technique to use in assisting her child with study of spelling words. The parent had always helped the student study spelling words at home, but, according to the parent, the student had always failed spelling anyway.

To facilitate communication and ensure that the home practice occurred, this consultant kept a frequent record of home contacts prior to implementation of the home project. She also made certain that the parent understood how to use the instructional technique by demonstrating, having the parent practice, and providing a guidesheet for referral to the steps involved in the technique. Once the program had begun, the consultant ensured that home instruction was occurring on Wednesday night by collecting the student's home spelling test on Thursday morning.

Some extraneous information about this project makes the results even more striking. This mother had four boys and did not have a lot of extra time for home instruction. It was essential to use a technique that did not require an inordinate amount of home instruction. Another factor was that the mother was a poor speller. She was initially concerned about identifying misspelled words in the home trial test. The consultant assured her that she could refer to the spelling lesson book, which was provided for home use, when correcting spelling errors. At the end of the project, this family moved from the community, but both mother and child stated that they wanted to continue to study weekly spelling words in this manner.

HOME CONSULTATION AND MATHEMATICS INSTRUCTION

Home instruction and practice for mathematics is another area that often fits naturally into what has already been initiated at school. Many students who have difficulty progressing at a normal rate through arithmetic curricula are weak in knowledge of math facts for either addition, subtraction, multiplication, or division. Some of these students may spend time at home trying to master basic math essentials and practicing with parents or siblings. Yet they continue to struggle through by counting on fingers or by responding in a sporadic pattern of sometimes correct, sometimes incorrect responses. Project 37 is an example of how a resource teacher, working as a home consultant, integrated home practice with resource instruction.

Project 37: Improving Speed of Saying Basic Facts with Home Instruction

R/CT: Mary Petry-Cooper

K. began receiving direct service in math in the resource room in March 1981, following a referral by his classroom teacher. Instruction was provided for mastery of basic multiplication and division facts, and for computational skills. K.'s mother was already helping him practice math flashcards at home, though they did not use a set procedure. The mother and the R/CT agreed that coordinating efforts at home and at school might help K. master math facts more quickly.

Home Instructional Program

K.'s mother and the R/CT met so the R/CT could explain and demonstrate the school program and so together they could decide on how to arrange a systematic home program. Fact practice at school consisted of a daily flashcard drill and a written timed test of the facts drilled. Three consecutive days of meeting mastery criteria were required before the student progressed to the next fact set. The procedure was continued through all 12 fact sets. K.'s mother agreed to practice flashcards and administer a written timed test at home each night, using the same facts and procedures that were used at school. The R/CT agreed to send home all necessary materials on a daily basis (flashcards and test blanks), monitor K.'s progress, and initiate communication with the mother and the classroom teacher to coordinate the home/school program. The student was asked to take the materials home each day, work with his mother or father for 10 to 15 minutes each night, and return the fact test to school the following day. On a few occasions when the student forgot to take the tests home, he and his mother still practiced the flashcards. He would then usually take two written tests at different times the following evening.

Results. Before initiating the home program, K. had worked on mastery of the first set of facts for 12 school days. Though he quickly met accuracy criterion (96 to 100 percent after the first day of instruction), consistently increasing his rate was a slower process (criterion was 20 correct facts per minute). K. met both criteria on the seventh day of instruction, but his rate then dropped for two days. He then again met criteria for two days, but fell slightly below on the third day. The R/CT considered lowering the rate criterion at this point, but instead obtained agreement with the mother to initiate the home program.

After implementing the home practice sessions, K. mastered the first fact set within five days. Both accuracy and rate criteria were met for mastery. The second set was mastered in five days and the third set within six days.

Discussion

The rate at which K. mastered facts doubled as a result of the home practice. What previously took 12 days to master was accomplished in five to six days after home practice. This program emphasizes the importance of coordinating efforts at home and school to provide the greatest benefits for the student. In this case, the parent was anxious to help her son at home, and had, in fact, been trying to do so already. She was willing to work with the R/CT and her son, and she did so consistently. Consequently, her son was able to progress at school at a much faster pace.

In examining the progress data for this student prior to home instruction, it was noted that he mastered the criteria by the end of the first week of instruction. However, since he was required to meet criteria for three consecutive days, daily testing continued to the following Monday. When presented with the same test that was mastered on Friday, the student did not pass. Daily drill was needed to maintain his skill level. Fortunately, his mother was willing and consistent in providing this needed daily practice. Because of K.'s need for daily practice, the R/CT and mother planned to continue a similar program for K. during the summer vacation.

This teacher consultant was successful in initiating a systematic, data-based home instruction program. The charted data were not only of obvious use to the consultant for program evaluation, but they proved to be a source of motivation for the student. He watched his progress chart closely and was enthused over the progress he was making.

These six home instruction projects have been reported to illustrate that teacher consultants can establish home instruction that complements school instruction. The subject areas for which this instruction was provided were reading, spelling, and mathematics. Of course, home programs can be used for many other subject areas as well. This may be a most useful programming strategy for students whose academic gains show decline over long periods of vacation from school.

SUMMARY

This chapter describes the job role of a teacher consultant who also works as a consultant to parents. This role includes actively involving parents in educational programming and giving them frequent and systematic feedback on their children's progress. The role can be expanded to include establishing home programs to manage children's behavior at home and school, and to train parents to offer complementary home instruction.

COMMUNICATION EXCHANGE

A useful source for developing improved communication with parents can be found in Kroth (1975). Kroth (1975) presented a listening paradigm that included four types of listeners: (1) passive listeners; (2) active listeners; (3) passive nonlisteners; and (4) active nonlisteners (pp. 28–35). A *passive listener* listens attentively, exhibits nonverbal signs of acceptance, makes parents feel comfortable about talking, and allows parents to do most of the talking. An *active listener* offers an attentive, nonverbal listening posture (frequent eye contact and leaning forward), and reflects back on what parents have said. The active listener is neither judgmental nor offers solutions to problems. Instead, focus is placed on helping parents clarify problems. The *passive nonlistener* seems to hear what the parent is saying, but gives no verbal or nonverbal cues to reassure that attention has been given to the speaker's message. The *active nonlistener* talks rather than listens. While the parent is talking, active nonlisteners are thinking about what they will say next.

Kroth pointed out that no person falls exclusively into one of these four categories, but instead moves from category to category depending on the situation. He encouraged teachers to analyze their own listening behavior to determine what kind of listener they are in parent conferences and what kind of listener they would like to be.

Chapter 10

Extending Consultation: Sharing Skills with Others

An essential element of the role of a teacher consultant is sharing ideas and skills with others. Much of the sharing process occurs during the actual consultation, where skills are shared primarily on an informal basis. Such sharing can also occur in a more planned and systematic fashion through formal training of others.

Teacher consultants who offer inservice training to other teachers provide two important services. First, they share their skills with other teachers, who can then implement alternative techniques for management and instruction in their classrooms. Second, they can have an impact on the number of problem students who are referred for special services. As classroom teachers gain expertise in managing and teaching special learners, they may be more likely to accommodate an increased number of these students in regular classroom learning situations.

RESEARCH IMPLICATIONS FOR INSERVICE PROGRAMS

Adult education literature has pointed out that the rate at which professional competence for teachers reaches obsolescence has become increasingly shorter. In 1940, a span of 12 years was expected to occur before new information for teachers became obsolete. By 1980, it was projected that this span would be reduced to a mere five years (Tunick & Holcomb, 1980). These authors emphasize that there is an imperative need for short-term inservice training.

Educational technology has boomed in the last several decades, as has the development of more precise teaching technologies. The impact that this has had on special education is impressive. Over the past 20 years, special educators have begun to experiment with precise, systematic methods of instruction that have produced substantial behavioral and academic achievements for handicapped students. These changes in student behavior have stimulated special educators to teach these children in less restrictive environments. For many students with mild academic and social behavior problems, the regular classroom is the least restrictive environment. These changes have created a need for special education teacher consultants to provide regular classroom teachers with inservice programs that provide information about and help develop expertise in using advanced technologies for management and instruction of exceptional learners.

There is also substantial support for using teachers to instruct other teachers in the inservice education literature. In a summarization of literature reviews on inservice education, Cruickshank, Lorish, and Thompson (1979) observed four major trends developing in inservice education. One was a movement from narrow control of inservice programming by school administrators and/or university professors to collaborative governance, which includes heavy teacher participation. This implies that teachers ought to be heavily involved in selection and presentation of inservice programs. The role of a teacher consultant providing inservice training fits well within this trend.

Cruickshank et al. (1979) emphasized that nearly all of the inservice literature reviews that they examined failed to consider the presence or absence of scientific support when summarizing results and implications. They cited one literature review (Nicholson, Joyce, Parker, & Waterman, 1976) that closely considered scientific evidence as a prerequisite for drawing any conclusions about what constitutes effective inservice programming. Nicholson et al. (1976) reviewed 2,000 books, periodicals, and unpublished papers produced between 1957 and 1976. The criteria for inclusion in this study were that the reports be from any college or school-based program for improving professional competencies of employed teachers and that they have experimental or at least quasi-experimental designs. Cruickshank et al. (1979) pointed out that these conclusions must be taken as possible indicators or reasonable hunches, rather than as absolute scientific evidence, because of several limitations. The shortcomings were that subgroups and sample sizes used for comparison were of disproportionate sizes; the quality of experimental designs across studies was disproportionate; and distinctive regional differences were not considered.

The conclusions from the Nicholson et al. (1976) review were the following:

- School-based and college-based inservice programs were equally successful in improving teachers' knowledge, but school-based programs were slightly more successful in improving teaching skills.

- Teacher attitudes were improved more often in school-based than in college-based programs.
- Minicourses emphasizing the development and application of teaching skills had a high rate of success in both college and school settings.
- No medium of instruction, for example, lecture/discussion, reading materials, and observation systems, was clearly superior to others. However, the following specific objectives were successfully taught by the following methods: classroom management skills by using video- and audiotapes or classroom verbal behavior by using an observation system.
- School-based programs in which teachers participated as helpers and planners of inservice activities tended to be successful more frequently than programs planned and conducted without teachers' assistance. When personnel other than teachers planned and conducted school-based inservice programs, school administrators' programs were successful more frequently than those planned and conducted by college or other outside agents.
- All programs in which teachers engaged in self-instruction by using prepared materials, objectives, and planned guidance were successful.
- Programs with conceptual or information objectives were successful frequently in meeting those objectives, while programs with teaching skill objectives were successful less frequently. Programs with affective objectives were successful least frequently.
- Programs that attempted to change teacher behavior only were successful more frequently than programs that attempted to change teacher behavior and, consequently, pupil behavior.
- Inservice programs that had different or individualized training experiences for different teachers were successful more frequently than programs that had common activities for all subjects.
- Inservice programs that required the teachers to construct and generate ideas, materials, and behaviors were successful more frequently than programs in which teachers accepted ideas and behaviors from the instructional agent.
- Programs that emphasized demonstration, supervised trials, and feedback were successful more frequently than programs in which teachers were expected to make unsupervised applications at some future time.
- Programs in which teachers shared ideas and provided material assistance to each other were successful more frequently than programs in which teachers did not.

- Teachers were more likely to benefit from inservice programs that were part of a long-term, systematic staff development plan than they were from "single-shot," short-term programs.
- Teachers were more likely to benefit from programs in which they chose their own goals and activities than from programs in which goals and activities were preplanned.
- Teacher self-initiated and self-directed activities were seldom used in inservice education programs; however, when used, they were successful in accomplishing objectives.

Although these conclusions must be taken as general indicators, some of them are supported by evidence gathered by others (Berman & McLaughlin, 1978; Hutson, 1979; Lawrence, 1974; Mazzarella, 1980; McLaughlin & Marsh, 1978). Berman and McLaughlin (1978) surveyed 852 administrators and 689 teachers, followed by a second survey of 100 of the original projects two years later. Their conclusions were the following:

- Specific, concrete training that provides hands-on experience is useful.
- Using local resource personnel was superior to having outside consultants.
- One-time sessions prior to expected implementation were not useful.
- Direct participation was helpful, including direct observation of exemplary projects.

Teacher participation and support were also found to be important by others (Lawrence, 1974; McLaughlin & Marsh, 1978). As far as the source of consultation was concerned, two other sources, in addition to Berman and McLaughlin (1978), favored expert consultation coming from within the system (Lawrence, 1974; Mazzarella, 1980).

In contrast to the importance of seeking resources from within the system are the findings of Joyce, McNair, Diaz, and McKibbin (1976). They interviewed 1,016 teachers, administrators, and college faculty members, and found that only 2 percent favored using local education agency personnel as resources for inservice programs. Fifteen percent chose consultants, and 20 percent chose college faculty as the best sources for inservice training. In other words, these findings indicate that, even though several investigations and literature reviews support the importance of using local resources, school personnel may not select this as the best choice for seeking experts. A contrastive observation implies that even though teacher consultants may be fairly confident that offering inservice to other teachers is a well-supported approach, their colleagues may not view it as favorable. Therefore, teacher consultants must do a good job of selling a teacher-based inservice model. Having a supportive staff (McLaughlin & Marsh, 1978), offering training in the school itself (Mazarella, 1980), and meeting regularly (McLaughlin & Marsh, 1978) may prove useful to consultants who are advocates of teacher-produced inservice programs. Teacher consultants can offer teachers a menu of topics which could be offered through inservice programs in an attempt to gain staff support. They can encourage other teachers to participate in inservice programming and presentation. They can assist teachers in planning a comprehensive series that extends over time and meets regularly. Especially important, they can make certain that the training is concrete and encourages direct teacher participation and observation. As teachers become more actively involved in inservice education, their attitude may begin to contrast the dismal findings of Joyce et al. (1976).

FRAMEWORK FOR CONDUCTING INSERVICE PROGRAMS

Teacher consultants who plan to offer inservice programs for their colleagues may find some general guides developed within the University of Illinois Resource/Consulting Teacher Program useful. Within this program, a general model for presenting inservice training to classroom teachers is followed. The general components of the model include the following:

- gaining administrative support
- selecting topics
- surveying teacher needs
- designing a workshop outline
- eliciting preliminary feedback
- conducting the workshop
- obtaining evaluative feedback

The following is a discussion of how to utilize each of these components to produce an inservice program.

Gaining Administrative Support

As with any innovative change in educational policy, the key to successful implementation is having enthusiastic administrative support. This is especially important for inservice teacher education programs. As trends indicate, successful inservice education is more likely to occur when teachers and administrators cooperatively plan and select educational programs. School systems that actively support teacher consultation models are more likely to support using teacher consultants to prepare other teachers to work with mainstreamed, handicapped students.

In Vermont, the degree to which the teacher consultant model has been supported by local education agencies is ideal. The Division of Special Educational and Pupil Personnel Services of the Vermont State Department of Education has worked cooperatively with the University of Vermont Consulting Teacher Program to develop a consulting teacher approach to special education (McKenzie et al., 1970). Specific examples of state support include the following: (a) providing 75 percent of the consulting teachers' and accompanying aides' salaries; (b) discouraging use of special classes for moderately handicapped in school districts where consulting services are available; and (c) approving workshops conducted by teacher consultants for recertification credit (Christie et al., 1972).

In some other states, support of consulting teacher programs has been established more often within local education agencies, rather than throughout an entire state. In some of these school districts that employ the teacher consultant model, providing inservice education is a defined subcomponent of the role of a consulting teacher. In some other school districts, provision of inservice education occurs more gradually as teacher consultants begin to define their job roles based on needs of their consultees.

As the mainstreaming movement has developed and increasing numbers of school districts are educating handicapped students in regular classes, these districts are identifying a need to educate classroom teachers about handicapped and problematic students. Administrative leaders in local education agencies must be made aware of the many advantages that can be gleaned through a special education program that employs consulting teachers. Information should be disseminated to these individuals reporting on teacher consultant and inservice education programs.

Teacher consultants and resource teachers should begin to examine their own job roles. Such an examination should include determining whether effectiveness would be more widespread if groups of classroom teachers were prepared to instruct and manage problems students, rather than always consulting with individual classroom teachers or tutoring individual students. If the response to this examination is in favor of group training, then these teachers must share their ideas with school administrators. Forming collective groups of teachers who are interested in providing inservice programming is one way to begin to gain support. Once a coalition of interested teachers is formed, then spokespersons could be selected to meet with building and district administrators. The spokespersons can indicate that several others are also interested in working together to provide teacher inservice education. Gaining administrative support is more likely when teachers define their plans positively and actively seek administrative input, rather than when reactive and defensive plans are used.

If teachers decide to develop inservice programs at the building level, then two essential guides should be followed. First, from the beginning stages of development, teachers should encourage and seek assistance and support from building administrators. Second, once a coalition is formed with the building administrator, the notion of forming inservice programs should be shared with all building teachers. There may be other teachers who are interested in working on this type of cooperative project and who may have skills or information that they would like to share through this same format.

Finally, gaining administrative support should include requesting that educational credit be given to participating teachers. Given the rapid rate at which information for teachers becomes obsolete, formal recognition and reinforcement for teacher willingness to learn new skills must be considered and advocated.

Selecting Topics

Topics for inservice should be extensive. They should probably also include areas for which classroom teacher expertise could be shared with other teachers and support personnel, as well as the reverse.

In the Vermont consulting teacher program (Christie et al., 1972), consulting teachers provide the following three levels of training for classroom teachers: (1) consulting with classroom teachers; (2) offering training workshops; and (3) teaching formal courses with university credit available. In the workshops, teachers are introduced to readings on applied behavior analysis, given a rationale for teacher consultant models; and required to individualize a program for at least one student with verification of results using return to baseline or multiple baseline designs (Hersen & Barlow, 1976). The formal courses include two on analysis of behavior and individualized instruction and two on writing terminal objectives, determining enabling objectives, and general instructional procedures for use with entire classes.

A teacher consultant who uses data-based curricular instruction and principles of applied behavior analysis can consider a large number of choices for inservice topics. The following is a categorization of several types of topics that R/CTs from the University of Illinois have used for inservice education programs:

- the role of a teacher consultant
- referring students for special service
- assessing student performance in the reading, math, spelling, and content area curricula
- assessing student performance with criterion reference tests
- assessing student performance in unestablished curricular areas, such as handwriting, written language, oral language, dictionary skills, and study skills
- devising instructional strategies for improving student performance in the reading, math, spelling, and content area curricula
- devising instructional strategies for improving student performance in unestablished curricular areas, such as handwriting, written language, oral language, dictionary skills, and study skills
- writing IEPs
- involving classroom teachers in the IEP process
- involving parents in the IEP process
- applying principles of data-based instruction
- measuring pupil performance directly and daily
- recording and reporting pupil progress
- using charts and graphs
- using data to make decisions
- establishing and monitoring a tutor program
- reporting pupil progress to parents
- using the basics of applied behavior analyses
- establishing classroom rules
- managing disruptive student behavior
- using home reinforcement programs
- establishing home instructional programs

This listing is certainly not exhaustive; it should serve as a stimulus for teacher consultants to consider more precise and varied topics. Also, each listed topic is a general topic area. Consultants will find that as they become involved with inservice they will generate several sub-areas within these general ones.

Surveying Teacher Needs

Once several topics have been identified, a needs survey of the potential workshop participants should be conducted. Potential participants should be asked to select a spokesperson to assist the consultant in determining a tentative list of needs. The topics can be listed in a memo asking participants to prioritize the listing. Figure 10–1 is an example of a needs survey that could be sent to classroom teachers. Previously the teachers were involved in establishing the inservice series. The memo was sent by the teacher consultant and the spokesperson selected by the teachers to represent their inservice needs. It includes both an attempt to identify teacher preferences and an option for adding new topics. Once the responses are obtained, the topical areas could be presented in the preferential order indicated by the majority of the respondents. A recommended practice would be to provide the respondents with the survey results so they will know that their requests have been taken into consideration.

Designing a Workshop Outline

A recommended step that follows topic selection is to design an outline of the proposed workshop or presentation. This outline should reflect a breakdown of the major points or areas to be covered. Approximate time lengths should be projected for each subtopic as well as for the entire workshop. Figure 10–2 is an example of an outline design for a behavior management workshop that was presented to elementary school personnel. The group included classroom teachers, special educators, school psychologists, and speech and language therapists. This particular outline also includes a listing of materials to be used and a reminder to participants of what they should bring to the workshop.

A design outline can be used not only to assist the consultant with organization, but also as a preliminary notice that is sent to participants. Providing participants with information content and projected time spans in advance will help assure participants that the workshop is well organized. It will also aid them in planning their own time schedules before the workshop. Finally, the outline should be given to participants to follow during the training session. Workshop participants agree that having an outline of the work session helps them know what to expect and what will be expected of them.

Eliciting Preliminary Feedback

To assist in generating teacher interest and commitment to the forthcoming workshop, an explanatory letter can be sent to participants before

Figure 10–1 Sample Needs Survey to Identify Participant Preference for Inservice Topics

TO: Building Teachers

FROM: The Inservice Chairperson and the Teacher Consultant

RE: Inservice Teacher Preparation Series

Thanks to support and cooperation from our faculty and administrators, we are now ready to begin our inservice teacher preparation series. The first segment of this series will focus on preparing to better accommodate students with learning or behavior problems in our classrooms.

The following is a list of topics that we could cover in the first segment. Please rate the list in terms of your own needs. You are welcome to add other suggestions.

Circle one number for each topic.

1 = top priority

2 = interested, but it can wait

3 = low priority

Topics

1)	Managing disruptive classroom behavior	1	2	3
2)	What to do with poor mathemeticans	1	2	3
3)	How to improve reading ability	1	2	3
4)	What to do with poor spellers	1	2	3
5)	Strategies for measuring pupil progress more frequently	1	2	3
6)	What should we do about IEP's?	1	2	3
7)	Working together to help parents of students who have problems	1	2	3
8)	Other: _____	1	2	3

Thank you for your assistance in this important matter.

Figure 10–2 Sample Outline for a Workshop on Behavior
Management

Estimated Time Length: Two hours*
  I. Examples of Behavior Management Projects in an Elementary School
     a) single subject project
     b) small group project
     c) large group project
     (30 minutes)
 II. Defining Observable and Measurable Behaviors
     a) examples provided by the facilitator
     b) group generated examples
     c) each participant completes a checklist of behaviors which are/are not observable
        and measurable
     (20 minutes)

10-Minute Break

5-Minute Question Period

III. Designing a Project
     The situations necessary to complete this project will be brought to the workshop
       by each classroom teacher.
     (40 minutes)
 IV. Group Discussion (20 minutes)
  V. Evaluation (5 minutes)
     Materials Needed
       To be provided:
         1. checklist of behaviors to be completed by the participants
         2. graph paper
       *To be brought to the workshop by each workshop participant:***
         1. a pencil and a pad of paper to be used to generate and describe ideas
         2. a. an example of an individual child who is exhibiting behavior problems in
               the classroom or school (or)
            b. an example of a group situation occurring any place in the school setting
               that is causing behavioral problems

*All time assignments are approximate and can be altered.
**Please bring actual examples of situations that are occurring in your classroom or
  school.

---

the workshop. The letter can be used to explain the general intent of the
workshop, as well as to obtain preliminary feedback on projected workshop content. It should be sent early enough to incorporate feedback
information within the workshop design. Figure 10–3 displays a letter that
was sent to participants before a training session on behavior management
was conducted. This letter accompanied the projected workshop outline
(Figure 10–2).

Figure 10–3 Sample Explanatory Letter Used to Inform Workshop Participants of a Forthcoming Training Session

Date

To Workshop Participants

The attached is a description of a sample workshop on behavior management. This workshop is designed to assist classroom teachers and all school personnel with child management problems. The length of the workshop is approximately two hours. This time frame can be manipulated in order to meet the needs of the workshop participants.

The content of the workshop is divided into two specific content areas. The first component is a time of information sharing. This area is indicated on the attached description by Roman numerals I and II. The second component is devoted to problem-solving activities. The workshop participants will design a behavior change project that they can use in their classrooms or within the school setting. This is indicated by Roman numeral III on the attached workshop description.

I hope this workshop can serve as a tool to assist you in further development of behavior management techniques. If you have suggestions for improvement or alternatives, please share this with me prior to the workshop.

(signed Teacher Consultant)

Attachment

Conducting the Workshop

There are many effective styles to use when presenting information to a group. The following list illustrates a number of techniques that may be useful when presenting:

Preliminary Pointers

- Provide sufficient time immediately preceding the workshop for making final arrangements and preparations.
- Select clothes to wear that help you feel confident and comfortable.
- Make arrangements for beverages and/or snacks.
- Arrange the seating so that it accommodates the size of the group. Avoid large group seating arrangements for a small number of participants.
- Select a seating arrangement that reflects the intent of the workshop. For instance, if group discussion and interaction are desired, seats could be arranged in a semicircle or circle position. If participants will be writing, choose tables where groups can be seated together.

School desks lined up in rows may not create a physical environment that speaks of teacher collaboration and cooperation.

- Prepare materials in advance, and make certain that they are collated in the correct order.
- Ask another person to distribute materials and/or manage technical arrangements, such as operating a film or slide projector, or turning on and off ceiling lights. If you have a participant that you fear will give negative reactions, ask that person to manage these tasks.
- Determine how you want materials distributed. Will they be given to participants as they arrive as a means of welcoming them, will they be distributed as topics are discussed, or will you use a combination plan?

Pointers for Use During the Session

- Ask participants to introduce themselves briefly by describing the type of work they do and stating why they are attending the workshop. Do not ask participants to stand unless the group is large.
- Introduce yourself by briefly describing the type of work you do. Teachers will probably be more interested in your experience than in your college degrees.
- Give a brief overview of what will be covered during the session.
- Explain the format that will be used for asking questions, for example, whether people should speak out, raise their hands, or wait until the end of the session or the end of each topic area, and so on.
- Form partnerships within the group so that each person has a teammate. For an odd-sized group, assign one group of three. Explain that these partnerships are to be used for asking questions and comparing perceptions. Ask the partnerships to check with one another during the break. This will encourage teacher collaboration and will help reduce the number of people who want to ask you questions during the break. You will need the break more than anyone else.
- Give participants an occasional break to stretch and obtain refreshments.
- Provide a few minutes after the break for any specific questions that were unresolved over the break.
- Select workshop content that you know well. You will feel more comfortable and will be more likely to talk about the topic rather than to deliver a formal speech.
- Use a brief outline to guide you through a workshop. Avoid reading your notes.

- Eliminate physical barriers between you and your audience. Move among the group as you are working, and sit with them at times.
- Match hand-out materials to overhead transparencies. In this way, the transparencies can become the vehicle to guide you through the workshop sequence. Also, the overhead projector display gives a referential point for you and the audience. The participants can read the details on their own hand-outs rather than strain their eyes by reading from the overhead projection screen.
- Use explanatory examples from your experiences and those of others. Indicate that the examples are real.
- Include examples of mistakes you have made and how you have or would remedy them.
- Generate solutions to problems presented by the participants.
- Encourage audience participation. Initially, ask people to respond whom you know will react favorably and positively. This could help set a positive tone for the group.
- Watch for nonverbal responses of participants. Frowns and quizzical looks may indicate that a participant has a question or is thinking about the issue. Ask the participant if there is a question. This technique will help you feel more comfortable, rather than worrying about what the frowning is about. It can also help send a message to your audience that says, "It's important to me that I communicate well with you."
- Maintain eye contact with groups. Look at all participants. If you have a negative participant, be careful not to pay extra attention to that participant by always looking or responding to this particular person. If you are feeling unsure or uncomfortable, look at a participant whom you view as being positive and enthusiastic.
- Provide a specific time for discussion at the end of the session. Remind participants that theoretical and discussion questions can be asked during this time.
- End the session at the indicated time.
- Be prepared to spend time with some participants after the session. You could indicate to the group that you would like to take a quick refresher break and then you will be available for after-session questions.

Obtaining Evaluative Feedback

Obtaining feedback information can be useful to you. Most important, this can reinforce you. It feels good to know when others think you have done a good job. Second, feedback information can help you refine your presentation format and your topic selections. The evaluation form should be designed to give you concrete and specific information that will be useful in the future. Evaluation forms should be brief and clearly written. They should contain more than one type of response. Figure 10–4 contains a sample of the evaluation form used for the behavior management workshop described earlier in this chapter. This particular example contains selective choice, rank-order, and open-ended questions.

Participants should be asked to fill in evaluation forms at the end of the session. Responses could be collected at the door as participants depart by the same person who distributed them. Some teacher consultants prefer to use a pre/post evaluation form. With this format, a measurement of participant knowledge can be taken at the beginning of the session and again at the session's end. All evaluative information can be used to encourage further administrative and building support for inservice education programs offered by teachers themselves.

Figure 10–4 Sample Evaluation Form Used to Elicit Feedback from Training Group Participants

Behavior Management Workshop

Evaluation:
1. The concepts I learned were:
   _____ a) new
   _____ b) exciting
   _____ c) a good review
   _____ d) boring
   _____ e) not applicable
2. Rate the workshop activities according to their value to you. (Ratings: *first, second,* and *third* most important)
   _____ examples of projects
   _____ defining and observing
   _____ designing a project
3. The most important concept I learned was:

4. The concept I am the foggiest on is:

5. The concept I am most skilled at is:

EXAMPLES OF TEACHER CONSULTANT WORKSHOPS

This section contains four examples of how teacher consultants have started with the basic framework for inservice and have then created training workshops for their colleagues. Project 38 is an example of a one-hour session on behavior management, which was presented to elementary classroom teachers. Project 39 was also presented to elementary classroom teachers and was designed to offer techniques for using data-based instruction in the regular classroom. Project 40 was an inservice project presented at a district conference. It demonstrated direct instruction techniques for teaching reading. The audience included special educators working in secondary schools. Project 41 is a demonstration of how a teacher consultant, employed as a supervisor for cross-categorical resource programs, developed a series of inservice training sessions.

Project 38: Classroom Behavior Management Workshop

R/CTs: Jill Cunningham and Anita Andrews

The workshop was offered to 27 teachers in an elementary school in a small town in a Midwest farming community. The workshop was held after school from 3:20 to 4:30 P.M. in the school cafeteria. A needs survey was sent to all teachers to determine the topic preferred by the majority of the teachers. This was followed by a letter, which was again sent to all teachers, announcing the selected topic and the time and place for the training session. Figure 10–5 contains both the needs survey and the follow-up letter. An announcement was then posted on the school bulletin boards to remind teachers of the training session.

Exhibit 10–1 is the design outline that was used for the workshop.

Upon arrival, teachers were given pencils and a basic outline of the workshop design. (See Figure 10–6.) This outline contained the major and minor subheadings, and space to jot down ideas and questions to be asked during the discussion section of the workshop. The consultants divided the outline so each covered specific sections. They were careful to provide concrete examples from their own experiences to illustrate each of the subtopics. Fresh fruit and lemonade were served during the workshop.

After the formal presentations, the audience was asked if they had any particular problems or successes they would like to share with the group. When little response was elicited, a paper listing behavioral situations that might (and do) occur in the classroom was passed out. The situations were used to stimulate discussions. The situations used were the following:

Figure 10–5 Sample Letter Sent to Survey Teacher Needs and Sample Follow-Up Letter Announcing Workshop Topic, Time, and Place

Dear Teachers:

I am going to be giving an inservice workshop in April and would like your feedback as to which topic I should speak on. Please check one of the possible topic items below. Suggestions of your own are more than welcome.

Possible topics:
____ Curriculum-based assessments in the regular classroom
____ Behavior management strategies
____ Direct instruction in reading
____ Training peer tutors
____ Strategies for teaching in the content areas
____ Other ideas:
Please return this to me or bring it to the resource room.

Thank you,

Jill Cunningham

Dear Teachers:

Thank you all for your response to my workshop questionnaire. From your responses, I have decided to conduct a workshop on Classroom Behavior Management. Anita Andrews, another resource/consulting teacher, will be doing the workshop with me. The workshop will be held on Thursday, April 23rd, from 3:20 to 4:30 pm in the cafeteria.

At this workshop we will be sharing some ideas on behavior management with you, but we will also provide time for group discussion of problems that concern you. We would also be interested in hearing about any successes you have had with controlling behavior problems.

We hope this workshop can serve as a tool to assist you in further development of behavior management techniques. If you have any suggestions for improvement or alternatives, please share these with me. Contact me in the resource room by Friday, April 10.

Sincerely,

Jill Cunningham

Exhibit 10–1 Classroom Behavior Management Workshop

I. Classroom environment—setting the occasion for good behavior
   A. Room arrangement
      1. Teacher's desk in relation to group tables
      2. Grouping of students' desks
   B. Lesson planning
      1. Overplanning
      2. Meaningful seatwork
      3. Students always knowing what to do next
   C. Rules
      1. State rules and consequences
      2. Consistency
      3. Repetition
      4. Make rules short and to the point
      5. Phrase rules positively
      6. Teacher models own rules
   D. Teacher circulates during seatwork time
II. Realizing that there are problem children . . .
   A. A few terms and starting places:
      1. Defining problem in observational terms
      2. Baseline
         a. purpose
         b. examples
      3. Observation techniques
         a. event recording
         b. permanent product
         c. partial time sampling
      4. Intervention
         a. examples
III. Management strategies
   A. Reinforcement
      1. Choosing the appropriate reinforcer
      2. Reinforcers
         a. praise
         b. ignore some behaviors
            1. teacher variance/different tolerance levels
         c. points, stars
         d. free time
         e. privileges
   B. Premack principle—"Grandma's Rule"
   C. Good behavior game
   D. Ways to decrease behavior
      1. Response cost
      2. Reinforcement of other behaviors—omission training
IV. Discussion and questions
   A. Teacher's own problems and successes
   B. R/CTs present own successful management projects
   C. Group problem solving of given situations
V. Evaluations

Figure 10–6 Sample Outline Given to Workshop Participants with Space Provided for Note Taking

Classroom Behavior Management Workshop

I. Classroom environment—setting the occasion for good behavior
   A. Room arrangement
   B. Lesson planning
   C. Rules
   D. Teacher circulates during seatwork time
II. Realizing that there are problem children . . .
   A. Defining problems in observational terms
   B. Baseline
   C. Observation techniques
   D. Intervention
III. Management strategies
   A. Reinforcement
      1. Premack principle
      2. Good behavior game
   B. Ways to decrease behavior
IV. Discussion and questions
V. Evaluation—Please complete evaluation form and return to Anita or Jill.

THANK YOU!

- In your class, you have found it necessary to have five different reading groups in order to meet the needs of your students. When you are in the reading group, the rest of the class tends to be out of their seats, talking loudly, and doing everything but their assigned tasks. You have tried establishing rules and making sure that they know what their assignment is, but this is to no avail. You decide you must do something, because the only work that is getting done is in the reading group. Design an intervention for the class during reading time (all morning).

- Jimmy is a new student in your class who seems to be having trouble adjusting. He especially has problems working independently at his desk while you are in reading group. Instead of working, he stares off into space or wanders around the room disturbing other students. What might you do to change Jimmy's behavior?

- Robert is a child in your class who is a source of continual problems. His main problem is talking out in class. Whenever there is a class discussion, Robert rarely raises his hand, but continually talks out, interrupting other students or you, with comments that are seldom relevant. What might you do to change Robert's behavior?

To aid teachers in thinking of new ways to manage student behavior, a paper with some suggestions for improving class management was also disseminated at this time. A reproduction of this paper is contained in Figure 10–7.

Evaluation forms were distributed at the end of the session. The evaluative questions are contained in Figure 10–8. All of the responses were positive. Some of the specific comments were the following:

- very well organized
- informal atmosphere—put people at ease
- easy to understand and hear
- brief, precise, clear
- entertaining
- complicated task presented in a simple manner
- materials are applicable to situation

Several teachers suggested topics for future workshops. The topics were reading comprehension, creative writing, acquisition of math facts, and ideas for languge arts. One teacher suggested that more group interaction would be desirable.

To improve group interaction for future sessions, the consultants planned to divide the audience into three groups and have each group take one of the behavioral situations that were provided. Each group would discuss the situation within the group and determine several solutions. After approximately ten minutes, the groups would reconvene and a spokesperson for each group would summarize the discussion. Although more audience participation would have been welcomed and was encouraged, the consultants did not feel that this hampered the overall effectiveness of the workshop. Most important, they were prepared for lack of group response by using classroom situations and listing behavior management strategies to encourage group discussion.

Project 39: Data-Based Instruction: Application in the Classroom

R/CTs: Marianne Abbey-Smith, Barb Bobek, and Marjorie Heintz

This inservice program was offered to 13 elementary classroom teachers. Again, it was a collaborative effort shared by three teacher consultants. It was presented during a midyear inservice conference for teachers in one school district.

The teacher consultants projected two goals for their workshop. The goals were for participants to leave with (1) an interest in obtaining class-

Figure 10–7 Sample List of Suggestions for Improving Classroom Management Used as a Reference during Group Problem Solving

1. Catch kids being good.
2. Use list of positive statements and actions as an aide in increasing teacher praise:

   Statements:
   —Good remembering.
   —I like the way you said that.
   —You're catching on now.
   —Good for you.
   —You are really getting smart.
   —You sure are a hard worker.
   —Great!
   —Super!
   —Fantastic!
   —That's better.
   —Keep working, you'll get it.

   Actions:
   —Touch children.
   —Tickle children.
   —Smile at children.
   —Tell children to "clap for themselves."
   —Suggest that they pat themselves on the back.
   —Shake someone's hand.
   —Give someone a spaghetti handshake.

3. Expect good behavior.
4. List classroom rules in positive terms.
5. Praise students for following rules.
6. Praise *after* a task has been completed, not in the middle of it.
7. Praise students for listening, for following directions, and completing tasks.
8. Break work down into short easy tasks.
9. Break teacher directions down into fewer steps that are easier to follow.
10. Reprimand in private.
11. Classroom seating—place difficult students close to you.
12. React to children's mistakes *and* to their correct responses.
13. Use classroom routines and praise students for adhering to them.
14. Give certificates of merit.
15. Good Newsletter.
16. Win reinforcers for whole class.
17. Praise model behavior.
18. Good Behavior Contest (game).
19. Have fun with children.
20. If the children have been grinding away at a task, or seem to be getting tired, Don't Give UP, just stop for a minute or two, and do something different.

    Suggestions:
    —Have children stand up, sit down, turn around, etc.
    —Tell children "wiggle your arms, touch your ear, touch your knees," etc.
    —Let the children talk for a couple of minutes, then get back on-task.
    —Have children close eyes for about 30 seconds.
    —Change your voice. Talk fast, slow, very softly, etc.
    —Let a child be teacher for a minute or two.
21. Daily report cards sent home to parents.

Figure 10–8 Sample Evaluation Form Used to Collect Feedback
from Workshop Participants

1. The workshop was:
   _____ excellent
   _____ a waste of time
   _____ a good learning experience
   _____ applicable to my situation
2. The presenters were:
   _____ well prepared
   _____ hard to follow
   _____ entertaining
   _____ confusing
3. What were things that were good about the workshop?

4. What were some things that should be changed?

5. I would like another workshop on . . .

---

room performance data and (2) a knowledge of how to collect data for at least one academic behavior. With these goals in mind, they presented information as simply as possible. They directed charting procedures toward activities that they knew teachers normally used, such as math facts tests, oral reading accuracy, and daily worksheets.

The design outline that they used is shown in Exhibit 10–2.

The participants were given a brief agenda outline, which included a listing of the first five major topics and the subtopics for the first three major areas. They were also provided with a packet that included the following:

- a procedure for taking an accuracy count for reading (See Figure 10–9.)
- a procedure for recording reading errors (See Appendix 7–A.)
- a sample multiband chart (See Figure 7–3.)
- a listing of reading and math behaviors to measure (See Figure 10-10.)
- a sample raw data sheet for recording reading performance data
- a sample raw data sheet for recording math performance data
- a list of references (See Figure 10–10.)
- an evaluation form (See Figure 10–11.)

The evaluation form is displayed in Figure 10–11, along with the response data from the 13 participants. As indicated, everyone found the session of

Exhibit 10–2 Workshop Design Outline

I. Rationale
  A. Characteristics of data-based instruction
    1. Observable behavior
    2. Direct, frequent measurements
    3. Progress charted
    4. Behavior measured before you try something
    5. Decisions based on data trends
    6. Teaching techniques systematically applied
    7. Continuous monitoring and evaluation
    8. Positive reinforcement
  B. Application to regular classroom
    1. Accountability
    2. Use with special children
    3. Data shows what is or is not effective
II. Reading: practical application
  A. Some examples of activities for which data can be taken
    1. Oral reading accuracy (percent correct)
    2. Sound blending
    3. Isolated words
    4. Comprehension (percent correct)
    5. Daily skill papers or workbook pages (percent correct, number of papers completed)
  B. Oral reading accuracy
    1. 100-word sample
    2. Definition of errors
    3. Calculating percent correct
  C. Demonstration of plotting data
    1. Explain and demonstrate raw data sheet
    2. Chart on multiband chart
  D. Application
    1. Practice filling in raw data sheet
    2. Practice charting on multiband chart
  E. Summary
III. Math: practical application
  A. Activities for which data can be taken
    1. Mastery of skills
    2. Basic fact mastery
    3. Timed fact tests
    4. Percent correct on worksheets
  B. Data-based instruction process
    1. Set level of mastery (criterion level)
    2. Assess (three days)
    3. Record data
      a. Raw data sheet
      b. Multiband chart
    4. Make data-based decision
    5. Chart more data
    6. Make another data-based decision

Exhibit 10–2 continued

```
      C. Other activities to chart
          1. Flash card drill
          2. Daily worksheets
      D. Summary
  IV. Summary
      A. Review rationale
      B. Practical use in classrooms
          1. Reading
          2. Math
          3. Spelling
          4. Behavior management
   V. Questions and answers
  VI. Evaluation
```

use, and no one gave a negative rating for any item. Participants requested information on how to obtain charts that R/CTs typically use. These can be ordered from: Graphics Company, 1107 West University Avenue, Urbana, Illinois 61801.

Projects 38 and 39 were both examples of inservice sessions that teacher consultants have offered to classroom teachers in elementary schools. In the following example (Project 40), a teacher consultant presented a session on instructional techniques for teaching reading to secondary school students.

Figure 10–9 Sample Procedure for Taking a Reading Accuracy Count Included in an Inservice Workshop on Data Collection Procedures

1. Count out a 100-word passage from the story to be read.
2. Mark the beginning and ending of the passage.
3. Have the child read the passage.
4. Tally the errors made on the data sheet.
5. Subtract the errors from 100. The result of this is the percentage of words read accurately.
6. Variations:
    a) On a 50-word sample, multiply the errors by two and subtract from 100.
    b) On a 25-word sample, multiply the errors by four and subtract from 100.

Example:

Sample	Date	Story	Errors	% Correct
100 words	3/3/80	#8	(6)	94%
50 words	3/14/80	#16	$(4 \times 2 = 8)$	92%
25 words	5/2/80	#34	$(3 \times 4 = 12)$	88%

Figure 10–10 Sample Hand-Out for Workshop on Data-Based Classroom Instruction Listing Academic Areas for Measurement and Reference Sources

I. Reading
  A. Oral reading accuracy—percent correct
  B. Isolated words—percent correct
  C. Workbooks—percent correct, percent completed
  D. Daily worksheets—percent correct
II. Math
  A. Flashcards
    1. Percent correct
    2. Number correct in one minute—keep the number of facts constant
  B. Worksheets—percent correct, percent completed
  C. Time tests—percent correct

References
Phyllis K. Mirkin and Stanley L. Deno, *Basic Procedures in Data-Based Instruction*, Department of Special Education, University of Minnesota, 1974.
M. Stephen Lilly, *Children With Exceptional Needs, A Survey of Special Education*, Holt, Rinehart & Winston, 1979.
Norris G. Haring, Thomas C. Lovitt, Marie D. Eaton, and Cheryl L. Hansen, *The Fourth R, Research in the Classroom*, Charles E. Merrill Publishing Company, 1978.

Project 40: Direct Instruction Reading

R/CT: Julie Haizman

The teacher consultant is one of several teachers responsible for preparing special education students at the secondary level to be integrated into more normal classroom environments. The students had previously received instruction in self-contained, special classes for the educable mentally retarded. The intent of this inservice session was to demonstrate to teachers that these students can make substantial reading progress when direct instruction techniques are used (Idol-Maestas, Lloyd, & Lilly, 1981; Idol-Maestas, Lloyd, & Ritter, 1982).

The outline that the consultant followed is shown in Exhibit 10-3.

Fourteen teachers and one program supervisor attended the session; all were special educators. The teacher consultant provided them with a packet, which included the following:

- procedures for giving a curricular-based assessment (CBA) in reading (See Chapter 7 and Appendix 7-A.)
- a CBA placement form (Appendix 7-A)

Figure 10–11 Sample Evaluation Form and Response Data for an Inservice Workshop on Using Data-Based Instruction in the Classroom

Title of session: _____ DATA-BASED INSTRUCTION _____

Presenter: ___ MARIANNE ABBEY-SMITH, BARB BOBEK, AND MARJORIE HEINTZ ___

A. Did session contribute to your professional growth?

n=7	n=4	n=2	n=0
Very Much	Much	Some	None
1	2	3	4

B. Was the content relevant to your teaching area?

n=6	n=5	n=2	n=0
Very Much	Much	Some	None
1	2	3	4

C. Was the overall content and method of presentation satisfactory?

n=13	n=0
Yes	No

D. Would you recommend this presentation for future inservice?

n=13	n=0
Yes	No

E. Comments: Some sample comments were:

"Excellent"

"I would like more information on setting up the curriculum so that you can use data-based instruction more easily."

"Very good presenters"

"Every teacher in our district should see this session. I'm sure they could apply it to some area of their instruction—for their own knowledge, for parent conferences, etc."

- a sample story with accompanying soundsheet (Chapter 7)
- a set of directions for using multiband charts (See Figure 10-12.)
- a daily progress chart and accompanying directions (See Chapter 4.)
- a sheet for practicing charting information
- error correction procedures for misreading words and for sounding out words (See Chapter 7.)
- procedures for studying sound/letter relationships (See Chapter 7 and Figure 10-13.)
- procedures for using drill cards for spelling and studying sight words (See Figure 10-14.)
- strategies for improving reading comprehension (See Figure 10-15.)
- procedures for building a transition between oral and written reading comprehension (See Figure 10-16.)
- a procedure for using contingent skipping and drilling (See Figure 10-17.)

Exhibit 10–3 Outline Consultant Followed for Project 40

1. Introduction and rationale
   a. Find out who is in the audience.
   b. Tell how the consultant started using direct instruction.
   c. Demonstrate the need for direct instruction.
   d. Report on supportive research.
   e. Discuss versatility and use of this approach.
   f. Talk about materials used.
   g. Tell why students like this approach.
2. Placement testing
   a. Explain.
   b. Practice.
3. Basic format of a lesson
   a. Practice sounds.
   b. Practice words.
   c. Read stories.
   d. Use a consistent error correction procedure.
4. Tape recording of student reading
5. Charting
   a. Multiband chart
   b. Daily progress charts
6. Individual instruction interventions
7. Program adaptations
   a. Small group instruction
   b. Peer tutor instruction
8. Questions and comments

The evaluation form for this session contained open-ended questions. The overall responses are summarized after each question and are displayed in Figure 10-18.

Project 41: Learning Adjustment Inservice Yearly Plan

Program Supervisor and Teacher Consultant: Barb Bobek

This example demonstrates how a teacher consultant implemented inservice teacher education for large numbers of teachers. This teacher consultant was employed as a supervisor for Learning Adjustment Programs, which is a type of noncategorical resource program.

The supervisor/consultant developed a yearly plan to prepare teachers in Learning Adjustment Programs (LAP) to provide better service to mildly handicapped students in noncategorical resource rooms and their regular classroom teachers. Initially, she developed a set of overall goals for

Figure 10–12 A Set of Directions for Using a Multiband Chart to Monitor Student Performance Used in an Inservice Training Packet

THE MULTI-BAND CHART*

The Multi-band chart is designed to monitor up to 5 separate skills at one time. Each band on the chart is used to record information (data) about a specific behavior as time passes. These behaviors may be related, or may be completely separate from each other. The multi-band chart monitors behaviors by a single subject. By keeping track of behaviors on separate bands, we can monitor the improvement that the student is making in each area, apart from anything else that the student may be doing.

Each band of the Multi-band Chart looks like this:

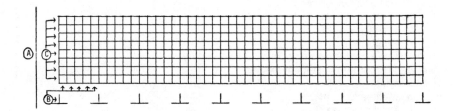

All of the places on the band above that have circled letters next to them provide separate pieces of information about the behavior that is being monitored on that band.

(A) Name of Behavior: On this line you put the name of the bahavior that you are monitoring. Also included can be the criteria for passing.

(B) Date of Observation: The first line (thick line) in each section represents the Monday of that week. The date for that Monday is placed on the ___ below it. The following lines, then, represent the following days of the week, excluding Saturday and Sunday. In this way, we can observe how the behavior changes over time, during the course of tutoring.

(C) Expected Range of Data: During instruction, it is expected that a student's level of performance will vary. Therefore, it is necessary to predict a range of possible scores that will accommodate these changes. To show the range of possible scores we give numerical value to each horizontal line on the band. These values can be either percentages, or numbers, depending on the skill and method of measurement. For example, if you are measuring rate of reading, and your student reads at approximately 45 words per minute, you may set up the range to go from 40 - 75, with each box representing 5 words per minute. If you are measuring comprehension, you would set your range to accommodate 0% - 100%, with each box representing 10% intervals.
You can see, then, that the range for each band of the chart is set depending upon the measured behavior, and the predicted levels of behavior that will be observed.

Criterion Line: When a criterion for passing a particular skill has been set, it is a good idea to mark this level on the band. This allows the instructor to see easily whether the student has passed the skill. This can be marked in colored pen, and can also change as the student's skill increases during direct instruction.

For reading instruction, the criteria are:

Accuracy: 95% correct words (from 100 word timed sample)

Rate: _____ correct words per minute (varies with reading level, about 10 x grade level)

Comprehension: 80% correct (4 of 5 questions answered correctly)

Individual skills criteria will be set by the instructor, to determine mastery.

* This handout was designed by Resource/Consulting Teacher, Charlie Davis.

Figure 10–13 Sample Procedures for Studying Sound/Letter Relationships Using Soundsheets for Practice— Included in an Inservice Training Packet

SOUND SHEETS

Many students will work on a phonetic approach to learning new words as part of their instruction. To teach work-attack skills, sound sheets will be used. These teach a number of sounds (usually 10-20 per sheet) taken from words in the stories that the students are working on. These can include single letter sounds, blends, different sounds for the same letter, etc. Students needing letter-sound instruction will use sound sheets daily, and data from this instruction will be charted daily on 1 band of the multi-band chart.

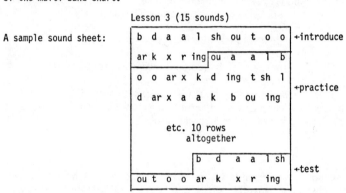

The same error correction procedure is used if the student does not know the sound, or pronounces the wrong sound:

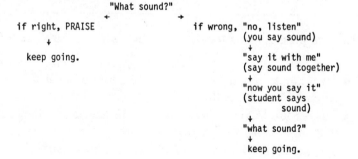

Students are tested on last section of sounds at the end of sound sheet instruction each day. Their % correct is determined

$$\left(\frac{\text{\# correct sounds}}{\text{\# total sounds}} \right)$$

and charted on a band of the multi-band chart.

CRITERIA: Student must get 100%, 5 consecutive days, to move to a new sound sheet.

Figure 10–14 Sample Procedures for Using Drill Cards to Practice Spelling Words and Sight Words Included in an Inservice Training Packet

Spelling Words

1. Using a list of commonly-used words, identify 10 words that the student cannot spell (beginning level is 0 percent).
2. Student writes each of the 10 words on a flashcard, spelling words aloud as he or she writes them.
3. Practice—teacher giving word, student spelling it (either aloud or on paper). Go through list several times, until student is spelling all correctly.
4. Again, if a word is misspelled, use the same error-correction procedure:

    "no, listen" (you say word, spell word)
    ↓
    "do it with me" (both say word, spell word)
    ↓
    "now you do it" (student says word, spells word)
    ↓
    give word again, student responds correctly.
5. Each day, beginning spelling instruction, student is tested on words. Results are graphed on a band of the multiband chart.
    Criteria: 100 percent, 3 consecutive days.

Sight words

This method can be used to teach students sight words. Words can be chosen from the Dolch list or comparable ones, practiced daily from drill cards, and tested to determine acquisition. An appropriate criteria might be 100 percent, three consecutive days.

---

inservice programming for the 1981–1982 school year. The overall goals were the following:

- To promote an understanding of the role of an R/CT so that LAP teachers function in their buildings more effectively;
- To give R/CT skills to the existing LAP teachers so they can function in their buildings as R/CTs;
- To give LAP teachers specific skills in direct instruction so they are better able to enhance pupil outcomes

She then designed a yearly plan to reflect the topical areas to be covered. This plan is shown in Exhibit 10-4.

Goals for Individual Inservice Sessions

The teacher consultant then projected goals arranged by dates for each of the topical areas for the plan.

Figure 10–15 Sample Strategies for Improving Reading Comprehension—Included in an Inservice Training Packet

When an incorrect answer is given to a question, a similar error correction procedure is used to help the student find the correct answer. This is followed for each incorrectly answered question, after all five questions are asked.

1. Reread the question. (See if the student can now answer correctly.)
2. "What is the question asking you?"   (Student rephrases question. See if he or
                                                  ← she now can answer it.)
    ↓
3. If he or she can rephrase it, but still   If student can't rephrase it, you model an
   can't answer it: appropriate response. Have him or her repeat
   "Look for the paragraph that tells   it. "It asks . . . . Now you tell me." Student
   you."   rephrases the question.
          ↓

   (If he or she can't find it, you point
   to it, and say, "Here, now you find
   the answer.")
          ↓

   (If he or she still can't find the
   answer, point to the sentence, say,
   "Here, read this." Student reads,
   see if he or she can answer.)
          ↓

   (If he or she still can't, you model
   an appropriate response, and have
   him or her repeat.)

Other strategies:

1. After working on the key words, but before reading the story, tell the student the five questions you will ask.
2. Do same as above, and as student reads, if a question is answered in the text, stop and ask, "Did that give an answer to a question?"
3. Have student predict the questions that may be asked about the story.
4. After the student reads a paragraph of the story, stop and have him or her answer a question about that particular paragraph. Then go on.

These are all strategies that should be faded as the student becomes more proficient at comprehending what he or she is reading.

October 2, 1981. The participant will identify the three roles of the R/CT model, so that the participant will be able to gain an understanding of the model.

October 26, 1982. The participant will identify the philosophy of curriculum-based assessment (CBA) so that the LAP teachers will have a unified pedagogical base.

Figure 10–16 Sample Procedures for Building Transition Between Oral and Written Reading Comprehension—Included in an Inservice Training Packet

As students begin achieving near grade level, it is necessary to work on their ability to respond in a written manner to comprehension questions, since this is the method most used in regular classes. This can be incorporated into the reading lesson in a variety of ways:
1. Students may answer a number of the five comprehension questions on paper.
2. The comprehension questions can be increased to 10, with the students answering the additional five questions on paper.
3. Students can respond orally to the five comprehension questions, and then write out their answers to those questions.

When requiring students to write the answers to the questions, criteria should compare to that used by regular teachers for similar exercises.

The participant will identify the characteristics of a CBA so that the LAP teachers will be able to collect data and place the student in the appropriate basal reader.

The participant will construct a CBA using the basal series employed in this district so that the LAP teachers have a consistent pedagogical instrument for purposes of assessment.

November 19, 1981. Objectives will be determined by the October 23 Vocational Education Conference.

February 11, 1982. The participant will be able to use a six-year chart so that the LAP teachers have an accurate measure of the amount of

---

Figure 10–17 Sample Procedure for Using Contingent Skipping and Drilling—Included in an Inservice Training Packet

Very often students will rapidly improve reading skills once they become familiar with the instruction procedure and excited by the progress they are making. Skip and drill can be used as a motivator to increase students' drive to excel and improve in areas of difficulty. The teacher makes an agreement with the student, that a number of stories can be skipped for reaching a particular level of achievement, which is above the passing criterion levels.

For example, a student who has trouble with comprehension may be more motivated to recall information if the following agreement is made: For any story that the student reaches accuracy and rate criteria and earns 100 percent on comprehension, the next two stories may be skipped. Although 80 percent is passing criteria, he or she will only advance to the next story if 80 percent is reached. One hundred percent will result in two skipped stories, further increasing rate of progress.

This strategy works particularly well with a student who was placed low in the curriculum because of poor comprehension skills or low oral reading rate.

Figure 10–18 Sample Evaluation Form and Response Data for Workshop in Direct Instruction Reading

1. What kind of class do you teach?
   Response summarization: Eight resource rooms (LD, BD, EMH, or Title I reading)
   Three occupational education classes (health, English, social studies, or math)
   One self-contained class (Trainable Mentally Handicapped)
   One special education supervisor
   Two student teachers
2. Do you feel this approach could be used in your class?
   Response summarization: Twelve participants said yes. The math teacher said she would use it in the future. The social studies teacher said yes, if she taught an English class. One student teacher did not respond.
3. Do you feel the material was organized clearly and explained adequately?
   All participants responded positively.
4. How would you evaluate the overall session?
   Response summarization: Fourteen respondents gave positive remarks (i.e., "excellent, good, wonderful, very interesting, helpful"). The math/social studies teacher said it was good for a teacher of reading.
5. Comments
   Response summarization: All comments were positive and highly reinforcing.

---

material the LAP student needs to learn, in order to be placed back into the classroom with his or her peer group.

The participant will be able to use a semester chart so that the LAP teacher has a daily record of progress through the basal curriculum.

The participant will be able to identify the elements of direct instruction so that LAP teachers may enhance pupil outcomes.

February 17, 1982. The participant will be able to identify the eight major characteristics of data-based instruction. The participant will be able to identify an appropriate procedure for daily data collection for each of four sample situations.

March 5, 1982. The participant will be able to identify assessment and instructional strategies for teaching spelling and handwriting.

This final project demonstrates the extent to which inservice preparation can be carried when full administrative support lies behind the intent. A special education supervisor developed an intensive plan for reeducating resource teachers to become data-based teachers who also serve as teacher

Exhibit 10–4 LAP Inservice Yearly Plan

Friday, October 2 1:00–3:30	Introduction to Resource/Consultant Model
Monday, October 26 8:30–3:30	Philosophy, Characteristics, and Construction of a Curriculum-Based Assessment
Thursday, November 19 1:00–3:30 (LAP grades 7-12)	Report on Vocational Education Secondary Conference
Thursday, February 11 9:30–3:30	Placement in the Curriculum Six-Year Charts Semester Charts Estimating Progress, Drawing Projection Lines Elements of Direct Instruction
Wednesday, February 17 1:00–3:30	Data-Based Instruction Daily Measurement Components of Daily Measurement
Friday, March 5 8:30–3:30	Curricular Assessment and Academic Intervention Techniques for Handwriting and Spelling
Tuesday, March 30 1:00–3:30	Procedures for Consulting with Regular Classroom Teachers

consultants. The same general format for training could be used to prepare classroom teachers to accommodate special needs learners in their classrooms.

SUMMARY

This section has focused on how teacher consultants have taken a set of guidelines for offering inservice education and have creatively applied them in a variety of situations. These teacher consultants also experimented with various forms of delivery including inservice programs within a building and programs at the district level. The examples also included instances where both voluntary and mandatory inservice programs were established. In all programs, the teacher consultants adhered to the practices of using detailed outline plans, providing participants with packets of materials, actively engaging participants in the training process, and seeking evaluative participant feedback.

COMMUNICATION EXCHANGE

Teacher consultants may find that the specialized vocabulary they use creates a communication gap with regular classroom teachers. The problem may be especially evident for consultants who are data-based instruction teachers and/or behavior analysts. Three strategies used by R/CTs at the University of Illinois may help alleviate this potential problem.

Strategy 1

Use clear and mutually agreed-upon definitions of behavior. Whenever two collaborating teachers work together, they must make certain that they are talking about the same behavior. The agreed-upon definition of a behavior should stem from both teachers' observations, rather than reflecting the opinions of the teacher consultant.

Strategy 2

Provide guidance for defining pupil problems with objective and measurable language. Consultants can offer classroom teachers examples of definitions of behaviors that are observable, measurable, and reliable. If a second individual were to observe the same behavior monitored by a first observer, a high agreement of occurrence and nonoccurrence of the behavior would occur.

Examples of precise behavioral definitions can be contrasted to less specific or nebulous behavioral definitions. Figure 10-19 contains a sample checklist of behavioral definitions that can be given to teachers to help them see the difference between specific and nonspecific behavior definitions. Giving the list to teachers and asking them to indicate which behaviors meet the standards for observability, measurability, and reliability is recommended. Comparisons and discussion should follow the rating completion so that all parties agree on the outcome rating of each behavioral definition.

Strategy 3

Use behavioral terminology and educational jargon in a guided fashion to ensure effective understanding. Consultants must be cautious not to overwhelm consultees with a barrage of behavioral terminology and a specialized vocabulary. Others can be guided to know and use new vocabulary and concepts by describing the process first in common language and then attaching the special label to speed conversation. For example,

Figure 10–19 Sample Exercise for Teachers to Determine
Observable and Measurable Behaviors

Place a + by the behaviors that are observable and measurable.
Place a − by the behaviors that are not observable and measurable.

_____ learn to have respect
_____ not be aggressive
_____ increase reading level by one year in five months' time
_____ be cooperative
_____ decrease thumb-sucking behavior
_____ not be so dependent
_____ be more independent
_____ learn to work independently in class
_____ spell ten different consonant-vowel-consonant–consonant patterns
_____ increase oral reading rate
_____ be polite
_____ pay attention when someone calls his or her name
_____ learn safety rules for the playground
_____ decrease the frequency of number of times out of seat during reading period
_____ increase oral reading accuracy
_____ learn to do things on his or her own
_____ complete 15 single digit addition problems in 15 minutes' time
_____ have a higher self-esteem

---

a teacher consultant might say, ''Let's find out how much of his classroom work John is currently finishing.'' Later the consultant can refer to this process as ''obtaining a baseline measurement.''

References

Affleck, J. Q., Lehning, T. W., & Brow, K. D. Expanding the resource concept: The resource school. *Exceptional Children,* 1973, *39,* 446–453.

Aho, M. Teaching spelling to children with specific language disability. *Academic Therapy,* 1967, *3,* 45–50.

Ainsworth, S. J. An exploratory study of education, social, and emotional factors in the education of educable mentally retarded children in Georgia public schools (U.S. Office of Education, Cooperative Research Program, Project Number 171). Athens, Georgia: University of Georgia, 1959.

Ascare, D., & Axelrod, S. Use of a behavior modification procedure in four "open" classrooms. *Psychology in the Schools,* 1973, *10*(2), 243–248.

Axelrod, S., & Paluska, J. A component analysis of the effects of a classroom game on spelling performance. In E. Ramp and G. Semb (Eds.), *Behavior analysis: Areas of research and application.* Englewood Cliffs, N.J.: Prentice-Hall, Inc., 1975.

Baldwin, W. D. The social position of the educable mentally retarded in the regular grades in the public schools. *Exceptional Children,* 1958, *25,* 106–108.

Ballard, K. D., & Glynn, T. Behavior self-management in story writing with elementary school children. *Journal of Applied Behavior Analysis,* 1975, *8*(4), 387–389.

Barnes, E. J. Cultural retardation or short comings of assessment techniques. In R. L. Jones & D. L. MacMillan (Eds.), *Special education in transition.* Boston, Mass.: Allyn & Bacon, Inc., 1974.

Barrish, H. H., Saunders, M., & Wolf, M. M. Good behavior games: Effects of individual contingencies for group consequences on disruptive behavior in a classroom. *Journal of Applied Behavior Analysis,* 1969, *2,* 119–124.

Bartholome, L. Using the typewriter for learning: Spelling, *Balance Sheet, 1977. 58,* 196–200.

Becker, W. C., Madsen, C. H., Jr., Arnold, C. R., & Thomas, D. R. The contingent use of teacher attention and praise in reducing classroom behavior problems. *Journal of Special Education,* 1967, *1,* 287–307.

Bennett, A. *A comparative study of sub-normal children in the elementary grades.* New York: Teachers College, Columbia University, 1932.

Berman, P., & Mclaughlin, M. W. *Federal programs supporting educational change, Volume VIII: Implementing and sustaining innovations.* Santa Monica, Calif.: The Rand Corporation, 1978 (ED 159 289).

329

Blankenship, C., & Lilly, M. D. *Mainstreaming students with learning and behavior problems*. New York: Holt, Rinehart & Winston, 1981.

Blatt, B. The physical, personality and academic status of children who are mentally retarded attending special classes as compared with children who are mentally retarded attending regular classes. *American Journal of Mental Deficiency*, 1958,.*62*, 810–818.

Bloom, B. S. Learning for mastery. In B. S. Bloom, J. T. Hastings, & G.F. Madaus (Eds.), *Handbook on formative and summative evaluation of student learning*. New York: McGraw-Hill Book Co., 1971.

Bloom, B.S. Time and learning. *American Psychologist*, 1974, *29*, 682–688.

Bradfield, R. H., Brown, J., Kaplan, P., Rickert, E., & Stannard, R. The special child in the regular classroom. *Exceptional Children*, February 1973, *39*, 384–390.

Broden, M., Bruce, C., Mitchell, M. A., Carter, U., & Hall, R. V. Effects of teacher attention on attending behavior of two boys at adjacent desks. *Journal of Applied Behavior Analysis*, 1970, *3*, 199–203.

Broden, M., Hall, R. V., & Mitts, B. The effect of self-recording on the classroom behavior of two eighth-grade students. *Journal of Applied Behavior Analysis*, 1971, *4*, 191–199.

Brown, V. Yes, but . . . *Journal of Special Education*, 1977, *11*(2), 175.

Brown, V. Independent study behaviors: A framework for curriculum development. *Learning Disability Quarterly*, 1978, *1*(2), 78–83.

Bruininks, R. H., & Rynders, J. E. Alternatives to special class placement for educable mentally retarded children. *Focus on Exceptional Children*, 1971, *3*(4), 1–12.

Budoff, M., & Gottlieb, J. Special class students mainstreamed: A study of an aptitude (learning potential) X treatment interaction. *American Journal of Mental Deficiency*, 1976, *81*, 1–11.

Cantrell, R. P., & Cantrell, M. L. Preventive mainstreaming: Impact of a supportive service program on pupils. *Exceptional Children*, April 1976, *42*(7), 381–386.

Carnine, D., & Silbert, J. *Direct instruction reading*. Columbus, Ohio: Charles E. Merrill Publishing Co., 1979.

Carroll, A. W. The effects of segregated and partially integrated school programs on self-concept and academic achievement of educable mental retardates. *Exceptional Children*, 1967, *34*, 93–99.

Carroll, J. B. A model of school learning. *Teachers College Record*, 1963, *64*, 723–733.

Cassidy, V., & Stanton, J. An investigation of factors involved in the educational placement of mentally retarded children (U.S. Office of Education, Cooperative Research Program, Project Number 43). Columbus, Ohio: Ohio State University, 1959.

Cegelka, W. J., & Typer, J. The efficacy of special class placement for the mentally retarded in proper perspective. *Training School Bulletin*, 1970, *66*, 33–66.

Christie, L. S., McKenzie, H. S., & Burdett, C. S. The consulting teacher approach to special education: Inservice training for regular classroom teachers. *Focus on Exceptional Children*, October 1972, *4*(5), 1–10.

Clanton, P. The effectiveness of the letter-close procedure as a method of teaching spelling. Unpublished doctoral dissertation, University of Arkansas, 1977.

Corman, L., & Gottlieb, J. Mainstreaming mentally retarded children. A review of research. In N.R. Ellis (Ed.), *International review of research in mental retardation* (Vol. 9). New York: Academic Press, 1978.

Cruickshank, P. R., Lorish, C., & Thompson, L. What we think we know about inservice education. *Journal of Teacher Education*, 1979, *30*(1), 27–32.

Culkin, W., Mooney, J. A., & Tremulis, B. The child development program: Label-free teaching. *Journal of School Psychology*, 1972, *10*(2), 165–170.

Deno, E. Special education as developmental capital. *Exceptional Children*, 1970, *37*(3), 229–237.

Deno, S., & Gross, J. The Seward-University project: A cooperative effort to improve school services and university training. In E. Deno (Ed.), *Instructional alternatives for exceptional children*. Reston, Va.: The Council for Exceptional Children, 1973.

Deno, S. L., & Mirkin, P. K. *Basic Procedures in Data-Based Instruction*, Department of Special Education, University of Minnesota, 1974.

Deno, S. L., & Mirkin, P. K. *Data-based program modification: A manual*. Reston, Va.: The Council for Exceptional Children, 1977.

Deno, S. L., & Mirkin, P. K. Data-based IEP development: An approach to substantive compliance. *Teaching Exceptional Children*, 1980, *12*(3), 92–98.

Dolch, E. W. A basic sight vocabulary. *Elementary School Journal*, 1936, *36*, 456–460.

Dollar, B., & Klinger, R. A systems approach to improving teacher effectiveness: A triadic model of consultation and change. In C. A. Parker (Ed.), *Psychological consultation: Helping teachers meet special needs*. Reston, Va.: The Council for Exceptional Children, 1975.

Dunn, L. Special education for the mildly retarded—is much of it justifiable? *Exceptional Children*, 1968, *35*, 5–22.

Eaton, M., & Haisch, L. A comparison of the effects of new vs. error word drill on reading performance. Unpublished paper, Working paper No. 23, Experimental Education Unit, Child Development and Mental Retardation Center, University of Washington, Seattle, Washington, 1974.

Education for All Handicapped Children Act (PL 94-142). *Federal Register*. Washington, D.C.: August 23, 1977.

Elenbogen, M. L. A comparative study of some aspects of academic and social adjustment of two groups of mentally retarded children in special classes and regular classes. *Dissertation Abstracts*, 1957, *17*, 2496.

Ellis, J. C., & Idol-Maestas, L. Lunchroom behavior change in rewarded children: A consultation project. Unpublished manuscript, Department of Special Education, University of Illinois, April 1981.

Engelmann, S. Relationship between psychological theories and the act of teaching. *Journal of School Psychology*, 1967, *5*, 93–100.

Englemann, S., Becker, W. C., Hanner, S., & Johnson, G. *Corrective reading series*. Chicago, Ill.: Science Research Associates, Inc., 1980.

Englemann, S., & Bruner, E. *DISTAR reading level 1*. Chicago, Ill.: Science Research Associates, Inc., 1974.

Epstein, M. H., & Cullinan, D. Social validation: Use of normative data to evaluate LD interventions. *Learning Disability Quarterly*, 1979, *2*(4), 93–98.

Evans, S. The consultant role of the resource teacher. *Exceptional Children*, 1980, *46*(5), 402–403.

Fisher, C. W., Berliner, D. C., Filby, N. N., Marliave, R., Cahen, L. S., & Dishaw, M. M. Teaching behaviors, academic learning time, and student achievement: An overview. In

C. Denham and A. Lieberman (Eds.), *Time to learn*. Washington, D.C.: U.S. Government Printing Office, 1980.

Fitzgerald, J. *The teaching of spelling*. Milwaukee, Wis.: Bruce Publishing Co., 1951.

Forness, S. R. Educational prescription for the school psychologist. *Journal of School Psychology*, 1970, *8*, 131–138.

Forness, S. R. Implications of recent trends in educational labeling. *Journal of Learning Disabilities*, 1974, *7*(7), 445–449.

Foster, G. G., & Salvia, J. Teacher response to the label learned disabled as a function of demand characteristics. *Exceptional Children*, 1977, *43*, 533–534.

Foster, G. G., Schmidt, C. R., & Sabatino, D. Teacher expectancies and the label "learning disabilities." *Journal of Learning Disabilities*, 1976, *9*(2), 58–61.

Fox, W. L., Egner, A. N., Paolucci, P. E., Perelman, P. F., McKenzie, H. S., & Garvin, J. S. An introduction to a regular classroom approach to special education. In E. Deno (Ed.), *Instructional alternatives for exceptional children*. Reston, Va.: The Council for Exceptional Children, 1973.

Fry, E. A readability formula that saves time. *Journal of Reading*, 1968, *11*(7), 513–516; 575–578.

Fry, E. Fry's readability graph: Clarifications, validity, and extension to level 17. *Journal of Reading*, 1977, *21*(3), 242–252.

Gajar, A. H. Educable mentally retarded, learning disabled, emotionally disturbed: Similarities and differences. *Exceptional Children*, 1979, *45*(6), 470–472.

Gajar, A. H. Characteristics across exceptional categories: EMR, LD, and ED. *Journal of Special Education*, 1980, *14*(2), 165–173.

Gillung, T. B., & Rucker, C. N. Labels and teacher expectations. *Exceptional Children*, April 1977, *43*(7), 464–465.

Gilstrap, R. Development of independent skills in the intermediate grades. *Elementary English*, 1962, *39*, 481–482.

Glavin, J. P. Follow-up behavioral research in resource rooms. *Exceptional Children*, 1973, *40*, 211–213.

Glavin, J. P. Behaviorally oriented resource rooms: A follow-up. *Journal of Special Education*, 1974, *8*, 337–347.

Glavin, J. P., Quay, H. C., Annesley, F. R., & Werry, J. S. An experimental resource room for behavior problem children. *Exceptional Children*, 1971, *38*, 131–137.

Glusker, P. An integrational approach to spelling. *Academic Therapy*, 1967, *3*, 51–61.

Goldstein, H., Moss, J. W., & Jordan, L. J. The efficacy of special class training on the development of mentally retarded children (U.S. Office of Education, Cooperative Project Number 619). Urbana, Ill.: University of Illinois, 1965.

Graham, S., & Miller, L. Spelling research and practice: A unified approach. *Focus on Exceptional Children*, 1979, *12*(2), 1–16.

Grandy, G., Madsen, C., & deMersseman, L. The effects of individual and interdependent contingencies on inappropriate classroom behavior. *Psychology in the Schools*, 1973, *10*, 448–493.

Graubard, P. S., Rosenberg, H., & Miller, M. B. Student applications of behavior modification to teachers and environments or ecological approaches to social deviancy. In E. A. Ramp & B. L. Hopkins (Eds.), *A new direction for education: Behavior analysis*. Lawrence, Kan.: University of Kansas, 1971, 80–101.

Greenwood, C. R., Hops, H., Delaquardi, J., & Guild, J. Group contingencies for group consequences in classroom management: A further analysis. *Journal of Applied Behavior Analysis*, 1974, 7(3), 413–424.

Guskin, S., & Spicker, H. Educational research in mental retardation. In N. O. Ellis (Ed.), *International review of research in mental retardation* (Vol. 3). New York: Academic Press, 1968.

Hall, R., Fox, R., Willard, P., Goldsmith, L., Emerson, M., Owen, M., Davis R., & Porcia, E. The teacher as observer and experimenter in the modification of disrupting and talking-out behaviors. *Journal of Applied Behavior Analysis*, 1971, 4, 141–149.

Hall, R. V., Lund, D., & Jackson, D. Effects of teacher attention on study behavior. *Journal of Applied Behavior Analysis*, 1968, 1(1), 1–12.

Hall, R. V., Panyan, M., Rabon, D., & Broden, M. Instructing beginning teachers in reinforcement procedures which improve classroom control. *Journal of Applied Behavior Analysis*, 1968, 1(4), 315–322.

Hallahan, D. P., & Kauffman, J. M. *Introduction to learning disabilities: A psychobehavioral approach*. Englewood Cliffs, N.J.: Prentice-Hall, Inc., 1976.

Hallahan, D. P., & Kauffman, J. M. Labels, categories, behaviors: ED, LD, and EMR reconsidered. *Journal of Special Education*, 1977, 11(2), 139–149.

Hammill, D. D., & Wiederholt, J. L. *The resource room: Rationale and implementation*. Fort Washington, Pa.: Journal of Special Education Press, 1972.

Haring, N. G., & Krug, D. A. Placement in regular programs: Procedures and results. *Exceptional Children*, March 1975, 41, 413–417.

Haring, N. G., Lovitt, T. C., Eaton, M. D., & Hansen, C. L. *The fourth R: Research in the classroom*. Columbus, Ohio: Charles E. Merrill Publishing Co., 1978.

Harris, V. W., & Sherman, J. A. Use and analysis of the "good behavior game" to reduce disruptive classroom behavior. *Journal of Applied Behavior Analysis*, 1973, 6(3), 405–417.

Hersen, M., & Barlow, D. H. *Single case experimental designs*. New York: Pergamon Press, 1976.

Hewett, F. M. Handicapped children and the regular classroom. In H. Dupont (Ed.), *Educating emotionally disturbed children: Readings*. New York: Holt, Rinehart & Winston, 1975.

Hill, C., & Martinis, A. Individualizing a multisensory spelling program? *Academic Therapy*, 1973, 9, 77–83.

Hobbs, N. *The process of re-education*. Paper presented at First Annual Re-ED Workshop. Gatlinburg, Tennessee, September 1963.

Hops, H., & Cobb, J. A. Survival behaviors in the educational setting: Their implications for research and intervention. In L. A. Hamerlynck, L. Handy, and E. Mash (Eds.), *Behavior change: Methodology, concepts, and practice*. Champaign, Ill.: Research Press, 1973, 193–208.

Horn, E. Principles of methods in teaching spelling as derived from scientific investigation. In *Eighteenth yearbook, National Society for the Study of Education*. Bloomington, Ind.: Public School Publishing Co., 1919.

Horn, E. *Teaching spelling*. Washington, D.C.: American Educational Research Association, 1954.

Houghton, R. V., Morrison, E., Jarvis, R., & McDonald, M. The effects of explicit timing and feedback on compositional response rate in elementary school children. *Journal of Applied Behavior Analysis*, 1974, 7(4), 547–555.

Hutson, H. *Inservice best practices: The learnings of general education.* Bloomington, Ind.: National Inservice Network, 1979.

Iano, R. P. Shall we disband special classes? *Journal of Special Education,* 1972, *6*(2), 167–177.

Idol-Maestas, L. A teacher training model: The resource/consulting teacher. *Behavioral Disorders,* 1981, *6*(2), 108–121.

Idol-Maestas, L., Givens-Ogle, L., & Lloyd, S. *The role of resource/consulting teachers: Strategies and outcomes,* 1981. (ERIC Document Reproduction Service No. ED 204 960)

Idol-Maestas, L., & Jackson, C. An evaluation of the consultation process. Unpublished report, Department of Special Education, University of Illinois at Urbana-Champaign, April 1981.

Idol-Maestas, L., & Jensen-Browne, K. Individual oral reading performance within data-based group instruction. Unpublished manuscript, Department of Special Education, University of Illinois at Urbana-Champaign, August 1980.

Idol-Maestas, L., Lloyd, S., & Lilly, M. S. Implementation of a noncategorical approach to direct service and teacher education. *Exceptional Children,* 1981, *48*(3), 123–219.

Idol-Maestas, L., Lloyd, S., & Ritter, S. A model for direct, data based reading instruction. Unpublished manuscript, University of Illinois at Urbana-Champaign, 1982.

Ito, H. R. Long-term effects of resource room programs on learning disabled children's reading. *Journal of Learning Disabilities,* 1980, *13*(6), 322–326.

Jenkins, J., Deno, S. L., & Mirkin, P. K. Measuring pupil progress toward the least restrictive environment. *Learning Disability Quarterly,* 1980, *2*(4), 81–91.

Jenkins, J. R., & Jenkins, L. M. *Cross age and peer tutoring: Help for children with learning problems.* Reston, Va.: The Council for Exceptional Children, 1981.

Jenkins, J. R., & Larson, K. Evaluating error-correction procedures for oral reading. *Journal of Special Education,* 1979, *13*(2), 145–156.

Jenkins, J. R., & Mayhall, W. F. Development and evaluation of a resource teacher program. *Exceptional Children,* September, 1976, *43*(1), 21–29.

Johnson, G. O. A study of the social position of mentally handicapped children in the regular grades? *American Journal of Mental Deficiency,* 1950, *55,* 60–89.

Johnson, G. O., & Kirk, S. A. Are mentally handicapped children segregated in the regular grades? *Exceptional Children,* 1950, *17,* 65–68, 87–88.

Joyce, B. R., McNair, K. M., Diaz, R., & McKibbin, M. D. *Interviews: Perceptions of professionals and policy makers.* Stanford, Calif.: Stanford Center for Research and Development in Teaching, Stanford University, 1976. (ERIC Document Reproduction Service No. ED 142 546)

Kaufman, M. *Reading in content areas.* West Lafayette, Ind.: Kappa Delta Pi Publication, 1980.

Kaufman, M. E., & Alberto, P. A. Research on efficacy of special education for the mentally retarded. In N. R. Ellis (Ed.), *International Review of Research in Mental Retardation* (Vol. 8). New York: Academic Press, 1976.

Kirk, S. A. Research in education. In H. A. Steven & R. Heber (Eds.), *Mental retardation.* Chicago, Ill.: University of Chicago Press, 1964.

Knapczyk, D. R., & Livingston, G. Self-recording and student teacher supervision: Variables within a token economy system. *Journal of Applied Behavior Analysis,* 1973, *6*(3), 481–486.

Knight, M. F., Meyers, H. W., Paolucci-Whitcomb, P., Hasazi, S. E., & Nevin, A. A four-year evaluation of consulting teacher service. *Behavioral Disorders,* 1981, *6*(2), 92–100.

Kroth, R. L. *Communicating with parents of exceptional children.* Denver, Col.: Love Publishing Co., 1975.

Kroth, R. L., & Simpson, R. L. *Parent conferences as a teaching strategy.* Denver, Col.: Love Publishing Co., 1977.

LaForge, J., Pree, M., & Hasazi, S. The use of minimal objectives as an ongoing monitoring system to evaluate progress. In E. Ramp and G. Semb (Eds.), *Behavior analysis: Areas of research and application.* Englewood Cliffs, N.J.: Prentice-Hall, Inc., 1975.

Lahey, B. B., Gendrich, J. G., Gendrich, S. I., Schnelle, J. F., Gant, P. S., & McNees, M. P. An evaluation of daily report cards with minimal teacher and parent contacts as an efficient method of classroom intervention. *Behavior Modification,* 1977, *1*(3), 381–394.

Lates, B. J., & Mesch, D. *Generic consulting teacher program.* Report to the Massachusetts Board of Education, Book V. Unpublished manuscript, Education Department, Simmons College, April 1981.

Lawrence, G. *Patterns of effective inservice education: A state of the art summary of research on materials and procedures for changing teacher behaviors in inservice education.* Tallahassee, Fla.: Florida State Department of Education, 1974. (ERIC Document Reproduction Service No. ED 176 424)

Lew, M., Mesch, D., & Lates, B. J. The Simmons College generic consulting teacher program: A program description and data based applications. *Teacher Education and Special Education,* Spring 1982 (in press).

Lilly, M. S. Special education: A teapot in a tempest. *Exceptional Children,* 1970, *37,* 43–49.

Lilly, M. S. A training based model for special education. *Exceptional Children,* 1971, *37,* 745–749.

Lilly, M. S. *Children With Exceptional Needs: A Survey of Special Education.* New York: Holt, Rinehart & Winston, 1979.

Little, T. L. *The consultation progress in special education: Trainers' program manual.* Cedar Falls, Iowa: Division of Special Education, University of Northern Iowa, 1975.

Lock, C. *Study skills.* West Lafayette, Ind.: Kappa Delta Pi Publication, 1981.

Lovitt, T. C., & Hansen, C. L. Round one—Placing the child in the right reader. *Journal of Learning Disabilities,* 1976a, *9*(6), 18–24.

Lovitt, T. C., & Hansen, C. L. The use of contingent skipping and drilling to improve oral reading and comprehension. *Journal of Learning Disabilities,* 1976b, *9*(8), 481–487.

Lovitt, T., Schaff, M., & Sayre, E. The use of direct and continuous measurement to evaluate reading materials and pupil performance. *Focus on Exceptional Children,* 1970, *2,* 1–11.

Madsen, C. H., Becker, W. C., & Thomas, D. R. Rules, praise, and ignoring: Elements of elementary classroom control. *Journal of Applied Behavior Analysis,* 1968, *1*(2), 139–150.

Mazzarella, J. A. Synthesis of research on staff development. *Educational Leadership,* November 1980, *38,* 182–185.

McGeorch, J., & Irion, A. *The psychology of human learning.* New York: Longmans, Green, 1952.

McGlothlin, J. E. The school consultation committee: An approach to implementing a teacher consultation model. *Behavioral Disorders,* 1981, *6*(2), 101–107.

McKenzie, H. S. Special education and consulting teachers. In F. Clark, D. Evans, & L.

Hammerlynk (Eds.), *Implementing behavioral programs for schools and clinics*. Champaign, Ill.: Research Press, 1972.

McKenzie, H. S., Egner, A. N., Knight, M. F., Perelman, P. F., Schneider, B. M., & Garvin, J. S. Training consulting teachers to assist elementary teachers in management and education of handicapped children. *Exceptional Children*, October 1970, *37*(2), 137–143.

McKinney, J. D., & Feagans, L. Learning disabilities in the classroom. Final report submitted to Bureau of Education for the Handicapped, U.S. Office of Education, U.S. Department of Health, Education, and Welfare, 1980, Grant No. G00-76-05224.

McLaughlin, M. W., & Marsh, D. D. Staff development and school change. *Teachers College Record 80*, September 1978, 69–94. EJ 195 497.

Medland, M. B., & Stachnick, T. J. Good-behavior game: A replication and systematic analysis. *Journal of Applied Behavior Analysis*, 1969, *2*, 3–13.

Mercer, J. R. Sociological perspectives on mild mental retardation. In H. C. Haywood (Ed.), *Social-cultural aspects of mental retardation*. New York: Appleton-Century-Crofts, 1970.

Mercer, J. R. The labeling process. Paper presented at the Joseph P. Kennedy Jr. Foundation International Symposium on Human Rights, Retardation, and Research, Washington, D.C., October 1971(a).

Mercer, J. R. The meaning of mental retardation. In R. Koch & J. C. Dobson (Eds.), *The mentally retarded child and his family*. New York: Brunner/Mazel, 1971(b).

Mercer, J. R. *Labeling the mentally retarded*. Berkeley, Calif.: University of California Press, 1973.

Meyen, E. L. A statewide approach to inservice training for teachers of the mentally retarded. *Exceptional Children*, 1969, *35*, 353–357.

Meyers, C. E. The school psychologist and mild retardation. *Mental Retardation*, 1973, *11*, 15–20.

Meyers, C. E., MacMillan, D. L., & Yoshida, R. K. Correlates of success in transition of MR to regular class (Final Report, Grant No. OEG-0-73-5263). Pomona, Calif.: U.S. Department of Health, Education, and Welfare, 1975.

Meyers, J. A consultation model for school psychological service. *Journal of School Psychology*, 1973, *11*(1), 5–15.

Miller, T. L., & Sabatino, D. A. An evaluation of the teacher consultation model as an approach to mainstreaming. *Exceptional Children*, 1978, *45*(2), 86–91.

Mowrer, D. E. Accountability and speech therapy in the public schools. *American Speech and Hearing Association*, March 1972, *14*(3), 111–115.

Moyer, S. B. Readability of basal readers and workbooks: A comparison. *Learning Disability Quarterly*, 1979, *2*(1), 23–28.

Mullen, F., & Itkin, W. The value of special classes for the mentally handicapped. *Chicago Schools Journal*, 1961, *42*, 353–363.

Muller, A. J., Hasazi, S. E., Pierce, M. M., & Hasazi, J. E. Modification of disruptive behavior in a large group of elementary school students. In E. Ramp and B. Semb (Eds.), *Behavior analysis: Areas of research and application*, Englewood Cliffs, N.J.: Prentice-Hall, Inc., 1975, p. 275.

Nelson, C. M., & Stevens, K. B. An accountable model for mainstreaming behaviorally disordered children. *Behavioral Disorders*, 1981, *6*(2), 82–91.

Newcomer, P. Special education for the mildly handicapped: Beyond a diagnostic and remedial model. *Journal of Special Education*, 1977, *11*(2), 153–165.

Nicholson, A., Joyce, B. R., Parker, D., & Waterman, F. T. *The literature on inservice teacher education: An analytic review*, ISTE Report III. Palo Alto, Calif., 1976. (Monograph Sponsored by National Center for Educational Statistics and Teacher Corps) (ERIC Document Reproduction Service No. ED 129 734)

O'Connor, P. D., Stuck, G. B., & Wyne, M. D. Effects of a short-term intervention resource-room program on task orientation and achievement. *Journal of Special Education*, 1979, *13*(4), 375–385.

O'Leary, K. D., & Drabman, R. Token reinforcement programs in the classroom: A review. *Psychological Bulletin*, 1971, *75*, 379–398.

Osborn, J. The purposes, uses, and contents of workbooks and some guidelines for teachers and publishers. Unpublished manuscript, Center for the Study of Reading, University of Illinois at Urbana-Champaign, Reading Education Report No. 27, August 1981.

Parker, C. *Psychological consultation: Helping teachers meet special needs*. Reston, Va.: The Council for Exceptional Children, 1975.

Pertsch, C. F. A comparative study of the progress of subnormal pupils in the grades and in special classes. Bound manuscript, New York: Teachers College, Columbia University, 1936.

Phillips, V. The effect of a mode of presentation of spelling on reading achievement. Unpublished doctoral dissertation, University of Illinois at Urbana-Champaign, 1975.

Piercey, D. *Reading activities in the content areas*. Boston, Mass.: Allyn and Bacon, Inc., 1982.

President's Committee on Mental Retardation. *The six-hour retarded child*. Washington, D.C.: The President's Committee on Mental Retardation, 1969.

Quay, H. C. Academic skills. In N. R. Ellis (Ed.), *Handbook of mental deficiency*. New York: McGraw-Hill, 1963, 664–690.

Quay, H. C., Glavin, J. P., Annesley, F. R., & Werry, J. S. The modification of problem behavior and academic achievement in a resource room. *Journal of School Psychology*, 1972, *10*, 187–198.

Reger, R., & Koppmann, M. The child-oriented resource room. *Exceptional Children*, 1971, *37*, 460–462.

Reynolds, M. C. Categories and variables in special education. In M. C. Reynolds & M. D. Davis, (Eds.), *Exceptional children in regular classrooms*. Minneapolis, Minn.: University of Minnesota, 1970, 30–38.

Reynolds, M. C., & Birch, J. W. *Teaching exceptional children in all America's schools*. Reston, Va.: The Council for Exceptional Children, 1977.

Sabatino, D. A. An evaluation of resource rooms for children with learning disabilities. *Journal of Learning Disabilities*, 1971, *4*(2), 26–35.

Sabatino, D. A. Resource rooms: The renaissance in special education. *Journal of Special Education*, 1972, *6*(4), 335–347.

Seaton, H. W., Lasky, E. Z., & Seaton, J. B. Teacher specialist—A communication gap. *Education*, 1974, *95*(1), 90–91.

Semmel, M. I., Gottlieb, J., & Robinson, N. M. Mainstreaming: Perspectives on educating handicapped children in the public school. In D. C. Berliner (Ed.), *Review of Research in Education* (Vol. 7). Washington, D.C.: American Education Research Association, 1979.

Sindelar, P. T., & Deno, S. L. The effectiveness of resource programming. *Journal of Special Education*, 1978, *12*(1), 17–28.

Skinner, B. F. *The behavior of organisms*. New York: D. Appleton Century, 1938.

Smith, D. D. *Teaching the learning disabled*. Englewood Cliffs, N.J.: Prentice-Hall, Inc., 1981.

Smith, H. W., & Kennedy, W. A. Effects of three educational programs on mentally retarded children. *Perceptual and Motor Skills*, 1967, *24*, 174.

Stallings, J., Gory, R., Fairweather, J., & Needles, M. *Early childhood education classroom evaluation*. Menlo Park, Calif.: SRI International, 1977.

Stallings, J. A., & Kaskowitz, D. *Follow through classroom observation evaluation, 1972–73*. Menlo Park, Calif.: Stanford Research Institute, 1974.

Stokes, T. F., & Baer, D. M. An implicit technology of generalization. *Journal of Applied Behavior Analysis*, 1977, *10*(2), 349–367.

Stowitschek, C., & Jobes, N. Getting the bugs out of spelling—or an alternative to the spelling bee. *Teaching Exceptional Children*, 1977, *9*, 74–76.

Tharp, R. The triadic model of consultation: Current considerations. In C. A. Parker (Ed.), *Psychological consultation: Helping teachers meet special needs*. Reston, Va.: The Council for Exceptional Children, 1975.

Tharp, R., & Wetzel, R. *Behavior modification in the natural environment*. New York: Academic Press, 1969.

Thomas, B. *Rhymes and reasons*, MacMillan, Series r, 1980.

Thomas, D. R., Becker, W. C., & Armstrong, M. Production and elimination of disruptive classroom behavior by systematically varying teacher's behavior. *Journal of Applied Behavior Analysis*, 1968, *1*(1), 35–45.

Thurstone, T. G. An evaluation of educating mentally handicapped children in special classes and in regular grades (U.S. Office of Education Cooperative Research Program, Project Number 6452). Chapel Hill, N.C.: University of North Carolina, 1959.

Tunick, R. H., & Holcomb, T. F. Professional renewal: The person and the process in inservice education. *Contemporary Education*, 1980, *51*(4), 189–192.

Vaac, N. A. A study of emotionally disturbed children in regular and special classes. *Exceptional Children*, 1968, *35*, 197–204.

Vaac, N. A. Long term effects of special class intervention for emotionally disturbed children. In H. Dupont (Ed.), *Educating emotionally disturbed children: Readings*. New York: Holt, Rinehart & Winston, Inc., 1975.

Valett, R. E. The evaluation of basic learning abilities. *Journal of School Psychology*, 1968, *6*, 227–236.

Walker, H., & Hops, H. *The use of group and individual reinforcement contingencies on the modification of social withdrawal. Report No. 6.* Unpublished manuscript, Oregon University, Department of Special Education (CORBEH), May 1972.

Walker, H. M., & Hops, H. Use of normative peer data as a standard for evaluating classroom treatment effects. *Journal of Applied Behavior Analysis*, 1976, *9*(2), 159–168.

Walker, V. S. The efficacy of the resource room for educating retarded children. *Exceptional Children*, January 1974, *40*, 288–289.

Westerman, G. *Spelling and writing*. San Rafael, Calif.: Dimensions, 1971.

Westland, D. L., Koorland, M. A., & Rose, T. L. Characteristics of superior and average special education teachers. *Exceptional Children*, 1981, *47*(5), 357–363.

Wiederholt, J. L. Planning resource rooms for the mildly handicapped. *Focus on Exceptional Children*, 1974, *8*(5), 1–11.

Wildman II, R. W., & Wildman, R. W. The generalization of behavior modification procedures: A review—with special emphasis on classroom applications. *Psychology in the Schools,* 1975, *12*(4), 432–448.

Wixson, S. E. Two resource room models for serving learning and behavior disordered pupils. *Behavioral Disorders,* 1980, *5*(2), 116–125.

Wrightstone, J. W., Forlano, G., Lepkowski, J. R., Sontag, M., & Edelstein, J. D. A comparison of educational outcomes under single-track and two-track plans for educable mentally retarded children (U.S. Office of Education, Cooperative Research Program, Project Number 144). New York: New York City Board of Education, 1959.

SUPPLEMENTARY REFERENCES THAT WOULD BE USEFUL FOR A TEACHER CONSULTANT

Carnine, D., & Silbert, J. *Direct instruction reading.* Columbus, Ohio: Charles Merrill Publishing Co., 1979.

Carnine, D., Silbert, J., & Stein, M. *Direct instruction math.* Columbus, Ohio: Charles Merrill Publishing Co., 1981.

Kaufman, M. *Reading in content areas.* West Lafayette, Ind.: Kappa Delta Pi Publication, 1980.

Piercey, D. *Reading activities in the content areas.* Boston, Mass.: Allyn & Bacon, Inc., 1982.

TEXT REFERENCES

Economy Co.: Keys to reading. Oklahoma City, Oklahoma: The Economy Co., 1975.

Harcourt Brace: The Bookmark Library. New York: Harcourt, Brace, Jovanovich, Inc., 1976.

Holt, Rinehart and Winston: The Holt basic reading system. New York: Holt, Rinehart and Winston, 1977.

Laidlaw: The Laidlaw Reading Program, River Forest, IL: Laidlaw Brothers Publishers, a division of Doubleday & Co., 1976–1978.

Macmillan: The new Macmillan reading program. New York: Macmillan Publishing Co., Inc., 1975.

Macmillan: Series R. New York: Macmillan Publishing Co., Inc., 1980.

Scott, Foresman: Scott, Foresman basics in reading. Glenview, Illinois: Scott, Foresman and Company, 1978.

REFERENCE NOTES

1. Jenkins, J. R., & Pany, D. *Some resources to help teachers manage classroom behavior problems.* Unpublished manuscript, Department of Special Education, University of Illinois at Urbana-Champaign.

2. Wilcox, B., & Pany, D. *Use of group contingencies in classroom management: A review and evaluation of research.* Unpublished manuscript, Department of Special Education, University of Illinois at Urbana-Champaign.

Index

Note: Italicized numbers indicate references to tables and figures.

About the Author

Dr. Lorna Idol-Maestas is an assistant professor in the department of special education at the University of Illinois, Champaign-Urbana. She coordinates the Resource/Consulting Teacher Program, which is designed to prepare Master's level teachers to work as teacher consultants to classroom teachers.

Dr. Idol-Maestas completed her Ph.D. in special education at the University of New Mexico in 1979, an M.Ed. in special education in 1974, and a B.S. in special education and elementary education in 1969. Both of the earlier degrees were earned from the University of Nevada, Reno. She also studied at the University of Denver in Colorado.

Dr. Idol-Maestas worked as a classroom teacher and a resource teacher before pursuing doctoral studies. She has worked in special education teacher preparation for five years and has published several articles pertaining to academic, language, and behavioral problems of mildly handicapped students as well as articles on teacher consultation and teacher preparation.